THE WRITE

FANTASY L

D0567554

THE WRITER'S GUIDE TO

FANTASY LITERATURE

FROM DRAGON'S LAIR TO HERO'S QUEST

HOW TO WRITE FANTASY STORIES OF LASTING VALUE

EDITED BY PHILIP MARTIN

❋

THE WRITER BOOKS

The Writer Books is an imprint of Kalmbach Trade Press, a division of Kalmbach Publishing Co. These books are distributed to the book trade by Watson-Guptill.

For all other inquiries, including individual orders or details on special quantity discounts for groups or conferences, contact:

Kalmbach Publishing Co.
21027 Crossroads Circle
Waukesha, WI 53187
(800) 533-6644

Visit our website at http://writermag.com
Secure online ordering available

This is a work of criticism to help writers better understand the nature of well-written fantastic literature. For acknowledgements of permissions granted to quote from critical works by others, see pages 237 and 238; those pages are considered a continuation of this copyright page.

Front cover artwork © Greg & Tim Hildebrandt (All Rights Reserved). For original Hildebrandt art and collectibles, visit: http://www.spiderwebart.com.

Printed in Canada

02 03 04 05 06 07 08 09 10 11   10 9 8 7 6 5 4 3 2 1

Publisher's Cataloging-in-Publication
(Provided by Quality Books, Inc.)

    The writer's guide to fantasy literature : from dragon's
      lair to hero's quest / edited by Philip Martin. — 1st ed.
        p. cm.
      Includes bibliographical references and index.
      ISBN 0-87116-195-8

      1. Fantasy fiction—Authorship. 2. Authors—
    Interviews. 3. Fantasy fiction—History and criticism.
    I. Martin, Philip, 1953-

    PN3377.5.F34W75 2002   808.3'8766
                      QBI01-201382

Book design by Mighty Media, Minneapolis

CONTENTS

PART III: TECHNIQUES OF WRITING FANTASY

PART IV: RESOURCES

INTRODUCTION

by Philip Martin

MILLIONS OF US HAVE BEEN ENCHANTED with fantasy literature since we were old enough to encounter the original Potter books—Beatrix Potter, that is—whose vest-wearing, tea-drinking rabbits charmed young and old alike. Others were first swept away by Lewis Carroll's tales of Alice, the sane child amused by the antics of demented adults. In my family, we started with *The Wizard of Oz*, with its wholesome Midwestern themes, my father reading out loud that first book and then many of the sequels, a chapter a night, to me and my younger sister. Later, as a growing young reader in the 1960s and '70s, I discovered for myself the worlds of fantasy: the books of Lloyd Alexander, Susan Cooper, and Andre Norton; the imaginary lands of C.S. Lewis and J.R.R. Tolkien; the soaring fiction of Ray Bradbury, the comic earthiness of Fritz Lieber, the mythic depths of Ursula Le Guin. I was hooked.

As a teenager, with a paper route to provide the cash, I bicycled nearly every week past farmers' fields to the new mall on the outskirts of Evansville, Indiana, to scour the bookstore's Science Fiction and Fantasy shelves. A new fantasy book would suck the paper-route dollars right out of my pocket, and I would race home to crack the spine and plunge into a wondrous adventure, usually finishing late that same night, turning the pages feverishly until the plucky young hero had defeated the last dark lord.

The purpose of this book is help you write such fantastic stories, whether for children or for adults. At first, many authors will tell you that this ability is instinctive, something either you already have (a talent) or absorb somehow (like language); it just springs out of you when the time is right. Some authors believe that authors discover stories, like lost continents, or that stories find them, as Madeleine L'Engle has said. Ray Bradbury says that stories aren't built, they explode. Jane Yolen claims that she writes her stories to find out what happens. Good authors are always surprising themselves, it seems, by what happens when they sit down to write.

Can this be learned? Perhaps not entirely. Yet these same authors proceed to talk about how they work—how they put themselves into the right frame of mind to allow such epiphanies to happen: how they research and read widely; how they solve particular problems; how they develop the discipline to keep writing, even when Bradbury-like explosions are not detonating on the page.

O fantasy, that at times does so snatch us out of ourselves that we are conscious of naught, even though a thousand trumpets sound about us.
—Dante, The Divine Comedy

This advice is folk wisdom. Like other cultural knowledge, it is carried forward in the experiences of elders—and in the experimental testing of those patterns by younger generations. Through the test of time, the best stories and the best ways of writing prevail.

In Ursula Le Guin's first *Earthsea* novel, *A Wizard of Earthsea*, young Ged leaves his village to travel with his new master, a magician. He expects to begin training immediately. But nothing happens. After walking through the hills for days, Ged has not heard a single spell or incantation. Worst of all, "The mage's oaken staff that Ged had watched at first with eager dread was nothing but a stout staff to walk with." After three or four days of this, Ged asks his master:

> "When will my apprenticeship begin, Sir?"
> "It has begun," said Ogion.
> There was a silence, as if Ged was keeping back something he had to say. Then he said it: "But I haven't learned anything yet!"
> "Because you haven't found out what I am teaching," replied the mage, going on at his steady, long-legged pace. . . .

This is not a ten-easy-steps book. Rather, it tries to share the words and thoughts of great writers. If you listen to them carefully, perhaps you will understand what they are teaching. They gladly share their knowledge, but you need to find your own path. You need to figure out how to make fantasy fiction work for *you*. There are secrets to be shared. And sometime an oaken staff is just that.

The first bit of advice: Read as many of the works cited as you can. Like Ged, learn to listen. By following good advice, writing every day, and continuing to listen and grow, you will become ready for the stories that are looking for you.

Perhaps your words will hold fast the next generation of followers, listening to their fathers or mothers reading your story aloud, or will cause a solitary kid to hold a flashlight long into the night, turning pages to find out what happens to *your* plucky hero as he or she approaches the fortress of the last dark lord.

PART I

ON THE FIELD OF FANTASY

CHAPTER ONE

POTTERMANIA

O N THE EVE OF THE 21ST CENTURY, a young lad named Harry Potter enchanted the world. In *Harry Potter and the Sorcerer's Stone* (U.S. edition, 1998), the first in a planned seven-book series, the youngster with unruly hair and a lightning-bolt scar on his forehead turned 11 years old and entered the Hogwarts School of Witchcraft and Wizardry, an odd boarding school for fledgling magicians located somewhere in Britain. The series promised to follow the boy's development, year by year, till he turned 18.

By the time the fourth book was released, Pottermania was a full-fledged craze. *Harry Potter and the Goblet of Fire* went on sale on July 10, 2000. At the stroke of midnight, children and adults waited in long queues winding from the front doors of booksellers. At 12:01, the doors opened.

By the close of the second day, Barnes & Noble had logged half a million copies sold. Amazon.com recorded almost 400,000 copies sold by the end of the weekend (most of those were advance orders). The combined first printing in the U.S. and Britain totalled over five million copies. After the first weekend, the American publisher, Scholastic, was already planning to go back on press soon to fill the incredible demand for hardcover copies of this children's book.

Surprisingly, many adults purchasing Potter books confessed they were buying them for their own reading pleasure. In Britain, the publisher, Bloomsbury, thoughtfully issued an edition with a more inconspicuous cover—so adults could sneak in a read on the subway and not feel too embarrassed. Embarrassed? How many other adults on the subway were doing the exact same thing: rattling along on the London underground while riding in their mind's eye a Nimbus 2000 (a high-tech flying broomstick used to play the aerial magician's sport, "Quidditch"), as they paged through the latest volume of Harry's exploits?

In a July 12, 1999, article in *The New York Times*, author Eden Ross Lipson quoted a mother, Sally Lodge of Wellesley, Massachusetts:

> I've been a mother for almost 18 years, and never in my parenting career have all three of my children read and even fought over the same book. But then my husband started the first book at the same time the 11-year-old was reading it, and he wanted it reserved for him. So he hid it under his pillow. But she found it.

In Britain, the appearance of the third book, Harry Potter and the Prisoner of Azkaban, starring 13-year-old Harry, knocked the book Hannibal (Lecter) off its number-one place on bestseller lists. In a parody of tabloid journalism, a British newspaper's headline proclaimed: "Hannibal eaten for breakfast by 13-year-old."

It was a worldwide love affair that brought together millions of readers young and old, a cast of endearing fictional characters, and a talented and lucky author named J.K. Rowling. Make that Dame Rowling; on March 2, 2001, she was invested as an Officer of the Order of the British Empire by Prince Charles for her contribution to children's literature. Queen Elizabeth II had told Rowling that her 11-year-old granddaughter, Princess Eugenie, was a fan—as, it was reported, was Prince Charles himself, who may have identified with the gangly young hero at boarding school, awaiting his anointed destiny.

Librarians and booksellers happily noted that Harry Potter's popularity created a strong spillover effect. Facing a year's wait until the next Potter installment and suffering from P.W.S. (Potter Withdrawal Syndrome), young readers turned to other books, devouring the magical epics of Lloyd Alexander, Susan Cooper, Diana Wynne Jones, and others. Significantly, the Potter series attracted not only girls, always voracious series readers, but also throngs of boys. That had not been seen since the *Goosebumps* series crested earlier in the 1990s. But the *Goosebumps* craze had not spread to other titles; the boys wanted *Goosebumps* and little else. Not so with the chronicles of young Harry; after consuming the latest installment, boys were inspired to seek out related fantasy titles, reading voraciously.

To the consternation of some, the Potter books skyrocketed onto the coveted *New York Times* bestseller lists; at times, two or three Potter titles appeared on it simultaneously. Some cried foul; children's books should not take up spaces reserved for respectably adult books!

However, Rowling's books were not the first fantasy titles ostensibly for children to land on adult bestseller lists. Twenty-five years earlier, *Watership Down* (think *Aeneid,* with rabbits) did the same. In 1952, E.B. White's tale of a talking pig and spider, *Charlotte's Web,* spun its magic on that list for three weeks. Many other children's book authors, from Maurice Sendak to A.A. Milne, have long had devoted followings in adults. Dr. Seuss's classic *Oh, the Places You'll Go!*, for instance, is a popular gift for college graduates. There has been a long tradition of children's books, from *Alice in Wonderland* to *The Wizard of Oz*, being eagerly embraced by large audiences of all ages in their day—and many of these favorites have gone on to become enduring classics.

Some dissenting voices, however, decried the Potter books for the seemingly non-Christian themes embodied in the tales of wizardry. By the end of 2000, according to the Office for Intellectual Freedom of the American Library Association, Rowling's books hit the top of another list: the "most challenged books" list. Fundamentalists found it appalling to jest with images of magic, witchcraft, and demons. Demanding that the books be withdrawn from school and public libraries, these critics feared the series might lure young readers to engage in pagan practices—or at least weaken their Christian resolve in some fashion.

Despite such debate, it's unlikely that books as good-humored and positive as Harry Potter will suck youngsters into Druidic cults (although what child wouldn't sometimes wish for a magic wand or cloak of invisibility?). In the long run, no more readers will be drawn to the black arts than previous generations reading books of fantasy had been tempted to jump through mirrors or down rabbit holes.

In fact, many moderate Christian commentators spoke up for the positive traits found in the Harry Potter stories; they recognized the young fellow as a good-hearted underdog crusading against evil nasties. *Christianity Today* columnist Charles Colson said that Harry and his friends at Hogwarts "develop courage, loyalty, and a willingness to sacrifice for one another—even at the risk of their lives. Not bad lessons in a self-centered world." Wheaton College professor Alan Jacobs noted that the stories promote a message of "spiritual warfare" and "a struggle between good and evil." Jacobs felt the books offered "the possibility for serious moral reflection . . . the question of what to do with magic powers is explored in an appropriate and morally serious way."

As concerned parents read more closely, most tended to like what they saw. For better or worse, Harry Potter was getting kids reading. Most parents felt this was an improvement, that the books were more challenging than yet another *Goosebumps* novel, more thought-provoking than endless video games.

C.S. Lewis received a letter from the mother of a 9-year-old boy, asking for advice; her child was concerned that he loved the fictional lion Aslan in Narnia more than he did Jesus. Lewis wrote back, "I don't think he need be bothered at all. God knows all about the way a little boy's imagination works (He made it, after all) and knows that at a certain age the idea of talking and friendly animals is very attractive." —in the book, C.S. Lewis Letters to Children, edited by Dorsett & Mead, 1985

What is it that we find so enchanting in stories like these? Perhaps Harry Potter, like many heroes of fantasy, is endearing because he is rather ordinary. Surrounded by magic, he is the quintessential young, insecure schoolboy, seeking friendship from peers and respect from adults, learning to trust others, trying to stand up for what he thinks is right. While engaging in ongoing struggles with evil creatures of darkness, he is also fond of sports heroes (Quidditch players, of course), wizard trading cards, and jelly beans of every (yes, every) flavor.

In the best of fantasy, the world is infused with magic—but victory comes in the end, after all is said and done, from very human values of faith, courage, and perseverance. J.K. Rowling understands this. In an interview with Judy O'Malley for the American Library Association's *Book Links* (July, 1999), Rowling said:

> The book is really about the power of imagination. What Harry is leaning to do is to develop his full potential. Wizardry is just the analogy I use.

In fantasy, magic *is* the analogy; it is the spark that lights our imaginations, that fires up our dreams. Fantasy allows us to return for a few precious moments to that luminous realm of childhood, to a time when our unlimited powers of imagination and our hopes to discover our place in the real world were all one. From tales of Harry Potter's escapades at a school for young magicians to the adventures of hobbits battling orcs and ringwraiths in Tolkien's great epic, *The Lord of the Rings*, these are stories of our highest aspirations—to "touch that larger dream, that greater vision, that infinite knowing," as author Jane Yolen has said in her book on fantasy and fairy tales, *Touch Magic*.

Hopefully, these dreams of imagination do not leave us entirely once we become adults.

> The amazing thing about storytelling is that it has a universal pattern; the elements of "story" are the same for an American, a Frenchman, and a Pathan from faraway Hind.
> —George H. Scithers, et al., in On Writing Science Fiction: The Editors Strike Back, 1981

EIGHT REASONS WHY HARRY IS A SUCCESS

Harry Potter is the hobbit of the new millennium, the small individual drawn into a great quest. In many ways an ordinary fellow, young Potter is dropped into a maelstrom of eccentric characters, mysterious doings, and grand conflicts. In the cadences of these tales, we hear echoes of that same sense of wonder we felt when we read Tolkien's marvelous books. As they sweep across thousands of pages, these stories of hobbits and Hogwarts schoolboys recall something inside us hard to express—except in fantastic images of dragons we fear, magic we don't fully control, and heroes who step forth when called.

Author J.K. Rowling has committed to write seven books following this young apprentice magician and his schoolmates at Hogwarts School of Witchcraft and Wizardry. The success of the series has resounded around the globe—from Scotland to South Africa, from Canada to China. The enormous popularity of the Potter books (they reached the 100-million-sales mark in Spring 2001; in comparison, Tolkien's books have sold 50 million copies) is due to a remarkable convergence of elements that suggest some proven touchstones for success in writing fantasy stories.

1. THE FANTASY HERO MEETS THE SCHOOLBOY

Would you rather see a hero defeat Dark Lords of Evil, or school bullies? Why not both? In a famous essay, C.S. Lewis wrote that two types of stories were invariably popular with children: fantasy stories and schooldays stories. In fantasy tales like *Alice in Wonderland*, children could develop their individual imaginations as they fantasized about being in their own private worlds. On the other hand, Lewis recognized the appeal of popular stories like *Tom Brown's Schooldays* that chronicled the rise of immature striplings to gain the highest position of respect, the rank of the boarding school's Head Boy.

In his review of *Harry Potter and the Prisoner of Azkaban* (Book 3), fantasy author Gregory Maguire recalled that essay by Lewis and noted how the Potter books succeeded in combining the two threads: individual expressiveness and tribal allegiance. "While desiring heroic distinction, children also have to find their places in the herd."

A great deal of attention in the Potter books is given to Harry's social concerns, so crucial to any schoolchild. Harry is teased by bullies, builds a circle of close friends, and has bonding escapades. He discovers whom he can trust, whom to avoid, and whom he must stand up to. Readers feel the same sympathy for Harry and his friends when House Cup points are deducted unfairly by teachers, when opponents cheat at Quidditch, and when school bullies pester him as they do when Harry is faced with the classic fantasy mélange of ogres, dragons, and evil lords.

> Fantasy is hardly an escape from reality. It's a way of understanding it.
> —Lloyd Alexander

2. THE ENDEARING ORPHAN

Why do we love Harry Potter, and Taran the Assistant Pig-Keeper, and Dorothy in Oz? Because they are small, fairly ordinary, and often innocent in the ways of the world. And they are often orphans.

Sometimes in fantasy stories the main character has lost just one parent, usually at the beginning of a story. Cinderella loses her mother; her father remarries and Cinderella is neglected. Hansel and Gretel lose their mother; her father remarries and is pressured to abandon the young children in the woods. Then there's poor little Peter, in Beatrix Potter's *The Tail of Peter Rabbit*, whose father was shot by Farmer MacGregor!

In the realm of fantasy, the state of being an orphan has a greater purpose than just to tug at the heartstrings of sympathetic readers. The orphaned young hero has more opportunity to go out into the world alone. Parents are not around to limit this exploration.

If not killed off, parents are often simply left behind for most of the story, as in Peter Pan when the Darling children go to Never Never Land, or when Alice falls down the rabbit hole, or when Will in Susan Cooper's *The Dark is Rising* finds his family frozen in time as he is drawn into battle with evil forces. In the Narnia books, the children go through the wardrobe and are on their own. In Harry Potter, not only is Harry an orphan but all the students are far removed from parents, off in the world of the boarding school.

Yet one more plot twist is presented when a character is an orphan: the possibility that a surprise of parentage or family ties may be revealed later.

3. THE HERO'S QUEST

Harry Potter's tale fits the classic form of the Hero's Journey. Harry is separated from his home and brought up at first without knowledge of his powers. He bears a visible mark that sets him apart from others. He passes through a portal to enter another world, where he endures a series of trials, winning them one by one, each taking him closer to an ultimate test. Along the way, he gains friends—both animal and human helpers—and magical tools. He advances in knowledge and wisdom. He may be forced to sacrifice something precious to him for the greater good. In the end, his quest fulfilled, he returns home changed, although always not recognized as such by those left behind.

The key aspects of the Hero's Journey, as defined by the famous scholar of myths, Joseph Campbell, are repeated time and again in stories around the world. These are powerful stories of archetypal myth, what Campbell called "the one, shape-shifting yet marvelously constant story." The commonality of the stories gives them great power to hold our attention, as they also represent, according to psychologist Carl Jung, the story of our own inner growth, of our own private quests to conquer secret dragons inside us.

Natalie Babbitt, author of *Tuck Everlasting*, was surprised at how often the elements of the Hero's Journey turn up in fantasy stories—including, somewhat to her surprise, throughout her own book. Rereading Campbell, she realized how strongly these invisible patterns are imprinted on writers in the field.

> It is annoying in the extreme to find that one's work, struggled with for so long and finally finished after trying and discarding numberless bits of detail, can be found to have been summed up—parts of it, anyway—by [Joseph Campbell] years before one even began, and described as "typical." . . .
>
> Still, we have to come to the conclusion that all fantasy stories are fundamentally alike. Their patterns are immutable, and as writers we must follow them willy-nilly or suffer the consequences of a plot line gone askew. It is annoying, but it is miraculous, too.

Myths are the "masks of God," through which men everywhere have sought to relate themselves to the wonders of existence.
—Joseph Campbell

We are trapped, but it is a kind of confinement that joins us together in a brotherhood, writers and readers alike. . . . For the questions have never changed, and the answers are always the same.

—From "Fantasy and the Classic Hero," in *Innocence and Experience: Essays & Conversations on Children's Literature*, 1987, edited by Barbara Harris & Gregory Maguire

4. HARRY AS INTERNET PHENOMENON

Harry Potter's unique success has been created in part by avid young readers who, for the first time, have been able to communicate directly with each other around the world through the magic of the Internet. Countless websites have sprung up devoted to Potter discussion and trivia. Harry Potter's success can be attributed in part of the incredible power of the World Wide Web, as young Potterites gathered in virtual chat rooms to discuss the finer points of raising dragons from eggs or the architecture of Hogwarts School— or to speculate about whom Harry might eventually fall in love with.

As the Potter series spread across the world, with editions of the first three books by mid-2000 in 40 languages in 100 countries, the Internet became the town square for the community of fans, allowing them to converse with similar-minded folk, to share their personal opinions about the work and pass the excruciating time between the release of each volume in the series.

Kathleen Horning, a librarian at the Cooperative Children's Book Center at the University of Wisconsin, is convinced that the Internet fluency of today's cyber-literate kids has contributed to the swelling Potter phenomenon:

The home computer has had a big role in Harry's success. As children began to discover Harry Potter for themselves a few years ago, they spread the news to other children, not just on the playground but through cyberspace. Today it's not at all unusual to find a boy in Canada discussing the finer points of Harry's latest Quidditch match with a girl in Indonesia. Children around the world are inventing their own Hogwarts histories; drawing pictures of characters; writing stories, poems, and songs about Harry Potter; and sharing it all with each other through the Web.

—In *On Wisconsin* (UW alumni magazine), Winter 2000

5. FANTASY SERIES AND BLOCKBUSTER BRANDING

For publishers and booksellers, it is far easier to print, promote, and sell many copies of a single bestselling title than to reap the equivalent dollars spread across lots of lesser-known titles. The Yellow Brick Road to financial success is to develop brand-name recognition for authors. Whether the author is J.K. Rowling or Stephen King, mass-market branding is in full force when the name of the author appears on the front cover in type as large as, if not larger than, the title of the book.

The effect snowballs as more titles in a series are released. Successive titles sell better and also boost sales of past works; new readers quickly consume earlier titles to catch up with the story.

In fantasy, this is reinforced by the effort it takes an author to invent a highly imaginative world, with unique characters and special rules. Once done, it is always easier to revisit that world than to make up another. Series have become so dominant in fantasy today that the single "stand-alone" title is now the exception.

The pressure from fans and editors for sequels is hard to withstand even if an author wants to quit. L. Frank Baum, the author of the *Oz* series, did not want to continue the series, but endless letters from fans finally impelled him to write many more *Oz* books. If an author dies, publishers may negotiate with heirs to be allowed to continue the saga with other authors; Tor did this with the *Conan* novels; HarperCollins is planning the same with C.S. Lewis's tales of Narnia.

Besides buying the book and movie rights for Harry Potter, Warner Bros. is reportedly considering a theme park and a weekly television series (animated or live). Coca-Cola paid in the vicinity of $150 million for exclusive global partnership rights in conjunction with the first movie, its video, and the sequel.

The brand value of characters created, especially for children, can be immense. In Spring 2001, Disney bought all rights to Winnie-the-Pooh for a lump sum of $350 million, the corporate accountants realizing the long-term value of securing the charming bear—lock, stock, and honey pot.

As the gatekeeper to Oz's Emerald City at the end of the Yellow Brick Road exclaimed in amazement, "That's a horse of a different color!"

I knew that, at some point during that first lunch meeting, I would have to say, very tentatively, "Do you think you might want a sequel ... or two? Because, basically, I have planned seven." ...
Thank God, after the first course, he turned to me and said, "So, obviously we're thinking sequels."
—J.K. Rowling, interview with Judy O'Malley, in *Book Links*, July 1999

6. HUMOR GALORE

While Rowling has profited from the convergence of many forces that catapulted her books to bestseller status, she is the one who got it going by writing terrifically entertaining stories. Besides drawing on a mix of European mythology and classic fantasy, her books pack a solid punch of imaginative situations and laugh-out-loud humor.

The comical touches are a real pleasure: the odd ghosts who roam the halls; the quaint titles of magical textbooks; interactive diaries that write back; school songs that everyone sings together at their own pace and to their own tune; student assignments in classes like Defense Against the Dark Arts—or the History of Magic, taught by a ghost teacher who drones on about the Werewolves Convention of 1638 but is so absent-minded that he never noticed that he died one day; a three-headed hell-hound named Fluffy. . . . You get the picture. Rowling knows how kids would have a blast being a magician—setting off magical fireworks or riding in a flying car—and she milks these situations for all they are worth.

Other humor is drawn directly from the mind of the adolescent, with jelly beans in appalling flavors like spinach and tripe, threats to stick peoples' heads down toilets, and adventures that involve crawling through slimy places. In one scene, Harry, with the help of faithful companions Hermione Granger and Ron Weasley, fights a battle against a particularly gruesome mountain troll. In desperation, Harry jumps on the troll's back.

> The troll couldn't feel Harry hanging there, but even a troll will notice if you stick a long bit of wood up his nose, and Harry's wand had still been in his hand when he'd jumped—it had gone straight up one of the troll's nostrils.
>
> Howling in pain, the troll twisted and flailed its club, with Harry clinging on for dear life; any second, the troll was going to rip him off or catch him a terrible blow with the club.
>
> Hermione had sunk to the floor in fright; Ron pulled out his own wand—not knowing what he was going to do, he heard himself cry the first spell that came into his head: *"Wingardium Leviosa!"*
>
> The club flew suddenly out of the troll's hand, rose high, high up into the air, turned slowly over—and dropped, with a sickening crack, onto its owner's head. The troll swayed on the spot and then fell flat on its face, with a thud that made the whole room tremble.

With Harry Potter, there's no mention of Minerva McGonagall's unmet needs as a witch. .... The adults are not lecturing. In his new book, Bobos in Paradise, David Brooks comments that the offspring of baby boomers are "awash in moral instruction to an extent unprecedented even at the height of the Victorian era." In the Potter books, "there isn't one section about why they should recycle." Moreover, it's good vs. bad. Draco Malfoy isn't misunderstood, he's mean.
—Deirdre Donahue, in USA Today, June 8, 2000

Harry got to his feet. He was shaking and out of breath. Ron was standing there with his wand still raised, staring at what he had done.

It was Hermione who spoke first.

"Is it—dead?"

"I don't think so," said Harry, "I think it's just been knocked out."

He bent down and pulled his wand out of the troll's nose. It was covered in what looked like lumpy gray glue.

"Urgh—troll boogers."

He wiped it on the troll's trousers.

—*Harry Potter and the Sorcerer's Stone*, 1998, by J.K. Rowling

Maybe it's not Dickens, but a lot of readers will find themselves laughing out loud while reading Harry Potter books. No wonder children love this stuff; Rowling talks their language fluently. And adults find themselves realizing how much they would have enjoyed reading stories like these when they were young.

What is Dickensian are cleverly named secondary characters, a delightful mixture of evil schemers and dim-witted dunderheads. The most luscious are the dreadful Dursleys, Harry's unmagical stepparents who are completely mean-spirited and eternally clueless. At first, the Dursleys make Harry, left on their doorstep as an infant with a note, live in a spidery closet under the stairs and try to ignore him. Meanwhile, they dote absurdly on their doltish bully of a son, Dudley.

The contrast between Dudley and Harry is delightfully drawn in a deadpan style.

> Dudley looked a lot like Uncle Vernon. He had a large pink face, not much neck, small, watery blue eyes, and thick blond hair that lay smoothly on his thick, fat head. Aunt Petunia often said that Dudley looked like a baby angel—Harry often said that Dudley looked like a pig in a wig.
>
> Harry put the plates of egg and bacon on the table . . . . Dudley, meanwhile, was counting his presents. His face fell.
>
> "Thirty-six," he said, looking up at his mother and father. "That's two less than last year."
>
> "Darling, you haven't counted Auntie Marge's present, see, it's here under this big one from Mommy and Daddy."

Very often I get asked, "Who do you have in mind when you write? Is it your daughter or is it the children you've met?" No. It's for me. . . . The humor in the books is really what I find funny.
—J.K. Rowling, in interview with Linda Richards, January Magazine

"All right, thirty-seven then," said Dudley, going red in the face. Harry, who could see a huge Dudley tantrum coming on, began wolfing down his bacon as fast as possible in case Dudley turned the table over.

Aunt Petunia obviously scented danger, too, because she said quickly, "and we'll buy you another *two* presents while we're out today. How's that, popkin? *Two* more presents. Is that all right?"

Dudley thought for a moment. It looked like hard work. Finally he said slowly, "So I'll have thirty . . . thirty . . ."

"Thirty-nine, sweetums," said Aunt Petunia.

—Harry Potter and the Sorcerer's Stone

In contrast, Uncle Vernon and Aunt Petunia's mean, meager gifts to Harry for Christmas or a birthday are ridiculous items like a rubber band or a cast-off pair of Uncle Vernon's socks.

7. PAGE-TURNING SUSPENSE

Besides the ample humor, Rowling offers up a plot bursting with cliff-hanging suspense. Rowling shamelessly tantalizes and tips us off about things to come, revealing quite a bit but not all of what is around the corner. There is always something brewing, something worrying Harry. Mischief is afoot, as Harry and his friends struggle to figure out how to foil the nefarious plans of the bad guys.

We also know from the start that Harry is special. In the first chapter of Book One, *Harry Potter and the Sorcerer's Stone*, we are told he is destined for greatness, as the orphaned infant is left on the Dursleys' doorstep with a letter from Headmaster Dumbledore.

"A letter?" repeated Professor McGonagall faintly, sitting back down on the wall. "Really, Dumbledore, you think you can explain all this in a letter? These people will never understand him! He'll be famous—a legend—I wouldn't be surprised if today was known as Harry Potter day in the future—there will be books written about Harry—every child in the world will know his name!"

When Harry goes to Hogwarts, everyone stares at him in the halls; they know who he is and what he's done (survived the Evil Lord's deadly attack, which killed his parents). Plot points are laid out like a Persian carpet. A Quidditch match is coming. A three-headed hell-hound is guarding a trapdoor in a secret room in a forbidden corridor. A fellow student, the pure-blooded Malfoy, is out to get Harry. Hagrid is incubating a dragon's egg. One of the teachers is acting suspiciously. The forest beyond the school is forbidden. Oh, yes, and the Evil Lord is plotting to take over the world again.

When we reach chapters with titles like "The Midnight Duel" or "Through the Trapdoor," it is almost impossible to put down a Potter book. We want to find out what happens. Anticipation is one of the most delicious tastes of literature, and Rowling spoons out dollop after dollop, in a great banana-split dessert heaped with all the trimmings.

8. A HEART OF GOLD

The last piece of the puzzle is Rowling's heart of gold. She is truly fond of Harry and his friends, and she cares what happens to them. Touching moments occur in each book when Harry tenderly recalls his deceased parents. His relationships with his friends are very close. He spends time away from school with a big, rambunctious, surrogate family, the Weasleys. And his admiration for his patient mentor, Dumbledore, is genuine. Together, Harry and his friends stand up to hallway bullies and Evil Lords and always manage to carry the day, if by the skin of their teeth.

This pure love of an author for his or her own characters is impossible to ignore. Successful writers enjoy spending time with their creations. Tolkien had this fondness for his imaginary world of Middle-earth. He invented its runic language (which he could speak quite convincingly, as he was occasionally asked to do in interviews); he wrote its legends, he drew its maps.

Rowling clearly shares that passion, and successfully shares with us her loving concern for the student heroes of the Hogwarts School of Witchcraft and Wizardry.

THE HOLY GRAIL OF SUCCESS

Rowling herself is amazed at Harry's vast worldwide success—no author in her right mind would ever expect such things to happen. She has kept a fairly low profile, remaining committed to writing books that satisfy herself, sticking to her plan to write seven books to tell the story of Harry's amazing school years at Hogwarts.

One way to arouse curiosity ... is to imply that there must be a secret waiting to be revealed. What kind of secret? Well, it must be ... a crucial one, or it would not have been kept secret in the first place. The revelation then must be postponed for as long as possible.
—Joan Aiken, "Piquing the Reader's Curiosity," in The Writer, February 1996

As she told interviewer Linda Richards, for *January Magazine*, "I want to finish these seven books and look back and think that whatever happened ... I stayed true to what I wanted to write. This is my Holy Grail: that when I finish writing Book Seven, I can say, hand on heart, I didn't change a thing.

"Without permitting it to sound too corny, that's what I owe to my characters. That we won't be deflected—either by adoration or by criticism."

There has indeed been criticism—from those who feel that Rowling has borrowed too freely from the works of other fantasy authors. Certainly, many ideas found in the Harry Potter tales are not new. Consider a tale of a young lad who has just turned 11, with a bit of wizard's blood in him. He enters a school for fledgling magicians, held in a far-off castle with rather odd rooms, doors, and passageways, with pictures on the wall that wink back at him. He starts as a First Year student, forms friendships with a girl and a boy in his class, messes up some spells in classes like Curses and Transformations. Despite his unprepossessing experience, everyone knows when he arrives that he is destined to play a key role in saving the school from an evil lord.

Harry Potter? No, it's young Thornmallow, from Jane Yolen's 1991 novel, *Wizard's Hall*. Hints of Potter themes can also be found in the works of Diana Wynne Jones, whose *A Sudden Wild Magic* (1992) presents a Britain with a secret society of well-organized magicians going about their business in the midst of everyday life, or in the writings of British authors like C.S. Lewis, Roald Dahl, and Eva Ibbotson.

Yet as a series, Rowling's books promise to stand on their own in the annals of fantasy. Certainly they have already fulfilled Professor McGonagall's bold prophecy: that Harry Potter would be so famous that "nearly every child in the world will know his name." Today, that is amazingly close to the actual truth.

The message to aspiring writers is clear. Fantasy has been around a long time and is likely to remain in the forefront of popular literature for many years to come. As 21st-century biotechnology begins to tinker with the very building blocks of genetic life, the question of what truly makes us human—the stories we tell, the tales that touch our hearts—can only grow in significance.

[The rules of fiction] require that the author ... shall make the reader love the good people in the tale and hate the bad ones.
—Mark Twain

CHAPTER TWO

WHAT IS FANTASY?

W HAT EXACTLY IS FANTASY LITERATURE? To approach a working
definition, let's begin with this: Fantasy is "speculative fiction."
Fantasy creates a world imaginative to the highest degree,
populated with creatures, rules of magic, and places remarkably
different from the real world we see around us.

But science fiction is also "speculative fiction." Science fiction
clearly pushes the boundaries of imagination just as much as fantasy
does. Indeed, these two strands of fiction are often mingled freely
on bookshelves, in writer's organizations, and sometimes in the
pages of books themselves.

Science fiction, however, speculates in a very different manner.
The worlds of "SF" are based on an extrapolated aspect of real-life
natural laws. Jules Verne imagined submarines and space travel to
the moon. Asimov, Heinlein, and Clarke depicted space stations,
Mars exploration, supercomputers, artificial intelligence, and
genetic engineering. Such things were vaguely plausible, if far-
fetched at the time, yet much of it exists today. When we saw Neil
Armstrong set foot on the moon, we instantly recalled the stories of
Verne and H.G. Wells. Today, the technology set forth in George
Orwell's once-frightening novel, *1984*, where Big Brother uses sur-
veillance devices to eavesdrop on everyone, would hardly make
teenagers at the mall think twice.

SF turns science on its edge—pushes and twists it to the limits—
to create new futures or otherworlds, yet those imaginary worlds
are connected by a line of reasoning, however tenuous, back to
ours. Science-fiction authors strive to explain why these worlds
exist and how they work. The more inventive the explanation, the
better.

While science fiction looks outward, fantasy looks inward—into
ourselves, where wonder and wishes overcome knowledge, where
belief rules over science. The elves and fairies and dragons and

magicians of fantasy are not plausible. We will never find Alice's rabbit were we to peer down every dirt hole in England. Exploring with all our wishful hearts, we won't find the opening to Narnia hidden behind any piece of furniture. As adults and as children, we understand that fantasy is a trip to a purely imaginary place.

In fantasy, there is a rational disconnect between our real world and the fantasy world. We step through a magical portal and are in a place where things are different. There, magic happens with a wave of the wand or the chant of a spell. Of course, like all fiction, it needs internal rules and consistency. (The difference between fiction and reality, it has been noted, is that fiction needs to make sense.) Fantasy asks us to "believe," in a tolerant fairy-tale way. The more fanciful the story, the more delightful. Other times, what we savor is the eerie similarity of an incredible fantasy realm to our own real world.

We suspend rational assumptions and almost everything we learned in science class to enjoy Tolkien's hobbits as they strive to deal with a magical ring, the powers of which they do not fully understand. In the first Harry Potter book, we follow a young boy into a magic-wand store and are amused as a self-propelled tape-measure measures the space between his nostrils to determine "the proper fit," as the store's proprietor rummages through his stock for the right wand made of dragon's heartstrings and phoenix feathers.

Fantasy, then, is speculative fiction that takes one giant step inward. It is highly imaginative, wondrous fiction, rooted in inner beliefs and values. Fantasy is about good and bad, right and wrong. It startles us with wonder, yet soothes us like a familiar lullaby.

Fantasy easily gives birth to dragons and goblins, unicorns and hobbits, giants and talking animals. Magic is the coin of the realm, the force that replaces the natural laws of science fiction. Transformations happen by magic. A sword is pulled from a stone, or rises above a lake's surface, held aloft by a submerged lady's hand. Sleeping beauties slumber for eons in stone towers. Wraiths pass through solid walls. Talking spiders capture a band of dwarves and bind them fast, while an invisible hobbit ponders how to free them.

Fantasy celebrates the nonrational. Wrapped in a cloak of magic, it dares a rational reader to object to a frog suddenly being turned into a prince. Where an explanation would be required in science fiction, fantasy says: "Because it did." Though fantasy may offer some cause and effect—the prince probably did something wrong in

It has the general appearance of being science fiction, but it is not....There is mystery, mysticism, a feeling of indefinable, brooding horror ... this book quests for something it never touches.
—Saturday Review, in a review of Madeleine L'Engle's 1962 book, A Wrinkle in Time

the first place to cause him to be turned into a warty amphibian—no scientific rationale is required.

There is a *reason*, says science fiction. We *believe*, says fantasy.

Dorothy wishes to go home and clicks her heels, and she is home. There is no counter-cyclone that blows her back (or "worm-hole" or other vaguely Einsteinian explanation). There is only a pair of slippers (ruby in the movie, silver in the book), a little coaching from a kindly witch, and a belief that home is a good place.

This rootedness in belief and wonder is why fantasy is so often connected with religion. Some of the greatest fantasists like C.S. Lewis, George MacDonald, and Charles Williams were theologians. Fantasy is associated with core myths of religion. It also reflects a common wish to be able to escape the imprisonment of reality, to fulfill fantasies of the mind, if only in fiction. Most of all, it is closely connected with the innocence of childhood. For young children, life itself is belief and wonder. They have little proof of many things that they accept anyhow. Fantasy for children is as natural as the air, which they never see but breathe in and out nonetheless. Adults just have to try harder to achieve that naturalness.

"Having once believed wholeheartedly in something, we seldom lose the ability to believe. It is like learning to ride a bicycle."
—Lloyd Alexander, in "Wishful Thinking—Or Hopeful Dreaming?"

THE SOURCE OF BELIEF

Where does fantasy's belief start? It starts in the mind of the writer.

Peter S. Beagle, author of *The Last Unicorn* (1968), considered one of the great classics of 20th-century fantasy, commented on the effect of an author's own belief in his created world—so evident in the stories of J.R.R. Tolkien.

> . . . [T]here is one possible reason for Tolkien's popularity that I would like to put forward, because it concerns the real strength of *The Lord of the Rings*. . . .
>
> Tolkien believes in his world, and in all those who inhabit it. This is, of course, no guarantee of greatness—if Tolkien weren't a fine writer, it would not make him one—but it is something without which there is no greatness, in art or in anything else. . . . [The] failure of belief on the authors' part is, I think, what turns so many books . . . into the cramped little stages where varyingly fashionable marionettes jiggle and sing.

But I believe that Tolkien has wandered in Middle-earth, which exists nowhere but in himself, and I understand the sadness of the Elves, and I have seen Mordor.

—From "Tolkien's Magic Ring," 1966, by Peter S. Beagle

This river of belief emanates from the writer and draws the reader's imagination to its course, just as a divining rod is pulled down by invisible magnetism to trace a subterranean current of an underground stream.

Peter S. Beagle's own work shows the depth of a storyteller's belief in his own creations. He is able to fully imagine the fantastic and then to pull the reader into seeing what is happening. Here from his novel *The Folk of the Air* (1986) is a description of a character witnessing a magical transformation:

> Farrell had in his life seen more shape-changing than most people. Each time he handled the experience less well; it always left him feeling as wrenched and disoriented as if he were the one who had passed through the sweet, nauseating shudder in the molecules, to stumble into moonlight on four feet. He looked away, as always, when it happened with Aiffe, but not quickly enough.
>
> Her shoulders hunched and bulked, neck and legs shortening so quickly that she seemed to fall to her knees. The metamorphosis of her head was frightening enough—the bones visibly hollowing and streamlining, but the face itself plunging forward, not into a raptor's hooked beak, but becoming a kind of feathered muzzle, drooling through gray lips. The arms were the worst. They jolted up and out in electrical spasms, achieving magical angles, and Farrell heard them grinding in their sockets as they yanked Aiffe off the ground, even before rust-and-lichen colored feathers had fully formed. Her feet had turned to huge, yellow-gray talons, arthritically gnarled by their own massiveness. Even the scales on them looked like miniature claws.

—*The Folk of the Air*, Peter S. Beagle

In our rational society, we tend to be suspicious of the need for fantasy for adults. A book for adults labeled fantasy is usually shelved in a subsection of library or bookstore, safely segregated from mainstream fiction. Despite the quality, seriousness, and popularity of fantastic literature written for adults, fantasy is often considered legitimate only for children. Any fantasy book that has children as its protagonists, like Philip Pullman's trilogy, *His Dark Materials*, based loosely on Milton's epic poem *Paradise Lost*, is marketed as Young Adult fiction, despite the complexity of its philosophy.

Fantasy for children, however, is generally considered positive. We realize it stimulates the imagination—a good thing for most children. But some parents worry. Might children who read fairy tales grow up with unrealistic expectations? Will they harbor irrational fears of gingerbread houses or large black kettles? Might reading stories about dragons and magicians warp a child's mind to confuse fantasy with reality?

The answer is no. Fantasy is unmistakably metaphor—even to a child. As C.S. Lewis wrote:

> We long to go through the looking glass, to reach fairy land. . . . [But] Does anyone suppose that [a child] really and prosaically longs for all the dangers and discomforts of a fairy tale—really wants dragons . . . ? It is not so.
>
> It would be much truer to say that fairy land arouses a longing for he knows not what. It stirs and troubles him (to his lifelong enrichment) with the dim sense of something beyond his reach and, far from dulling or emptying the actual world, gives it a new dimension of depth.
>
> —C.S. Lewis, from "On Three Ways of Writing for Children," in *Of Other Worlds*, quoted in *The Game of the Impossible: A Rhetoric of Fantasy*, by W.R. Irwin

As one writer noted, it makes no more sense to believe that children will turn to witchcraft because of reading Harry Potter than that they would feel they need to talk to furniture after reading *Goodnight, Moon*.

Fantasy is an exercise machine for the young that develops their muscles of belief. It creates habits of the heart; it strengthens powers of creativity. Madeleine L'Engle wrote:

> I had a disturbed and angry letter from a young mother who told me that a friend of hers, with young children, gave them only instructive books; she wasn't going to allow their minds to be

"Goodbye," said the fox. "And now here is my secret, a very simple secret: It is only with the heart that one can see rightly; what is essential is invisible to the eye."
—The Little Prince (1943) by Antoine de Saint Exupéry

polluted with fairy tales. They were going to be taught the "real" world.

This attitude is a victory for the powers of this world. A friend of mine, a fine story-teller, remarked to me, "Jesus was not a theologian. He was God who told stories."

Yes. God who told stories.

St. Matthew says, "And he spake many things to them in parables. . . . and without a parable spake he not to them." . . .

The well-intentioned mothers who don't want their children polluted with fairy tales would not only deny them their childhood, with its high creativity, but they would have them conform to the secular world, with its dirty devices.

The world of fairy tale, fantasy, myth, is inimical to the secular world, and in total opposition to it, for it is interested not in limited laboratory proofs, but in truth.

—from "Healed, Whole and Holy," in *Walking on Water: Reflections on Faith & Art*, by Madeleine L'Engle

As a child, John Steinbeck was touched by the power of the British cycle of legends known as the tales of Arthur and the Knights of the Round Table. In the introduction to his own retelling of that saga, *The Acts of King Arthur and His Noble Knights*, Steinbeck recalled the lessons he had gleaned from his boyhood reading of those legends.

I think my sense of right and wrong, my feeling of noblesse oblige, and any thought I may have against the oppressor and for the oppressed, came from this secret book. . . . I was not frightened to find that there were evil knights, as well as noble ones. In my own town there were men who wore the clothes of virtue whom I knew to be bad. In pain or sorrow or confusion, I went back to my magic book. Children are violent and cruel—and good—and all of these were in the secret book. If I could not choose my way at the crossroads of love and loyalty, neither could Lancelot. I could understand the darkness of Mordred . . . and there was some Galahad in me. . . . The Grail feeling was there, however, deep-planted, and perhaps always will be.

—*The Acts of King Arthur and his Noble Knights*, 1952, John Steinbeck

It's a good thing to have all the props pulled out from under us occasionally. It gives us some sense of what is rock under our feet, and what is sand.
—Madeleine L'Engle, in The Summer of the Great-Grandmother, 1974

This from the man who wrote *The Grapes of Wrath*, one of the great crusading works of fiction fighting for the rights of the impoverished and unfortunate.

One of Britain's greatest mythic storytellers today, Brian Jacques, sees things much the same way. His beloved *Redwall* series is a colorful tapestry of seasonal celebrations, sumptuous feasts, and heroic feats of bravery and derring-do, all conducted by small forest creatures: mice, squirrels, moles, hedgehogs. Like the Arthurian tales, Jacques' books are also populated by truly evil characters—"foe-beasts" (predatory foxes, weasels, and stoats), each more sinister, cruel, and greedy than the last.

Children, Jacques feels, seek tales of heroes as small as they are.

> The child is trying to resolve something, to be better, to be a hero. If the little mouse can, why can't the child? This is what I wrote about. . . . There's a moral there somewhere, for them to pull themselves up by their bootstraps like Matthias and Mattimeo. They had to learn to do those things. They have to learn to be warriors.

—Brian Jacques, from an interview on British television

Once we believe—even if only within stories—in the chivalry of King Arthur's knights or in Harry Potter's struggles at Hogwarts, once we have stood with the brave small creatures of Redwall against the foe-beasts, or swayed with Frodo on the edge of the Crack of Doom, we begin to see the forms of good and evil. First as children, later as adults, we come to believe that even creatures as small as ourselves can play a role, that the world is affected by the actions we take.

What separates fantasy from much other fiction is the great import of decisions made by small folk. Will Narnia survive if the four children who have traveled through the wardrobe do not resist the guile of the Snow Queen who holds the world in her cold grip?

THE PURPOSE OF FANTASY

In a famous essay, "On Fairy Stories" (in *Essays Presented to Charles Williams*, ed. by C.S. Lewis, 1947), Tolkien offers three key aspects of stories set in the world of "Faerie": Recovery, Escape, and Consolation. By Recovery, he means recovering the power to see the world magically, with wonder, as we once had as children. Escape refers to leaving behind the restraints of a modernistic world (escaping what

Grown-ups never understand anything by themselves, and it is tiresome for children to be always and forever explaining things to them.
—From The Little Prince, by Antoine de Saint Exupéry, 1943

Tolkien derisively called "The Robot Age"); to momentarily be able to converse again with animals, for instance, as in the Garden of Eden before the fall from grace.

As Consolation, Tolkien points to the resolution of fairy stories in happy endings, in the return at the end to a normal world. These aspects of fantasy, says Tolkien, are not escapist. They embrace that which we most yearn for—an acute awareness of the beauty of the real world—by leaving it, imagining richly, and then returning.

Fantasy helps us develop good, if idealistic, goals. Fantasy stories reach for truth inside us, plumbing the deepest wells of belief and wonder. As children or adults, we still ache with pleasure when we read a story that reminds us that life is worthwhile and home precious, that the world is filled with good creatures as well as foe-beasts.

Fantasy is about journeying to strange worlds, but it is ultimately about arriving, in a state of surprise and grace, at a place inside ourselves. As Susan Cooper, author of *The Dark is Rising* trilogy, wrote in her 1981 essay, "Escaping into Ourselves":

> And I am always overcome by wonder . . . ; and I always think of Eliot:
>
> *We shall not cease from exploration*
> *And the end of all our exploring*
> *Will be to arrive where we started*
> *And know the place for the first time . . .*

[Fairy] tales say that apples were golden only to refresh the forgotten moment when we found that they were green. They make rivers run with wine only to make us remember, for one wild moment, that they run with water.
—G.K. Chesterton, "The Ethics of Elfland"

We will grow up to believe in something other than fairies and elves. But learning to believe—and to trust that belief will lead to good—is an important part of childhood.

Fantasy deals with Truths so large, so pure, that they can be expressed no other way. As we step through the looking glass with Lewis Carroll or gaze into the mirror of Erised (desire, reflected) in Rowling's books, when we don the enchanted rings of Tolkien or George MacDonald, or dodge the dragons of Le Guin and Stephen King, we are reminding ourselves that some things are too important to be kept in the silver cage of reason.

CHAPTER THREE

FIVE GOLDEN RINGS OF FANTASY

IN WRITING FANTASY, EVERY SINGLE THING, it seems, is on the table, open to re-thinking. This immense playing field can be daunting to a beginning writer. What if nothing in a story, even the concept of reality, can be taken for granted? Should a hero be threatened by trolls or vampires? Can they escape by moving by magic from one world to the next? What if time itself can be frozen? Should dragons weep, or pigs fly?

Despite the variety, fantasy takes shape in clusters of style. There are categories in fantasy—although everyone might not agree on exactly what to call them, or where one stops and another begins. To help fathom the secrets of successful books, we can begin by looking at fantasy as a set of five main styles—five golden rings of tradition. These rings are often interlinked. They are also elastic and flexible. They can be stretched to far limits, or they can be folded back on themselves, nested in any combination.

It is always risky to categorize creativity. Yet to the craftsperson, knowledge of traditional form is important. A quilter works inside a square frame, but has a nearly infinite choice of combinations of patterns, colors, and textures. In the same way, a writer never needs to feel restrained by fantasy's heritage—just informed by its time-tested success.

Often, categories of fantasy are based on a story's visible content: urban fantasy, time travel, ghost stories, humorous fantasy, and so on. But whether a given story involves speaking animals, knights in armor, time-traveling children, or modern characters is not the real question. Let's look inside stories to their core. How do different styles approach the issue of good and evil? How do they develop a sense of wonder and belief?

Some writers will follow forms closely; others will bend the rules and break the frame at every chance. Even then, knowledge of what is being bent and broken can help a writer succeed in the key act of

Affixing "labels" to writers, living or dead, is an inept procedure ... a childish amusement of small minds: and very "deadening," since at best it overemphasizes what is common to a selected group of writers, and distracts attention from what is individual (and not classifiable) in each of them, and is the element that gives them life....
—J.R.R. Tolkien, in The Letters of J.R.R. Tolkien, ed. by Humphrey Carpenter, 1981

writing: selecting from fantasy's immense choices. Making choices is ultimately what writing is about—facing the invisible dragon of the blank page.

HIGH FANTASY

When we say a book is "a fantasy story," most people think of what is described as "high fantasy." High fantasy tends to be set in feudal landscapes, with castles and baronial manors for the well-to-do, peasant cottages for the rest. The stories swarm with knights, kings and queens, and their consorts, retainers, ladies- and gentlemen-in-waiting, men-at-arms, falconers, jesters, clerics, and magicians. In high fantasy, these peaceful kingdoms are threatened by evil forces seeking to dominate, subjugate, and oppress.

High fantasy is about lofty purpose and great causes. It easily takes itself seriously, with its grand campaigns, gallant chivalry, and noble efforts. It also lends itself easily to parody, as in Mark Twain's story of the outsider, *A Connecticut Yankee in King Arthur's Court* (1889), as Twain's Yankee hero is transported across time and space to confound Merlin and the pompous knights of Merry Olde England.

In general, high fantasy is rooted in classical mythology and medieval European legends. It reflects the idiom of Crusade or Quest. With a sense of grand destiny, this ring of fantasy tackles head-on the question of Good and Evil.

High fantasy tends to view Evil as a great force, sometimes personified. The Dark Lord wages a relentless campaign against the beleaguered forces of Good. People (and animals) take sides; they enter the fray on one side or the other, sometimes covertly. Sometimes they find themselves fooled at first, or change sides in the course of the story. The back-and-forth struggle is clearly drawn, often in near-religious terms: right versus wrong.

In the plot, a small band of heroes are pulled into the sweep of history. These foolhardy and oddly matched characters chase about the countryside in search of powerful talismanic objects: rings and swords, books of enchantment, answers to riddles. Possession of these things will change the balance of power, causing whole kingdoms to wax glorious or collapse.

The diminutive, somewhat ordinary heroes are forced to battle with forces far more powerful than they. They struggle to come to grips with their own role in this great undertaking. Eventually, they must face a big decision: to do the right thing, often involving some

There is no such thing as a true tale. Truth has many faces and the truth is like the old road to Avalon; it depends on your own will and your own thoughts, wither the road will take you.
—Marion Zimmer Bradley, in The Mists of Avalon, 1982

sacrifice—to carry a ring to its rightful owner, or free a damsel from the tower, or fulfill a grand prophecy.

The "struggle" or "quest" may also take shape as a journey of enlightenment—searching for one's real identity, growing up, discovering hidden powers. Often, this personal quest is woven into the larger political or religious struggle.

At some point, although it may stretch out over several books, as does C.S. Lewis's *Narnia* series, high fantasy often comes down to a big battle or duel. Aslan the God-lion is killed, but is reborn to triumph in the end. The Ring is cast into the Crack of Doom, and the menace of Sauron is defeated, or at least averted. The course of the world is changed. Goodness triumphs, the Dark Lord is crushed— or forced to slink away ignominiously, evil teeth gnashing.

Tolkien stated, "I wanted a large canvas." His masterpiece, *The Lord of the Rings*, was intended to be one unified story; his publishers persuaded him to divide it into three volumes to accommodate readers' pocketbooks. Following in the footsteps of Tolkien, high fantasy today commonly runs to multiple volumes—but not an unlimited number. A trilogy or tetralogy is traditional, allowing the author to thread the loom in the first volume, then weave the ongoing pattern through the middle book (or books), and finally tie up all loose ends by the conclusion of the last volume. Many high-fantasy epics, for example, have drawn on the story of King Arthur, including *The Once and Future King*, by T.H. White (four volumes, published in the 1950s), and Mary Stewart's *The Crystal Cave* trilogy, popular in the 1970s.

> If you ask me, "What was the greatest story ever told?" I'd say, "King Arthur—with a little more emphasis on the girls."
> —Jane Yolen, interview in The Writer magazine, March 1997

ADVENTURE FANTASY

A second ring of fantasy is found in the popular form of the fantasy adventure. Unlike high fantasy, which tends to elevate the story to Crusade or Quest, this ring of fantasy accepts the notion of adventure for its own sake. The purpose of such books is to seek adventures, small and large, and to have a rollicking good time doing it.

The escapades in adventure fantasy are shaped mostly by the internal desires of their protagonists, rather than epic struggles between Good and Evil. Robert E. Howard's prototypical hulk, Conan, wants swordplay, loot, and maidens, and he goes looking for them. Fritz Lieber's duo, Fafhrd and the Gray Mouser, want money, banter, and maidens, and they too go looking for them.

They are not being swept into the current of great battles; they willingly step out onto the streets of Lankhar looking for a good time.

Adventure fantasy has long been popular in America. Perhaps this has to do with America's preference for self-made adventure over the ancient, rooted-in-place legends of the Old World. The American frontier spawned tall-tale heroes such as Mike Fink, Paul Bunyan, Pecos Bill, and others whose escapades were absurd and self-propelled, as endless as the teller's imagination.

The Wizard of Oz (1900), by L. Frank Baum, is one of those adventure classics linked to American populism. Leaving Kansas on the winds of a tornado, Dorothy has a grand adventure, wins friends, and returns home. While Wicked and Good Witches exist in Oz, the imaginary land is not really a place where good and evil are locked in a great struggle. The witches have their regions, the Wizard has his, and they all are living fairly happily together until Dorothy and her annoying little dog and motley friends upset the balance of power, defrock the great wizard, crush a few feudal witches, and leave Oz to fend for itself when Dorothy returns home to her Kansas plain folk.

Some adventure fantasy is called "sword and sorcery," a term attributed since the 1960s to author Fritz Lieber, University of Chicago graduate and creator of the Fafhrd and the Grey Mouser adventure series. Sword-and-sorcery flourished in the "pulp" magazines popular since the early 1900s, digest-sized magazines like *Weird Tales* and *All-Story*. Such magazines featured tales like those by Robert E. Howard, creator of Conan the Barbarian, who first appeared in 1932. This style was derived in turn from the earlier writings of fantastic-adventure storytellers like H. Rider Haggard (*King Solomon's Mines*, 1885, and *She*, 1887), Rudyard Kipling's *Jungle Books,* Arthur Conan Doyle's tales of lost worlds, and the novels of Edgar Rice Burroughs, such as *Tarzan of the Apes* (1912).

These quick-thinking, fairly violent, sometimes amoral, adventurous heroes still are popular today in fantasy novels by Michael Moorcook and others, as well as in the pages of super-hero (and anti-hero) comic books and graphic fiction.

Similar to high fantasy, adventure fantasy is awash in magicians and magical beasts, in quests for any and everything, with enchanted rings, amulets, and swords with cryptic inscriptions stacked high in every castle closet and treasure hoard. While adventure fantasy tends to assume male heroes, relegating females to stock roles as temptresses or damsels in distress, there is a healthy

When I was a boy, writers to me meant people with "Sir" in front of their name, and three or four names—Sir Arthur Conan Doyle and Robert Louis Stevenson. These were the type of books my Dad would give me to read. He would say, "Read this, son, it's a good yarn."
…I like my work to be termed "romantic adventure."…I think that bookshops, besides having a Fantasy section and a Science Fiction section…should have a Good Yarns section. You'd know right where to go!
—Brian Jacques, interview in Locus magazine, November 1995

strain of sword-wielding women heroes, the first of whom was "Jirel of Joiry" (who appeared in 1934 in *Weird Tales*). More recent authors like Tanith Lee and others have continued that tradition of sword-wielding heroines.

Beyond the "sword and sorcery" style, adventure fantasy also encompasses tales of more diminutive adventurers, often featuring animals and sometimes small children as heroes. Examples are mild-mannered stories like *The Wind in the Willows* or the Winnie-the-Pooh series, where exclamations no saltier than Pooh's "Oh, bother!" or Toad's "Hang spring-cleaning!" are interspersed with a series of innocuous adventures: getting stuck in a honey pot or driving recklessly in an old roadster.

> "What's the matter?" asked Piglet.
>
> "It's a very funny thing," said Bear, "but now there seem to be *two* animals now. This—whatever-it-was—has been joined by another—whatever-it-is—and the two of them are now proceeding in company. Would you mind coming with me, Piglet, in case they turn out to be hostile Animals?"
>
> Piglet scratched his ear in a nice sort of way, and said that he had nothing to do until Friday, and would be delighted to come, in case it really *was* a Woozle.
>
> "You mean, in case it really is two Woozles," said Winnie-the-Pooh, and Piglet said that anyhow he had nothing to do until Friday. So off they went together.

—*Winnie-the-Pooh*, 1926, by A.A. Milne

Adventure-fantasy yarns share a common goal: to satisfy the desires of their characters for interesting escapades. The adventures come in turn straight from our own wishful imaginations: to wield mighty swords, to seek out buxom maidens, and to exchange barbs with barrel-chested barbarians—or simply to indulge in little walks, tasty dinners, cozy homes, and visits from charming friends. This type of fantasy probably best represents the wish-fulfillment often attributed to fantasy in general.

These stories seldom offer the culminating quest or defining moment found in Tolkien or other high fantasists. Instead, the escapades often end with a return home—but you are left with the suspicion that the characters will venture out again soon. These stories lend themselves well to open-ended series, like the numerous

A partial list of sequels to the original Conan novels of Robert E. Howard, written by diverse authors and published by Tor Books:

Conan the Invincible
Conan the Defender
Conan the Unconquered
Conan the Triumphant
Conan the Magnificent
Conan the Destroyer
Conan the Victorious
Conan the Valorous
Conan the Fearless
Conan the Renegade
Conan the Raider
Conan the Champion
Conan the Defiant
Conan the Warlord
Conan the Marauder
Conan the Valiant
Conan the Hero
Conan the Bold
Conan the Indomitable
Conan the Freelance
Conan the Great
Conan the Formidable
Conan the Outcast
Conan the Relentless
Conan the Rogue
Conan the Savage ...

novels of Conan the Barbarian or the "Elric" tales by Michael Moorcock.

Evil in adventure fantasy is not grand Evil personified, but a more obscure cousin: Chaos. In adventure fantasy, forces of evil (or uncertainty) are everywhere in never-ending supply: dragons, sorcerers, scheming barbarians, stalking Heffalumps. Unlike big Evil, Chaos is fluid, constant. As one barbarian horde is defeated, another is looming just beyond the horizon, ready for the sequel. Even in the small adventures of the "Oh, bother!" sort, one small triumph or setback just leads to the next.

However, throughout the fantasy adventure tale runs a distinct thread: a moral code. Adventure fantasy glorifies the cult of the good knight (for Pippi Longstocking, that of freckled super-strong girl), gallivanting about to save those in distress, freeing all from the cruel yoke of monster, dragon, or pirate. Conan's code, while not something you'd call moral, at least had its principles: stubbornness and brute strength will prevail. For Ali Baba, there was honor among thieves. And Pooh felt there was a right way to go about things: with self-important nonchalance.

A moral code is what keeps the endless forces of chaos at bay. Like the samurai warrior or the knights of the Round Table, the heroes of adventure fantasy are chivalrous and charming, prone to honesty, willing to sacrifice to help the weaker. In the *Redwall* series, the code is clearly articulated at least once per novel to the young mice, voles, and squirrels of the community.

> "You were born in Redwall, you know the rules of our Abbey: to live in peace with others, never to harm another creature needlessly, to comfort, assist, and be kind to all."
>
> —*Mattimeo*, 1990, by Brian Jacques

FAIRY TALES

A third ring of fantasy—in many ways the direct opposite of the sweeping canvas of high fantasy and the rollicking escapades of adventure tales—is the delicate canvas of the fairy tale. While in many ways a smaller form, it is no less ambitious; think of a miniature painting, which still contains an entire world within its borders. Fairy tales range from "once upon a time" bedtime stories to the published collections of literary practitioners, from Charles Perrault in

"The first law the dreamthief obeys says, 'Offers of guidance must always be accepted but never trusted.' The second says, 'Beware the familiar,' and the third tells us, 'What is strange should be cautiously welcomed.'"
—Michael Moorcock, The Fortress of the Pearl, 1989

the 17th century to Hans Christian Andersen in the 1800s to stories by today's Jane Yolen, Patricia McKillip, Donna Jo Napoli, and others.

The name "fairy tale" is misleading; only a small number involve fairies. The German term is Märchen, freely translated as tales of wonder.

Fairy tales tend to deal with personal transformation. In fairy tales, people (or creatures) change in dramatic, often miraculous ways, and this is at the heart of the story. The ugly duckling is transformed into a beautiful swan, the toad into a prince, a cinder-maid into a princess, the fool into a wise person.

Also, fairy tales explore on a very individual level the invisible boundary between the safety of home and the dangers that lie beyond (and that occasionally force their way into the cottage). In their simplest forms, they make perfect bedtime stories for the child resting in the cozy bed, on the boundary between being awake and crossing over into the magical world of dreams.

Fairy tales look out from the warmth of the hearth—or cottage, village, or protective castle walls—to the unknown, possibly evil world of the dark forest—the foreign land, the big city, the land of the wealthy, the odd strangers, the wilderness realm of monsters. Set mostly at home, or out in the everyday world, these tales are easily recognized by their settings, close to home, full of detail.

A proper fairy tale is anything but an untruth; it goes to the very heart of truth. It goes to the very hearts of men and women and speaks of the things it finds there: fear, courage, greed, compassion, loyalty, betrayal, despair, and wonder.
—Terri Windling, from her introduction to Snow White, Blood Red, edited by Ellen Datlow and Windling, 1993

"I believe the Spring has come at last," said the Giant; and he jumped out of bed and looked out.

What did he see?

He saw a most wonderful sight. Through a hole in the wall the children had crept in, and they were sitting in the branches of the trees. In every tree he could see there was a little child. And the trees were so glad to have the children back again that they had covered themselves with blossoms, and were waving their arms gently above the children's heads. The birds were flying about and twittering with delight, and the flowers were looking up through the green grass and laughing. It was a lovely scene, only in one corner of the garden it was still winter. It was the farthest corner of the garden, and in it was standing a small boy.

—Oscar Wilde, "The Selfish Giant"

While fairy tales were banished in Victorian times to the nursery, earlier fairy tales were powerful, often gruesome cautionary tales. Even the fairies for whom the genre is named were once held to be dangerous, malevolent, annoyed if crossed, and prone to taking revenge in dreadful ways.

Perusal of even the smallest bit of fairy tale scholarship quickly reveals the archetypes lurking behind tales only known today as Disney remakes for children. Powerful older versions of Cinderella, Snow White, Beauty and the Beast, or Little Red Riding Hood have been gutted, with only a few hints of their original dark shadows and true passions.

When the little cupid in the gilt clock on the mantlepiece struck its miniature tambourine, she was astonished to discover it did so twelve times.
"So late! You will want to sleep," he said....
He drew back his head and gazed at her with his green, inscrutable eyes, in which she saw her face repeated twice, as small as if it were in bud.
Then, without another word, he sprang from the room and she saw, with an indescribable shock, he went on all fours.
—Angela Carter, in "The Courtship of Mr. Lyons," from The Bloody Chamber and Other Stories, 1979

[in Giambattista Basile's 17th-century collection of fairy tales, The Pentamerone], Sleeping Beauty, known as Talia, falls into a death-like sleep when a splinter of flax is embedded under her fingernail. She sleeps alone in a small house hidden deep within the forest. One day a King goes out hawking and discovers the sleeping maiden. Finding her beautiful, and unprotesting, he has sex with her—while Talia, oblivious to the King's ardent embraces, sleeps on. The King leaves the forest, returning not only to his castle but also to his barren wife. Nine months later a sleeping Talia gives birth to twins named Sun and Moon. One of the hungry infants, searching for his mother's breast, suckles her finger and pulls out the flax splinter. Freed of her curse by the removal of the splinter, Talia wakes up and discovers her children. After a time, the King goes back to the forest and finds Talia awake, tending to their son and daughter.

Delighted, he brings them home to his estate—where his barren wife, naturally enough, is bitter and jealous. As soon as the King is off to battle, the wife orders her cook to murder Sun and Moon, then prepare them as a feast for her unwitting husband. The kind-hearted cook hides the children and substitutes goat in a dizzying variety of dishes. The wife then decides to murder Talia by burning her at the stake. As Talia undresses, each layer of her fine clothing shrieks out loud. . . . Eventually the King hears the sounds and comes to Talia's rescue. The jealous wife is put to death, the cook reveals the children's hiding place, and the King and Talia are united in a proper marriage.

—"Sleeping Beauty," by Midori Snyder

Today's authors use resilient fairy-tale forms to explore modern relationships. Their stories blend fairy-tale mischief, malice, and moxie with contemporary issues of dysfunction, alienation, disenfranchisement. The evil stepparent, the child bride, the wicked witch, are reinterpreted to examine social injustices and evil deeds—from abject poverty to child abuse. They also explore the eventual redemption found in tales of wonder—the transformation or forgiveness needed to live "happily ever after" in today's uncertain world. As Midori Snyder notes, Sleeping Beauty today takes on new forms; "portrayed in many different guises: as a helpless 1950s stay-at-home girl, a bold space opera heroine, an oppressed time-traveling queen, a stoic Holocaust survivor, a sexually abused child, and myriad others."

Despite the attempts of Disney to undermine the power of fairy tales, today's mythic fiction writers claim its rightful power. As author and fairy-tale scholar Jane Yolen points out in her essay, "Once Upon a Time":

> Cinderella, until lately, has never been a passive dreamer waiting for rescue. The fore-runners of the Ash-girl have all been hardy, active heroines who take their lives into their own hands and work out their own salvations. . . .
>
> To make Cinderella less than she is, an ill-treated but passive princess awaiting rescue, cheapens our most cherished dreams and makes a mockery of the magic inside us all—the ability to change our lives. [The Disney film version] set a new pattern for Cinderella: a helpless, hapless, pitiable, useless heroine who has to be saved time and time again by the talking mice and birds because she is "off in a world of dreams." It is a Cinderella who is not recognized by her prince until she is magically back in her ball gown, beribboned and bejeweled.
>
> Poor Cinderella, Poor us.

—Quoted in "White as Snow: Fairy Tales and Fantasy," by Terri Windling, in *Snow White, Blood Red*, 1993

Where high fantasy promotes great causes, and adventure stories teach codes of behavior, the fairy tale often comes down in the end to a practical lesson, usually learned the hard way, of personal and practical household value—about the difference between foolishness

You always read about it: the plumber with twelve children / who wins the Irish Sweepstakes. From toilets to riches. That story.

Or the nursemaid, some lucious sweet from Denmark / who captures the oldest son's heart. From diapers to Dior. That story.

—Anne Sexton, from her poem, "Cinderella," in Transformations, 1971 and wisdom, cowardice and pluckiness, industry and lassitude, worthiness and dumb luck.

These truths belong in the nursery, surely, but not only there. The ancient images of wolves, toothless soothsayers, dim-witted ogres, and scheming in-laws—and their constant, ultimate defeat at the hands of clever Ash-lads and Ash-girls—belong at the heart of the world's first and best literature, to be shared from the cradle to the grave.

Fairy tales deal ultimately with choices we all make every day: to help a stranger, to face a fear, to conquer our base instincts—so that by the end of our second of three wishes, we don't have a sausage stuck on our nose and have to waste that precious third wish to remove it.

In fairy tales, indeed, we have met the enemy and he is us. Fairy tales have given us our most memorable villains: the jealous witch in Snow White, the stepsisters of Cinderella, the wolf of Little Red Riding Hood.

Are they not so villainous precisely because they reside so close to home?

MAGIC REALISM

The fourth ring of fantasy, magic realism, produces stories in which magical things happen, often unexpectedly, in the midst of very realistic, everyday settings and events. These marvelous occurrences may be mysterious, but often they are very clear in what they portend. In these stories, magic is more likely to act as an independent character than as a tool used by the other characters.

As Sheila Egoff points out in her study of fantasy literature, *Worlds Within* (1988), a characteristic feature of "enchanted realism" is that, unlike in classic fantasy or fairy tales: "The [protagonists] of enchanted realism do not change the world; instead they themselves are changed. . . ."

In Gabriel Garcia Marquez' novel, *One Hundred Years of Solitude* (1967), the people of José Arcadio Buendía's village are enchanted by a sudden onslaught of magical gypsies.

> . . . whose dances and music sowed a panic of uproarious joy through the streets, with parrots painted all colors reciting Italian arias, and a hen who laid a hundred golden eggs to the sound of a tambourine, and a trained monkey who read minds, and the

multiple-use machine that could be used at the same time to sew on buttons and reduce fevers, and the apparatus to make a person forget his bad memories, and a poultice to lose time, and a thousand more inventions so ingenious and unusual that José Arcadio Buendía must have wanted to invent a memory device so that he could remember them all. In an instant they transformed the village. The inhabitants of Macondo found themselves lost in their own streets, confused by the crowded fair.

—*One Hundred Years of Solitude*, Gabriel Garcia Marquez, 1967 (English transl. 1970)

Then, in a passage which reveals another trick of magical realism, the tables of magic are turned. Before the gypsies depart, they offer the townspeople one last wonder. Inside a tent, guarded by a giant with a shaved head and a copper nose-ring, sits a large treasure chest. Inside is nothing but an enormous translucent block of ice, revealed to all who will pay to touch its oddly fiery cold surface.

This, too, is magic realism: the fantastic is transmuted back into the ordinary. Surprises, revelations, visions, and paradoxes are the coins of magical realism. Everyday reality is magical when seen in proximity to the astounding. In this back-and-forth trapeze act, magic realism offers the "Consolation" that Tolkien found in fantasy—the amazing return home to normalcy—throughout the story, rather than only at the end of book.

Magic realism crosses over readily into modern "mainstream" fiction. The term is used to describe the writings of Gabriel Garcia Marquez, Jorge Luis Borges, Günther Grass, Milan Kundera, Isaac Bashevis Singer, Louise Erdrich, and many others whose works are seldom found in fantasy "ghettos" in bookstores or libraries. Yet these stories are clearly the literature of fantasy. They deal with the same issues of good and evil, seen through the filtered light of magic, wonder, and belief.

In magic realism, sometimes the magic is for the good, as characters are overwhelmed by moments of beauty or passion.

On her the food [quail in rose petal sauce] seemed to act as an aphrodisiac; she began to feel an intense heat pulsing through her limbs. . . .

[After eating] The only thing that kept her going was the image of the refreshing shower ahead of her, but unfortunately she was

The dolphin stood tall and naked on the sand, and the moon gave him a new body and new clothes. He went to the fiesta. He danced with his hat on, so no one would see the breathing hole in his head. And he left the crowd with their mouths open: everyone was astonished by his reddish skin with blue glimmers and by the look from his widely spaced eyes, and by his thirst that liters upon liters of pure cane liquor would not quench.
—Eduardo Galeano, Walking Words, 1993, (English transl. 1995)

never able to enjoy it, because the drops that fell from the shower never made it to her body: they evaporated before they reached her. Her body was giving off so much heat that the wooden walls began to split and burst into flame. Terrified . . . she ran out of the little enclosure just as she was, completely naked.

By then the scent of roses given off by her body had traveled a long, long way. All the way to town, where the rebel forces and the federal troops were engaged in a fierce battle. One man stood head and shoulders above the others for his valor; it was the rebel who Gertrudis had seen in the plaza in Piedras Negras the week before.

A pink cloud floated toward him, wrapped itself around him, and made him set out at a gallop toward Mama Elena's ranch . . . without knowing why he did so. A higher power was controlling his actions. He was moved by a powerful urge to arrive as quickly as possible at a meeting with someone unknown in some undetermined place. But it wasn't hard to find. The aroma from Gertrudis' body guided him.

—*Like Water for Chocolate*, by Laura Esquivel, 1989 (English transl. 1992)

In other stories, tricks are played that trip up human protagonists, playing on their greed or other foibles, bringing the high and mighty face down in a street puddle. Magic realism is the story form of ancient mythic tales, the literature especially of Trickster, known to different cultures as Coyote, Anansi, Loki, Hermes, and so on. Trickster is a complex shape-shifter. Terri Windling calls him:

. . . a paradoxical creature who is both very clever and very foolish, a cultural hero and destructive influence—often at one and the same time. In the legends of many societies, it's Trickster who is responsible for giving humans fire, language, hunting skills, or even life itself . . . but he's also the one who brought us death, hunger, difficult childbirth, illness, and other woes. Alan Garner (the great British fantasy writer and folklorist) calls Trickster: "the advocate of uncertainty. . . . He draws a boundary for chaos, so that we can make sense of the rest. He is the shadow that shapes the light."

—"Wile E. Coyote and Other Sly Trickster Tales," by Terri Windling, from *Realms of Fantasy* magazine, 1997

In magic realism stories, the world naturally contains black and white, waxing and waning, the yin and the yang. The world is permeated with magical forces, small and large. The line between reality and dreams is often blurred, as are the lines between history and story, events and truth, reality perceived and actual.

Magic realists raise the question that Jorge Luis Borges asked: What if the world we believe is reality is some sort of dream? And if so, who is dreaming it? Louise Erdrich echoes this question in the closing page of her World Fantasy Award-winning novel, *The Antelope Wife*, with its central image of beading (in the floral patterns of the Woodland Indian tradition) to signify life itself.

> Did these occurrences have a paradigm in the settlement of old scores and pains and betrayals that went back in time? Or are we working out the minor details of a strictly random pattern? Who is beading us? Who is setting flower upon flower and cut-glass vine? Who are you and who am I, the beader or the bit of colored glass sewn onto the fabric of this earth? All these questions, they tug at the brain. We stand on tiptoe, trying to see over the edge, and only catch a glimpse of the next bead on the string, and the woman's hand moving, one day, the next, and the needle flashing over the horizon.

> —*The Antelope Wife*, 1998, Louise Erdrich

In magic realism, abstract thoughts and concepts become real. Something intangible is given sudden visible form, like the pink cloud of passion in *Like Water for Chocolate* that pulls the revolutionary soldier to Gertrudis, or the concept of transformation, as when Gregor awakes in Kafka's novel to discover he is a big bug. But absurd it is not. These are not the melted shapes of surrealism. On the contrary, magic realism tends to refine and express concepts clearly, more purely than in the murkiness of real life.

One writer suggested that Tolkien fantasy is inherently Protestant, with its reliance on the profound meaning of each individual's actions. Magic realism on the other hand is more Catholic, with its belief in magical transformation from outside, mysterious powers. In any case, magic realism is fantasy, but one in which the key rules are often invisible to the humans involved.

Are we the beader—or are we a bit of colored glass following the dancing needle?

DARK FANTASY

The forms by which men and women are haunted are far more diverse and subtle than we knew.
—Ernest Rhys, editor, The Haunters and the Haunted: Ghost Tales and Tales of the Supernatural, 1921

The fifth important ring of fantasy is dark fantasy. Dark fantasy encircles the historic core of horror and gothic fiction, but has grown broader and harder to define, sidling up to dark themes of sharp satire, urban decay, erotic fiction, and other edgy, marginal topics.

In popularity, this branch of fantasy has seen a tremendous rise since the 1970s, with the burgeoning careers of masters of the craft Stephen King, Anne Rice, and other. But it has antecedents in the weird tales of New England's H.R. Lovecraft and his followers, like Wisconsin author August Derleth, in the earlier part of the 1900s. Before that, tales of the macabre were well established in literature in the novels of Mary Shelley (*Frankenstein*), Bram Stoker (*Dracula*), Wilkie Collins (*The Moonstone*), Edgar Allen Poe, Arthur Conan Doyle, and others in the late 1800s.

> . . . I saw something moving round the foot of the bed, which at first I could not accurately distinguish. But I soon saw that it was a sooty-black animal that resembled a monstrous cat. It appeared to me about four or five feet long, for it measured fully the length of the hearth-rug as it passed over it; and it continued to-ing and fro-ing with the lithe sinister restlessness of a beast in a cage. I could not cry out, although as you may suppose, I was terrified. Its pace was growing faster, and the room rapidly darker and darker, and at length so dark that I could no longer see anything of it but its eyes. I felt it spring lightly on the bed. The two broad eyes approached my face, and suddenly I felt a stinging pain as if two large needle darted, an inch or two apart, deep into my breast.

—from "Carmilla," by J.S. Le Fanu, from *In a Glass Darkly*, 1872

The roots of horror go much farther, to Beowulf, with the monster Grendel's attacks to gorge itself on human flesh, or to age-old tales of dragons and other fantastic creatures who wrought destruction and demanded human sacrifices. The fiends of Greek and Roman legend were a vicious lot: harpies, minotaurs, and the like. From Gilgamesh to the Bible, ancient writings are hard to beat when it comes to truly terrifying monsters.

. . . Before the gates there sat
On either side a formidable shape;
The one seemed woman to the waist, and fair,
But ended foul in many a scaly fold
Voluminous and vast, a serpent armed
With mortal sting: about her middle round
A cry of hell hounds never ceasing barked
with wide Cerberian mouths full loud, and rung
A hideous peal: yet, when they list, would creep
If aught disturbed their noise, into her womb . . .

—From *Paradise Lost*, John Milton

The field of dark fantasy has many sub-rings. One is an ever-popular wealth of ghost stories. From the galloping headless horseman in Washington Irving's tale to Hamlet's ghost in Shakespeare's drama to Oscar Wilde's comic ghost of Canterville, this ring of fantasy has always held a compelling fascination, with its questioning of the finality of death.

In the center of the picture was a great irregular patch of brown canvas, as fresh as when it was stretched on the frame. The background was as before, with chair and chimney corner and rope, but the figure of the Judge had disappeared.

Malcolmson, almost in a chill of horror, turned slowly round, and then he began to shake and tremble like a man in a palsy. His strength seemed to have left him, and he was incapable of action or movement, hardly even of thought. He could only see and hear.

There, on the great high-backed carved oak chair, sat the Judge in his robes of scarlet and ermine, with his baleful eyes glaring vindictively, and a smile of triumph on the resolute, cruel mouth, as he lifted with his hands a *black cap*.

—Bram Stoker, in "The Judge's House"

Closely linked to spectral stories of ghosts are gothic tales. Gothic is a peculiar form, what novelist John Gardner called a "systematically altered realism." These stories of desolate moors with lonely, crumbling gothic mansions (hence the name) follow tight patterns: the gloomy structure, the desolate location, the normal person drawn into the strange world, forced to defend his or her honor

We love and need the concept of monstrosity because it is a reaffirmation of the order we all crave as human beings ... it is not the physical or mental aberration in itself which horrifies us, but rather the lack of order which these aberrations seem to imply.
—Stephen King, in Danse Macabre, 1981

against the bizarre denizens of the place, the ghostly apparitions. The weird inhabitants are creatures of fantasy, although often human rather than phantoms—more or less.

The most merciful thing in the world, I think, is the inability of the human mind to correlate all its contents.
—Opening line of "The Call of Cthulhu," by H.P. Lovecraft, in Weird Tales, 1928

> Through daily proximity to the great slabs of stone, the faces of the Gray Scrubbers had become like slabs themselves. There was no expression whatever upon the eighteen faces, unless the lack of expression is in itself an expression. They were simply slabs that the Gray Scrubbers spoke from occasionally. . . . They were traditionally deaf. The eyes were there, small and flat as coins . . . thirty-six of them, and the eighteen noses were there, and the lines of the mouths that resembled the harsh cracks that divided the stone slabs, they were there too . . . . yet it would be impossible to perceive the faintest sign of animation, and even if a basinful of their features had been shaken together and if each feature had been picked out at random and stuck upon some dummy head of wax at any capricious spot or angle, it would have made no difference. . . .

> —*Titus Groan*, 1946, Mervyn Peake

Then there are tales of erotic fantasy, such as the vampire tales of Anne Rice. This ring of fantasy is rooted deeply in sensuality and morbid emotions. These tales wind down paths of strange desires and attractions; their realm is the dark and forbidden, and they play with readers' mores and inhibitions. Their charms are Byronic (the English poet who wrote of beauty, graveyards, and those who died young; and who kept a skull as a drinking cup). Delving into mystery, these tales are meant less to frighten than to allure. They embrace the bizarre and freakish, from vampires to voodoo sagas.

> The electric power had gone out that night with the storm, they told me. . . .
> Only oil lamps and candles illuminated the large square rooms. I had seen the flicker in the fanlight above the entranceway as we approached. Lanterns swayed in the wind in the deep galleries that wrapped the great square house about on its first and second floors. . . .
> She came down barefoot to meet me, in a lavender dress covered with pink flowers, scarcely the witch at all.
> . . . "David Talbot," she had said to me almost formally.
> . . . "Merrick Mayfair," I'd said warmly. I took her in my arms.

She had been tall for her fourteen years, with beautifully shaped breasts quite natural under her simple cotton shift, and her soft dry hair had been loose down her back. She might have been a Spanish beauty to anyone outside of this bizarre part of the Southland, where the history of the slaves and their free descendants was so full of complex alliances and erotic romance. But any New Orleanean could see African blood in her by the lovely café au lait of her skin. . . .

She had a temptress's poise as she sat there, small in the great winged chair of oxblood leather, a tiny tantalizing gold chain around her ankle, another with a small diamond-studded cross around her neck.

. . . Though the night had been only cool, there was a fire in the fireplace, and the room, with its shelves of books and its random Grecian sculptures, had been fragrant and comfortable, conducive to a spell.

—*Merrick,* 2000, by Anne Rice

It is the sense of nameless menace, unformulated threat, that really has power to chill the blood. . . . Horror is specific, fear is indefinite.
—Joan Aiken, "How to Keep the Reader on the Edge of the Chair," in The Writer, March 1973

In pure horror stories, anything goes—usually straight for the throat. Monsters attack the house, crawl down the chimney, slither or slouch in zombie ranks closer and closer with each step to the front porch. These fantastic creatures are evil to the core: from slurping, sucking alien monsters to cursed cars that kill their owners.

Early in these stories evil begins to appear, usually after a brief opening scene of calm and quiet tranquility, in small measures. The first insignificant signs—the solitary bird trapped in the house—will eventually become a throng of squealing, eye-pecking birds over-running the entire town. In horror, evil intensifies throughout the story to enormous proportions, tipping the scales until the very end. Sometimes it carries the day.

Some assume that the role of horror is to invoke fear or dread. But its roots lie in ancient tales wherein the matter of curses is closely linked to religion and taboos. Doing something wrong is bound to lead to awful consequences. These stories are morality plays; often the plot hinges on unraveling the mystery of just what was done wrong—and on discovering the manner in which this can be corrected or reversed. Horror explores the consequences of misguided action, just as the Old Testament of the Bible explores the sometimes horrific consequences of what happens to those who transgress the law.

Some theories of horror literature dwell on the beneficial catharsis of shock. We look into the darkness, sensing something coming nearer and nearer. We wait and shiver. It pounces. We scream—and then we laugh. The idea is that a good-natured teasing of our own irrational, deep-seated fears helps us deal with them; we diminish their power by fictionalizing them. Dark fantasy toys with our fears, investigates the magnetic power that draws foolish protagonists to stay the night in the haunted house, or go down in the cellar alone, or walk from the campfire into the woods—despite the fact that everyone else who has done so, up to that point in the story, has strangely disappeared.

Horror and fairy tales, at first glance opposites, are closely linked. Older fairy tales were quite gruesome, and modern ones often address horrific themes. Likewise, horror tales can be seen as fairy tales with one constant moral: don't go out in the dark alone.

FIVE BANQUET TABLES

The five rings of fantasy are not five pens in which to separate authors and stories like flocks of sheep. Perhaps we can also imagine these labels—*high fantasy*, *adventure fantasy*, *fairy-tale fiction*, *magic realism*, *dark fantasy*—as signs leading to five wooden doors, all opening into a great castle of imagination. Inside are five great halls. In each hall is a massive, sprawling banquet table, surrounded by throngs of feasting guests. The boisterous revelers fill the great halls—grabbing food, quaffing wine, telling stories, singing and laughing.

Some guests roam freely through the whole castle. Some visit more than one banquet, tasting the delicacies of more than one feast. Others meet by chance or appointment in halls or back rooms to talk and debate, to whisper and reveal secrets. There are revolving bookcases, hidden passages, chandeliers to swing from, balconies to climb to observe the patterns flowing below.

The important point: at each banquet table are some empty chairs, awaiting new guests. And there is an abundance of food and spirits. There is room for all at the tables of Fantasy. The five rings are really circles of true gold: the gold of good company.

WRITING HIGH FANTASY

by Patricia A. McKillip

Patricia A. McKillip is a winner of the World Fantasy Award. Her novels include The Riddle-Master trilogy, as well as The Book of Atrix Wolfe, Song for the Basilisk, and others. She is known for her richly textured writing style, full of beautifully crafted images which touch all five senses. Here, in an article first published in The Writer magazine, she talks about the challenges in writing high fantasy, where clichés await the unwary.

The formula is simple. Take one 15th-century palace with high towers and pennants flying, add a hero who talks like a butler, a wizard with fireworks under his fingernails, and a Lurking Evil that threatens the kingdom or the heroine, and there you have it: high fantasy in the making.

And there we have all had it up to the proverbial "here." How many times can you repeat the same plot? But how can you write high fantasy without the traditional trappings, characters, and plot that are essential for this kind of fantasy?

So I am forced to ask myself the same question when I begin a new fantasy: How can it follow the rules of high fantasy and break them at the same time?

THE HERO

In writing the *Riddle-Master* trilogy, my impulse was to be as deliberately traditional as possible: A ruler leaves the comforts of his castle to learn from wizards how to fight a Lurking Evil that threatens to destroy his land. The hero, the magic, the danger, are after all elements of fantasy as old as storytelling. But how do you give the Generic Hero—who only has to be high-born, look passable, and fight really well to be a hero—personality?

I discarded quite a number of auditioning heroes before settling on Morgon, Prince of Hed, ruler of a tiny island, who liked to make beer, read books, didn't own a sword, and kept the only crown he possessed under his bed. He did not talk like an English butler, he knew which end of a shovel was up, and only a penchant for wanting to learn odd things kept him from being a sort of placid gentleman farmer. That small detail—among all the details of a prosaic hard-headed life that included farming, trading, pig-herders, backyard pumps, and a couple of strong-willed siblings—became the conflict in his personality that ultimately drove him from his land and set him on his questing path.

Before I let him set forth, I placed him against as detailed a background as I possibly could. I wanted the reader to see the land Morgon lived in and how it shaped him before he left it and changed himself. So I let him talk about grain and bulls, beer and plowhorses, and his sister's bare feet, before I let him say fairy tale words like tower, wizard, harp, and king, and state his own driving motivation: to answer the unanswered riddle.

THE HEROINE

In *The Sorceress and the Cygnet*, my questing hero found himself falling literally into the path of my questing heroine. She is, in one sense, the princess in the tower whom my hero eventually rescues; in other words, she is very much a piece of the familiar storytelling formula. But she has imprisoned herself in a rickety old house in a swamp, trapped there by her own obsession with the darker side of magic.

As she defines herself: "I have been called everything from sorceress to bog hag. I know a great many things but never enough. Never enough. I know the great swamp of night, and sometimes I do things for pay if it interests me." She has pursued her quest for knowledge and power into a dangerous backwater of mean, petty magic, from which, it is clear to everyone but her, she must be rescued. The language she uses, like Morgon's, covers a broad territory between palace and pigherder's hut. Her wanderings have freed her tongue.

In the same novel, I also used a female point of view, that of a high-born lady, to contrast with the more earthy, gypsyish, view of my hero. She is a female version of the "friend of the hero"; she frets about the sorceress, gives advice, and fights beside the sorceress in the end. She is perhaps the toughest kind of character to work with: genuinely good, honest, and dutiful. Making a point-of-view character both good and interesting is a challenge. Traditionally, a "good" character has a limited emotional range, no bad habits to speak of, and a rather bland vocabulary. As the "friend of the heroine," she is also a sounding board for the heroine's more colorful character.

I deliberately chose that kind of character because I wanted to see how difficult it would be to make her more than just a device to move the plot along its necessary path. She turned out to be extraordinarily difficult. I wanted her to be elegant, dignified, calm, responsible. . . .

To keep her from fading completely into the plot, I constantly had to provide her with events that brought out her best qualities. Keeping her dialogue simple kept her uncomplicated yet responsive as a character; it also moved the plot forward without dragging along the unnecessary baggage of introspection. She is meant to observe and act; the language should not be more complicated than she is.

THE LURKING EVIL

Traditionally, the evil in fantasy is personified by someone of extraordinary and perverse power, whose goal in life is to bring the greatest possible misery to the largest number of good honest folk. Sauron of the *Lord of the Rings* trilogy, Darth Vader of the *Star Wars* trilogy, Morgan le Fay of *Le Morte D'Arthur*, are all examples of social misfits from whose destructive powers the hero and heroine must rescue humanity and hobbits and the world as they know it.

The problem with the Lurking Evil is that as social misfit, it might become far more interesting than the good and dutiful hero. Yet without proper background and personality, the Lurking Evil becomes a kind of unmotivated monster vacuum-cleaner that threatens humanity simply because it's plugged in and turned on. I have trouble coming up with genuinely evil characters who are horrible, remorseless, and deserving of everything the hero can dish out. I always want to give them a human side, which puts them in the social misfit category.

In my *Riddle-Master* trilogy, I used various kinds of misfits: the renegade wizard Ohm, who was motivated by an unprincipled desire for magical power; the sea-people, whose intentions and powers seem at first random and obscure, until they finally reveal their origins; and the ambiguous character Deth, who may be good and may be evil—and who keeps my hero off-balance and guessing until the end of the tale.

In *The Sorceress and the Cygnet*, I used much the same kind of device: allowing my hero to define characters as evil until, in the end, they reveal that the evil is not in them, but in my misguided heroine. I do this because evil as a random event, or as the sole motivation for a character, is difficult for me to work with; it seems to belong in another genre—to horror—or mystery.

Jung says that all aspects of a dream are actually faces of the dreamer. I believe that in fantasy, the vanquished evil must be an aspect of the hero or heroine, since by tradition, evil is never stronger than the power of the hero to overcome it—which is where, of course, we get the happy endings in high fantasy.

MAGIC

If you put a mage, sorceress, wizard, warlock, witch, or necromancer into fantasy, it's more than likely that, sooner or later, they will want to work some magic. Creating a spell can be as simple or as difficult as you want. You can write, "Mpyxl made a love potion. Hormel drank it and fell in love." Or you can do research into herb lore and medieval recipes for spells and write: "Mpyxl stirred five bay leaves, an owl's eye, a parsnip, six of Hormel's fingernails, and some powdered mugwort into some leftover barley soup. Hormel ate it and fell in love."

Or you can consider love itself, and how Mpyxl must desire Hormel, how frustrated and rejected she must feel to be obliged to cast a spell over him, what in Hormel generates such overpowering emotions, why he refuses to fall in love with Mpyxl the usual way, and what causes people to fall in love with each other in the first place. Then you will find that Mpyxl herself is under a spell cast by Hormel, and that she must change before his eyes from someone he doesn't want to someone he desires beyond reason.

The language of such a spell would be far different from fingernails and barley soup. The Magic exists only in the language; the spell exists only in the reader's mind. The words themselves must create something out of nothing. To invent a convincing love potion you must, for a moment, make even the reader fall in love.

WHY?

Why write fantasy? Because it's there. Fantasy is as old as poetry and myth, which are as old as language. The rules of high fantasy are rules of the unconscious and the imagination, where good quests, evil lurks, the two clash, and the victor—and the reader—are rewarded.

Good might be male or female, so might evil. The battle might be fought with swords, with magic, with wits, on a battlefield, in a tower, or in the quester's heart.

At its best, fantasy rewards the reader with a sense of wonder about what lies within the heart of the commonplace world. The greatest tales are told over and over, in many ways, through centuries. Fantasy changes with the changing times, and yet it is still the oldest kind of tale in the world, for it began once upon a time, and we haven't heard the end of it yet.

❄

The mountain-king, enveloped in fur, put a gentle hand on his shoulder. . . .

". . . Morgon . . . I wanted to give you something that might help you; I racked my brains trying to think what, when it occurred to me that there are times in your journey that you might simply want to disappear from enemies, from friends, from the world, to rest awhile, to think . . . . There's nothing less obvious than a tree in a forest."

"A tree." Something in his mind quickened. "Danan, can you teach me that?"

"You have the gift for shape-changing. . . . You must simply learn to be still. You know what kind of stillness is in a stone, or a handful of earth."

. . . Morgon followed him out of Harte, down the winding, quiet road, then into the forests high above Kyrth. Their footprints broke deep into the powdery snow; they brushed pine branches heavy with it, shook soft snow flurries loose that bared webs of wet, dark fir. . . . They stood there listening. The clouds, softly shaped by the wind, rested on the silence; trees were molded to a stillness that formed the whorls of their bark, curve of branch, the heavy, downward sweep of their needles and pinnacle of tip. A hawk floated in the silence, barely rippling it, dove deep into it and vanished. Morgon, after a long while, turned to Danan, feeling suddenly alone, and found beside him a great pine, still and dreaming . . . .

He did not move. . . . The trees circling him seemed to enclose a warmth like the stone houses at Kyrth, against the winter. Listening, he heard suddenly the hum of their veins, drawing life from deep beneath the snow, beneath the hard earth. He felt himself rooted, locked into the rhythms of the mountain . . . . Wordless knowledge moved through him, of slow measureless age, of fierce winds borne beyond breaking point, of seasons beginning, ending . . . .

The stillness passed. He moved, felt an odd stiffness as though his face were being formed out of bark, his fingers dwindling from fingers of twig. His breath, which he had not noticed for a while, went out of him in a quick, white flash.

Danan said, his voice measured to the unhurried rhythm of the silence, "When you have a moment, practice so you can fade in a thought from man to tree. Sometimes I forget to change back. . . ."

❄

—From Patricia McKillip's novel, The Riddle-Master of Hed (Book 1 of the Riddle-Master trilogy), first published by Del Ray, 1976. The trilogy was reissued as a single volume by Ace Books in 1999. Copyright © 1976, 1999 by Patricia A. McKillip.

WRITING ADVENTURE FANTASY

Interview with John Marco
by Claire E. White

John Marco's fantasy series, Tyrants and Kings, has been called "absorbing" and "deftly plotted" (Kirkus). The military-epic trilogy began with the release in 1999 of his debut novel, The Jackal of Nar, which won widespread praise for its action scenes and complex characters. Here, he talks with Claire E. White, editor of The Internet Writing Journal (www.writerswrite.com) about his epic series and offers some advice for aspiring authors. The interview was held April 1999, shortly after the release of Jackal.

(White) What did you like to read when you were a child?

(Marco) I started off with comic books. Even before I could read I was looking at the pictures, pretending I could tell what was happening. I was really into Spider-Man, and the other Marvel superheroes. As I got a little older I discovered science fiction and fantasy. I remember going to the library with my mother and scanning the shelves; anything with a really cool cover grabbed my interest. That's where I discovered some of the genre's greats, like Edgar Rice Burroughs and Fritz Leiber.

(White) How has your background as a technical writer affected your writing style and habits?

(Marco) Some people believe that any writing helps exercise the basic skills needed to write well. Others believe that technical writing is really a waste of time; that it has no bearing on the ability to write good fiction.

I think the truth is somewhere in the middle. I know my years as a technical writer helped me with basic writing skills. Really, the best way to get better at writing is simply to do it. Having been a technical writer has made me more disciplined. I get up, take a shower, check my email, and then it's business as usual.

(White) What was your inspiration for *The Jackal of Nar*?

(Marco) I wanted to tell a multilayered story—a war story—but also wanted to create a unique world and fill it with diverse people, all of whom had their own sets of goals and problems. I needed a really big template, so I looked to books with big stories, like *Shogun* and *Gone with the Wind*, to see how those authors dealt with the problem.

If I had to pick one major influence, I would have to say it's *All Quiet on the Western Front*, by Erich Remarque. I read that just before I started writing *Jackal*, and something clicked. I've never read a book that better describes the damage war can do to a person, and when I was done with it I knew where to start the story.

My main character, Richius Vantran, was going to be young and caught in the middle of a war. Like Paul, the main character in *All Quiet*, Richius keeps daydreaming about home. But he can't go home because he's stuck in a conflict that he didn't start. After the first few chapters, *Jackal* starts to look nothing at all like Remarque's book, but that kernel of an idea got me going.

(White) What was the most challenging aspect of writing the story?

(Marco) Finding the time. I was working full time while writing the book, and would do all of my writing at night when I came home from work. That went on for about two years, and it was really difficult. Fortunately I have a very supportive wife. Honestly, looking back, I'm not sure how I was able to do it.

As for the story, the most challenging part was creating believable characters. I wanted to avoid the archetype of the strong hero and the evil villain.

Jackal is definitely not a story about good versus evil. I tried to keep in mind that there are two sides to every conflict, and each side always believes that they're right. Usually the truth is somewhere in the middle.

Richius, for instance, isn't the perfect soldier, and he makes a lot of mistakes. I think that's much more realistic than having a hero that always knows what to do and does it perfectly.

Even the villains in the story aren't what they seem at first glance. I tried to give them motivations for the terrible things they do. I'm not excusing their actions, of course, but I did try to make them believable.

(White) Did you find it difficult to integrate the romantic elements into the story?

(Marco) Not really, because the romance was always meant to be a central story line. It's sort of a classic theme: having a man and a woman meet in a war zone, having them fall in love, then having them forced apart. That part of the story really wrote itself. All I had to do was imagine how horrible it would be to lose someone I really loved. Thinking about that set the events in motion.

There's that old cliche that "love conquers all," and in *Jackal* it really does. Maybe that's a bit naive, but after pages and pages of death and destruction, it's nice to know that two people who love each other can survive, and even thrive.

(White) The hero of the story is Richius Vantran, a complex man who faces some truly difficult decisions. How did you create Richius?

(Marco) To me, Richius represents the common man, the kind of person who always gets the worst duties in a war. Just about all the soldiers in every war are regular men who don't want to be there. They do their duty because they know they have to, but they would much rather be home living a normal life.

Richius is just like that. Even though he's a prince, he's really an ordinary fellow. But he's caught up in extraordinary circumstances, and things start getting out of his control. He's also the story's straight man. He's not as flashy or fascinating as some of the villains, but he's not meant to be. He's the character around which everyone and everything else revolves.

And despite all the things he goes through, he's still relatively normal by the end. I've gotten some interesting feedback from readers about the Richius character; a few don't like some of the decisions he makes in the story. But his circumstances are really overwhelming, and I don't think most people would react any differently.

Most readers realize that he's just a regular guy trapped in insane circumstances.

(White) Count Biagio really is quite frightening! How did you go about creating him?

(*Marco*) Creating Biagio was a lot of fun. He became my favorite character, and plays a major role in the second book.

The most interesting thing is that he was never intended to be a character. I write extensive outlines before I begin a writing, and nowhere in my outline for *Jackal* is the name Biagio. He just sprang up out of my imagination as I was writing. I needed another character—a liaison between Richius and the Emperor, someone who Richius could talk to about Nar and learn from. And because he Emperor is so old and feeble, I needed a character who could challenge Richius on his level, and who could travel.

So I started thinking about henchmen, and I remembered how Adolph Hitler had all kinds of cruel and fanatical people around him, an inner circle that knew him well and carried out his orders. That's how Biagio was born. He's the Emperor's spy-master. He is the head of a secret police force, and everyone fears him.

But even Biagio has his good side. He does some horrific things in the book, and he's certainly a villain, but he's also complicated, and even soft-hearted at times. Mostly this is seen in his love for the Emperor, whom he adores like a father. He desperately wants the Emperor's approval, and is willing to do anything for it. Such devotion makes him very dangerous.

(*White*) What do you see as the main themes of this series?

(*Marco*) Well, there's the war theme, and the romance. But there are also a couple of others that I wanted to explore.

One is the idea of beauty. I've always liked the story of Beauty and the Beast. In *Jackal* there's a character named Tharn, a magical holy man. He's been horribly mutated by his use of magic, and I wanted to explore the idea that he's unlovable because he's so grotesque. That always strikes me as profoundly sad. Tharn has the respect and adoration of his people, but he doesn't have the love of the one woman he has always adored, Dyana. And this is something that Tharn finds difficult to accept. He knows he's hideous, and having to live with his deformities shapes his personality.

The other major theme of the book is about growing old. The leaders of Nar take drugs to keep themselves young. They're all terrified of getting older and dying. This is particularly true of the Emperor, who has lived for over a hundred years and will do anything to become immortal.

For me, that's an interesting idea. Would I like to live forever? Or would I rather grow old gracefully and eventually die? All of us ask ourselves this question from time to time, and writing about Nar gave me a chance to examine it.

(*White*) The city of Nar is an incredible creation: dark, industrial and quite overwhelming. How did you go about creating the city, and the rest of the world in which this series is set?

(*Marco*) World-building is always an important aspect of fantasy writing, and many authors take a long time in creating their worlds and bringing them to life. It's one of the most fun aspects of fantasy writing, because it gives me a chance to put together little bits of knowledge I have about many different cultures and history.

To me, Nar City is like a cross between London and ancient Rome. It's a modern city. It's also the seat of imperial power, and I wanted it to have a fearsome quality. Yet even though it's a frightening place, it's also awe-inspiring. When Richius, the main character, travels to the city, he can't help being impressed by it, because he's from a little country of farms and ranches.

The other major setting of the book is Lucel-Lor, a vast land inhabited by a race called the Triin. I wanted to give it an Asiatic flavor, as in feudal Japan. Lucel-Lor is made up of many different regions, each ruled by a warlord. The Triin have been fighting amongst themselves for decades. They're not war-like, precisely, just caught up in years of regional conflict.

Unlike the Narens, who have one god, the Triin have many gods and diverse religious beliefs. They're also much less concerned with materialism. Because they're so different, they're feared and misunderstood by the people of Nar. The ignorance that the cultures have for each other plays a major role in the story.

(*White*) When reading a military epic, it is tempting to infer the author's views on current events. Are personal views of yours reflected in the book?

(*Marco*) I admit that *Jackal* leaves a lot of room for speculation. But I really don't have any hard answers. For me, it's all about the exploration of ideas, but I never come to any real conclusions. Like the reader, I'm just speculating about things. And they're always things that interest me, like politics, war, etc.

Really, I don't think I'm telling any profound truths in the book. Though I'm sure it's colored somewhat by my perceptions, it's just meant to entertain.

(White) What was your inspiration for Dyana?

(Marco) The character of Dyana came out of my need for a strong female love interest. She's the woman Richius meets and falls in love with during the war. He idolizes her. Of course, Dyana isn't perfect, but Richius doesn't see her imperfections.

Dyana was probably the hardest character for me to create. Even though there are long stretches of the story where she doesn't appear, she's the engine of the plot. Now, I know there are male writers who have no trouble writing about female characters, but I'm not one of them. It's hard for me to get into their heads, and perhaps that's why most of the characters in the book are men.

When I first submitted the book to Bantam, Dyana wasn't really a character that could stand on her own; she was just Richius' idealized view of womanhood. Anne Groell, my editor, made some suggestions on how I could turn her into something more than a young man's fantasy. She wanted Dyana to be more feisty, more independent.

At first it was difficult for me to make the changes, because I didn't want Dyana to interfere with Richius' characterization. But after reworking her character, I saw that Anne had been right. It really made her much stronger. Because Dyana grew so much, she plays a major role in the next book, *The Grand Design*.

(White) What's your advice to aspiring authors?

(Marco) First off, be sure writing is something they want to pursue. I don't want to sugarcoat it; getting a first novel published is difficult. I was very fortunate to find an agent, and even more fortunate to find an editor willing to take a chance on an unpublished author. That's not to say I didn't work hard, but hard work will only take you so far. Eventually, you're going to need that elusive bit of luck.

If at all possible, hook up with another writer, someone who shares your passion for writing and your desire to get published. Two heads really are better than one, and two people can learn how to write well faster than one person working alone. For me, working with a friend, Ted, was crucial. He gave me excellent feedback and was always honest with me, and I know that *Jackal* is a much better book because of his involvement.

Another thing that was really helpful to me was audio books. Reading is great, of course, but audio books were key to helping me understand the rhythm of writing. When something is well written, it has a distinct cadence, and I never realized that until I began listening to books on tape. It was really eye-opening, and helped me immensely.

I still try to capture that musicality every time I write.

❋

On summer evenings, when the sun threw long shadows across the city, High Street teemed with vendors and merchants; caterwauling slave traders peddling their captured flesh, traveling hunters with trussed-up game birds, beggars and thieves and harlots and prostitutes, and, amazingly, the occasional toy shop. There was money in this part of Nar, looted from a thousand successful campaigns, and the well-heeled of the city liked to spoil their greedy offspring. . . .

There were toy soldiers with silver guns and brass cannons, and dolls with luxurious hair and exquisite dresses. . . . There were stuffed animals with real fur; stringed instruments of polished wood; and fabric-covered flying machines that actually glided through the air, suspended from the ceiling by translucent wire. Grand vessels floated in basins of water. . . . A three-foot wooden model of an elf played on a flute, its animated fingers clicking with mechanical perfection as it blew out its endless tune. . . .

But although the Piper was famous for his mechanical wonders, there was one particular skill that brought eager girls to his toy shops. He was, without question, the Empire's peerless maker of dollhouses. . . . His replicas of the Black Palance were celebrated, and his skill was unmatched by any scientist or engineer. . . .

[Minister] Bovadin sat down cross-legged on the [toymaker's] workbench. He clapped his hands excitedly as his men set down the crate.

"Gently," he said. "Yes, right there."

The crate eased down to the floor. . . . Bovadin tossed the crowbar to one of his men.

"Open it," he ordered.

The man wedged the tool's clawed head beneath the sealed lid and gave a muscular pull. Slowly the nails crept outward, screeching free of the wood. The other men joined in. . . . Piper stared wide-eyed at the contents, trying to see past the wooden supports. He caught a glimpse of silver metal and a ganglia of snake-like hoses, all held together with ropes and leather straps. Whatever it was, Bovadin wasn't taking any chances. Once the walls of the crate were let down, the men stepped aside, letting the toymaker see.

Bovadin laughed. . . . "Take a good look, toymaker. You won't see anything like this again." He walked into the center of the crate and stroked the metal tubes lovingly. "Beautiful, isn't it?"

The Piper wasn't sure how to answer. It was amazing, certainly. But beautiful? It was unrecognizable, like some metal monster from the ocean.

. . . "Explain it to me," said Piper. "This is supposed to fit in my dollhouse, yes?"

"Yes," said the minister. He gave his men a scowl, the only gesture needed to send them scurrying out of the room. When he was sure they couldn't hear him, Bovadin continued . . .

"It's not armed yet," explained Bovadin, grinning. "But when it is, there will be only an hour before the device starts up. You can build the angel, can't you?"

Piper nodded. "I've already made him."

He went to his workbench and slid open a hidden drawer. Inside was an unpainted figure of an angel, an archangel with a trumpet to his lips. It was perfectly detailed in every facet, just like the real one above the cathedral's gates. Gingerly, he handed the figurine over to Bovadin, who cooed when he felt it in his small hands. . . .

". . . It's so detailed. So real."

"Of course," bragged the toymaker. ". . . That's what I do, Minister. I make dreams real."

Bovadin smirked at him. "That's an odd way to describe what we're about to do, don't you think?"

✵

—From John Marco's novel, The Grand Design (Book 2 of Tyrants and Kings), published by Bantam Books. Copyright © 2000 by John Marco.

WRITING FAIRY-TALE FICTION

Interview with Donna Jo Napoli
by Philip Martin

Donna Jo Napoli teaches linguistics and is the author of a number of popular and thought-provoking novels based on familiar myths and fairy tales. Her stories have found widespread audiences especially with middle-grade and young adult readers. Her award-winning books, which include Beast, Sirena, and The Magic Circle, are striking for their spellbinding imagery, psychological complexity, and fresh interpretation of the motivations of characters involved in these traditional tales.

(Martin) Your books take old fairy tales and myths and reshape them very inventively. What do you look for or consider when tackling a traditional story? And are you changing these stories, in your opinion, or retelling them?

(Napoli) I am never retelling in the sense of trying to tell it differently. Instead, I am respectful of the integrity of the original work. I love folk tales, fairy tales, myths, religious stories—all of them—because these have stood the test of time. They are powerful.

What I respond to are the psychological realities of these stories. And I look for parts of them that haven't been told. Those gaps free me to tell what I need to tell. But on every detail that was actually told in the original, I am faithful to the original.

For example, in the original Rapunzel story, we are told that a witch traded lettuce for a baby. We are not told why.

We know that witch raised the child lovingly and then put her in a tower when she came of age. We are not told why.

We know a young man found her and immediately tried to free her. Again, no hint of why his attachment to her was so fast and so sure.

Many details are given in the original (which takes about a page and a half), but without motivation.

I take the characters seriously. I believe the story. And that allows me to enter it and find the details that are the motivation.

I never really feel like I'm writing a story when I work on these traditional tales. I feel like I'm simply reporting more fully. I'm simply finding the truths.

(*Martin*) It seems that these stories turn in complex, unexpected ways, and touch feelings we all carry close to our hearts. They seem to deal with interpersonal relationships, questions of love, loss, risk, transformation—who to trust, who is telling the truth, the boundaries between home and hearth and the dark woods or stranger. Can you elaborate on this? Why do people feel so attached to such fairy-tale or mythic stories—yours in particular?

(*Napoli*) Your words are very much what I would say. Fairy tales deal with the evils we know exist in the world around us and in ourselves. Myths deal with the magic around us—the magic of natural phenomena like thunder and sunrise-sunset. Religious stories deal with the fact that our physical lives end—we are mortal—and that presents the question of whether or not our lives can be meaningful.

These questions and problems will always be with us. They are part of the human condition. I don't care how much science you study, the first time you hold your own newborn, you are overcome with the magic of it all. I say this as someone who considers herself a scientist (I am a linguist), so I am in no way casting aspersions on science. Much to the contrary. I am a person who has always cared more about why people do things than what they do.

These traditional stories are, I believe, explorations of behavior that begs us to consider why the characters do what they do. It is the characters that draw me—the way they face their plights.

(*Martin*) In reading some reader reviews of your novels on Amazon.com, I was struck with how your stories seem to strike a chord with today's teenage readers. Some gave wonderfully personal reviews of, for instance, *Zel*, describing how this mother wants to keep a girl away from a guy and so she locks her up. . . . It seems like the stories struck home!

What's your impression of how your stories affect your readers? Do you write for any particular audience? Are you trying to be "educational"—to deliver something "uplifting"—or are you trying to write a story to entertain and fascinate?

(*Napoli*) I wrote for 14 years before I finally sold something, so it is clear that I am not writing totally for an audience.

I need to write. And I never think of my audience as I write the first draft of a story. Instead, I just let the story come, all willy-nilly, and discover it as it appears on the computer screen.

Then I let my editor tell me what age the story is for. I let her help me see that. Rarely, though, do I ever change something just to make it more appropriate for my audience. Rather, I write what I have to write—and then I find out who might be interested in reading it.

The Magic Circle, for example, was said to be an adult story by many when it first came out. Dutton, the publisher, debated whether or not to bring it out as a children's book. *Albert*, my first picture book, which came out this spring, has been said to be an adult story. Harcourt, the publisher, feels it's a story for any age.

In both instances, I feel outside the debate. I don't really know what the difference is between children's literature, teens' literature, and adults' literature. But children have responded to these works positively, and the publishers published them, so I don't care about the debate.

Do you see what I mean? These are not academic questions; they are questions of emotional responses. If a reader responds to a story, then the story is appropriate for that reader, no?

And I am not only a fantasy writer. I write contemporary stories and I write historical fiction, as well. And in all cases, I do a tremendous amount of research.

Fantasy does not give license to make up things at will. Instead, it demands an even stricter adherence to the truth of the story. No details can be allowed that do not fit.

Coherence is the bible.

❄

"Oh, Mother, the goose is on her nest again." Zel rests her weight on the windowsill and leans out. Her feet dance on tiptoe. The goose stretches her neck forward and smacks the bottom of her bill on the rocky soil. "Goose!" Zel shouts. "Dear goose. You're terribly confused." Zel hears a thunk. She spins around.

Mother has just put a bowl of apricots on the center of the table.

. . . [Zel] sees that Mother wears her good shoes. "Oh, we're going to town today!" She laughs. And now her dancing feet take her around the table, around Mother, impelled by the rare joy of town. Zel sings, "Today today today today." . . .

Zel loves seeing people. No one ever comes to visit their alm [mountain pasture], but still Zel gets to see people often. So far this summer she has spied at least one of the herd boys every day. These are the boys who live in the lower hills in winter. But in fair weather they take up residence with the mountain people in their scattered cabins. Once a week each boy takes a turn driving the communal herd across the alms for grazing. Zel has always wished that she and Mother had a cow to contribute to the herd so that the boys would stop by their alm. But Mother prefers goats. And whenever a herd boy crosses their grasses, Mother shoos him away before they can even exchange names.

But in town Mother can't shoo people away. Zel will get to see everyone, talk with everyone. Oh, town is wonderful.

. . . Finally they pass through the covered bridge over the great river that empties into their lake, footsteps and voices resounding on the stone. When they emerge, the lake shines opaque green down to their left. It is long and flat this morning. Sometimes the lake moves from one end to the other like a thin good-weather quilt in a spring wing. . . .

At last, Zel and Mother arrive in town. They follow the cobblestones, winding through people and animals. The huge clock in the town tower seems to look down on the market square like an open eye. Zel and Mother stop at table after table—here piled high with paprika, bunches of parsley, savory, oregano; here covered with neat pyramids of cheese balls. . . .

Zel hums. She feels absorbed by the throng of people. She stops a moment, enjoying the sense of warmth and envelopment. But Mother nudges her along.

And here's the fruit stall they always visit. A girl Zel has talked with before hugs her warmly. A boy who looks to be the girl's brother sneaks strawberries into Zel's hand, the small, wild, exquisitely sweet kind. Mother grabs Zel by the wrist and the berries drop in the dust.

✳

—From the first chapter of Donna Jo Napoli's novel, Zel, published by Dutton Books, a telling of the story of Rapunzel set in Switzerland in the mid-1500s. Copyright © 1996 by Donna Jo Napoli.

WRITING MAGIC REALISM

Interview with Diane Schoemperlen
by Philip Martin

Diane Schoemperlen is a Canadian writer, author of the critically acclaimed novel In the Language of Love and collections of short stories, including Forms of Devotion, which won the Governor General's Award for Fiction, Canada's highest literary prize. In this interview, she discusses her novel Our Lady of the Lost and Found (2001).

(Martin) It seems to me your novel *Our Lady of the Lost and Found* fits into the magic-realism approach to fiction.

(Schoemperlen) Magic realism is indeed a type of fiction where the protagonists are the ones affected by the mysterious appearance of the fantastic. And that is what happens in my book. That was how I wanted to set it up: to have the Virgin Mary appear in the middle of the narrator's ordinary life and then take part in ordinary life.

I wanted to do that because all the things I read about Mary emphasized how she's considered to be both fully human and fully divine. But most of the readings focused on the divine side. I wanted to put her in our world. She wears regular clothes and does the dishes and goes to the mall and does all kinds of stuff that ordinary people do. Even though she is an apparition.

(Martin) I enjoyed especially the first scenes when Mary appears in the narrator's living room, next to the big potted plant.

(Schoemperlen) I had a lot of fun writing that first scene. It was a little hard at first to put words into her mouth. Who am I to be saying, well, the Virgin Mary said this and the Virgin Mary said that? In fact that is why I didn't use the standard quotation marks for punctuation. I used what we call here [in Canada] the French dash—a long

dash at the front of a spoken passage. That seemed a little less presumptuous on my part.

But once I got a voice for Mary then I really found it fun to imagine the kinds of things that she might say to this woman. Mostly, as I was working on it, I was just imagining ordinary things and then just taking it a step further.

I'd think about what it was like when you actually are unpacking a suitcase. Then I would think, okay, but how can I make this a bit magical? I thought, well, I could have her pull things out of this suitcase for a long time. While the narrator thinks about Pandora's Box and what might happen when she opened that suitcase.

(*Martin*) I was fascinated that there was a little golden lock on her suitcase. Does Mary worry about traveling like the rest of us?

(*Schoemperlen*) Well, whenever I travel, I always lock my suitcase with this little gold lock. I did kind of leave it open—what if she had come there the regular way, by plane? So, I wanted to play around with the connections between ordinary and extraordinary. I wanted to leave a little questions in the reader's mind, like did she actually just get on a plane or did she transport herself?

Having her flying there on an airplane could have been a whole scene in itself. Imagine finding yourself sitting beside the Virgin Mary on an airplane. But I didn't put that in.

And there were her shoes. I originally wanted them to be Nikes, for the simple reason that it's such a recognizable brand name. It was a part of making Mary just like everybody else. Then I remembered it comes from classical mythology—and it turned out even better than I could have planned. There were so many of those things in this book that I sometimes felt I was getting a little help from above or something.

(*Martin*) Maybe that's one of the things about writing in a way that touches on myths and divine symbols.

(*Schoemperlen*) I think so. This was a new experience for me. The other books I've written were all just set in the world as we know it. So for me, I learned a lot about how Mary fits into other kinds of mythology beyond the Christian story, and about the connections in so many things that we don't think about.

(*Martin*) Another thing about magic realism is that often it brings things full circle back to the ordinary.

(*Schoemperlen*)   Yes. Ordinary things are somehow transformed. There's one place towards the end where the narrator says she couldn't believe that the Virgin Mary had actually come to her to show her how to keep a cleaner house and enjoy it. And she *didn't* come to her just for that reason. But I do think one of the things that makes people unhappy is feeling that much of daily life is what Mary and the Catholic Church refer to as "ordinary time."

Most of our lives is ordinary time. Nothing big is happening, good or bad. Sometimes we get impatient or unhappy with that. We have that feeling of "Oh, I wish my life were more exciting" and "This is so boring." One of the things I wanted people to come away with was the feeling that there is a lot about daily life that can be appreciated if you can look at it in a different way.

(*Martin*)   So how was the protagonist changed by Mary's visit?

(*Schoemperlen*)   I think she was changed in two ways. Ironically, before Mary came to visit her, she thought that she was pretty happy and satisfied in her quiet, sort of isolated little life. But Mary's visit made her realize that she needs somehow to go forward. Mary has made her see that she needs to open herself to life more than she has been.

But also, the visit from Mary made her realize that there is a lot about her life that is really good. That it's not just going through the motions.

The changes she goes through are all pretty internal. Psychological things. I toyed with the idea of making it a bit more dramatic, then steered away from that, because I think that the changes that happen inside are the ones that are the most real.

(*Martin*)   So what is it that Mary represents in your novel?

(*Schoemperlen*)   One of the things I learned in doing my research was that what she represents has changed over the last 2,000 years. There's one school of thought that looked at Mary as being representative of the perfect, passive vessel.

In the 20th century, however, particularly in the Latin American countries, that really changed. She became looked upon as a real driving force for women—a positive role model for women who want to take charge of their lives.

(*Martin*)   So, is she a person or is she a concept?

(*Schoemperlen*) In my book, she's both. I'm sticking to the tradition of this fully human, fully divine thing. Not somehow half human and half divine, but all human and all divine. Which logically speaking, does not compute, because that adds up to 200%.

(*Martin*) You discuss a view of the universe that's much more complex than "either/or"—allowing something to be "200%."

(*Schoemperlen*) There's a lot about Heisenberg's Uncertainty Principle and quantum mechanics, allowing us to think "both/and" rather than "either/or." We limit ourselves by thinking that things can only be either/or—and that's what makes it hard understand Mary. Because she's both/and.

To me, she's the epitome of how thinking in opposites just doesn't begin to cover it. It's a really limited way of looking at the world and our own experiences. The more I thought about it, the more that became a really important theme in the book.

(*Martin*) Classic fantasy often is very strongly involved with the concept of Good and Evil—with very distinct capital letters.

(*Schoemperlen*) The white hats and the black hats.

(*Martin*) So magic realism offers a different viewpoint.

(*Schoemperlen*) Right. I mean, I did have to talk about evil. I really struggled with that. All the way through the book, I was conscious that a lot of the questions coming to me were not questions that I could possibly answer. And yet I still had to ask them in the book.

I don't know the answers. Why do evil, terrible things happen to good people? The narrator theorized about it, and I really wished that I could have had Mary give her the answers, but I couldn't.

And I worried about that because I thought, well, maybe people would assume that if the Virgin Mary came to your house, that you'd expect to sit her down and ask her those questions.

(*Martin*) Well, if you answered those questions, you should be charging a lot more for the book.

(*Schoemperlen*) [Laughs] Right. So there was a lot in this book that I really had to struggle with. But the "both/and" approach says that there's not necessarily one answer.

It also took me a while to figure out what my approach was going to be to all the historical accounts of Mary's appearances over centuries. I felt a real need to honor those narratives. I felt it was important that I didn't get fanciful about the documented events—that I stick to what people said they had seen and heard of Mary.

And that led me to the whole theme about fiction and nonfiction. Historically, what is truth and what are the stories that we believe? It's reflected in the way I tell the story—that Mary's one request is that the story not be told as fact, that it must be called a fictional novel. This also is a major aspect of magic realism, a blurring between the lines of history and story, between reality and miraculous events.

❊

Looking back on it now, I can see there were signs. In the week before it happened, there was a string of unusual events that I noticed but did not recognize. Seemingly trivial, apparently unconnected, they were not even events really, so much as odd occurrences, whimsical coincidences, amusing quirks of nature or fate. It is only now, in retrospect, that I can see them for what they were: eclectic clues, humble omens, whispered heralds of the approach of the miraculous.

These were nothing like the signs so often reported by other people who have had similar experiences. The sun did not pulsate, spin, dance, or radiate all the colors of the rainbow. There were no rainbows. There were no claps of thunder and no bolts, balls, or sheets of lightning. There were no clouds filled with gold and silver stars. The moon did not split in two, the earth did not tremble, and the rivers did not flow backward. A million rose petals did not fall from the sky and ten thousand blue butterflies did not flock around my head. There were no doves. There were no advance armies of angels. There was not even one angel, unless you care to count the squirrel.

Three mornings in a row a fat black squirrel with one white ear came and balanced on the flower box at my kitchen window. . . . On each of those three mornings, the squirrel sat at my window for exactly half an hour and then it scampered away.

On the fourth morning, I got up early, got dressed, and waited . . . but the squirrel never came.

That day, Thursday, turned out to be what I now think of as The Day of Mechanical Miracles.

The kitchen faucet, which had been dripping for a year and half, stopped.

The toaster, which for a month had been refusing to spit out the toast (thereby necessitating its extraction by means of a dangerous operation with a fork), repented. That morning the toast popped up so perky and golden, it fairly leaped onto my plate.

The grandfather clock in the living room, which I had bought on impulse at an auction six years before and which had not kept good time since, became accurate and articulate, tolling out the hours with melodious precision.

The answering machine, which had been recording my callers as if they were gargling underwater or bellowing into a high wind, recovered its equanimity and broadcast my new messages into the room in cheerful, dulcet tones.

I, of course, marveled extensively at these small miracles but had no reason to suspect they were anything but fortuitous gifts meant perhaps to finally prove my theory that if you just leave things alone and let them rest, they will eventually fix themselves. I had no reason to suspect that these incidents of spontaneous repair might be products or premonitions of the divine. . . .

The next day, Friday, I had several errands to run. I was hardly surprised to discover that my car, which had lately been suffering from some mysterious malady that caused it to buck and wheeze whenever I shifted into second gear, had quietly healed itself during the night, and it now carried me clear across town without complaint. There were parking spaces everywhere I needed them, some with time still on the meter.

At the bank, I got the friendliest, most efficient teller after a wait of less than five minutes. On a Friday afternoon, no less. While I waited, I noticed that all three of the women in line in front of me were wearing navy blue trench coats and white running shoes.

At the library, all the books I wanted were in and shelved in their proper places.

At the bakery, I got the last loaf of cheese bread.

At the drugstore, all the things I needed—toothpaste, shampoo, bubble bath, and vitamins—were on sale. . . .

That night I slept soundly and deeply, undisturbed by dreams, desire, or any prescient inkling of what was going to happen next.

※

—From the beginning of Diane Schoemperlen's Our Lady of the Lost and Found: A Novel (Viking, 2001). Copyright © 2001 by Diane Schoemperlen.

WRITING DARK FANTASY

by Elizabeth Hand

Elizabeth Hand has won both the World Fantasy Award and the Nebula Award for her stories. Her captivating novels, including Waking the Moon, Glimmering, and Winterlong, are filled with prose that has been called "hypnotically beautiful" and the work of "a latter-day Aubrey Beardsley." In this article, slightly condensed from its first appearance in The Writer (May, 1996), she talks about the techniques of writing supernatural fiction.

I've always thought that the oldest profession was that of story-teller—in particular, the teller of supernatural tales. A look at the cave paintings in France or Spain will show you how far back our hunger for the fantastic goes: men with the heads of beasts, figures crouching in the darkness, skulls and shadows and unblinking eyes. Take a glance at the current bestseller list, and you'll see that we haven't moved that far in the last twenty thousand years. Books by Anne Rice, Stephen King, Joyce Carol Oates, and Clive Barker, among many others, continue to feed our taste for dark wine and the perils of walking after midnight. But how to join the ranks of those whose novels explore the sinister side of town?

Unfortunately, unlike more stylized works such as *Dracula*, *The Turn of the Screw*, or *The Shining*, most horror novels lose their ability to chill the second time around—they just don't stand up to rereading. As Edmund Wilson put it, "The only horror in these fictions is the horror of bad taste and bad art."

More than other genres, supernatural fiction is defined by atmosphere and characterization. By atmosphere, I mean the author's ability to evoke a mood or place viscerally by the use of original and elegant, almost seductive language. The most successful supernatural novels are set in our world. Their narrative tension, their very ability to frighten and transport us, derives from a conflict between the macabre and the mundane, between everyday reality and the threatening other—whether revenant, werewolf, or demonic godling—that seeks to destroy it.

The roots of supernatural fiction lie in the gothic romances of the 18th and 19th centuries with their gloomy settings, imperiled narrators, and ghostly visitations. Even today these remain potent elements. Witness Anne Rice's vampire Lestat during a perambulation about prerevolutionary Paris:

> The cold seemed worse in Paris. It wasn't as clean as it had been in the mountains. The poor hovered in doorways, shivering and hungry, the crooked unpaved streets were thick with filthy slush. I saw barefoot children suffering before my very eyes, and more neglected corpses lying about than ever before. I was never so glad of the fur-lined cape as I was then. . . .

Much of the pleasure in Rice's work comes from her detailed evocations of real, yet highly romanticized, places: New Orleans, Paris, San Francisco. Stephen King has staked out rural Maine as his fictional backyard. The incomparable Shirley Jackson also turns to New England for horrific doings in *The Haunting of Hill House*, *The Bird's Nest,* and *We Have Always Lived in the Castle*.

Just about any setting will do, if you can imbue it with an aura of beauty and menace. My neo-gothic novel *Waking the Moon* takes place in that most pedestrian and bureaucratic of cities, Washington, D.C. By counterpointing the city's workaday drabness with exotic descriptions of its lesser-known corners, I was able to suggest that an ancient evil might lurk near Capitol Hill:

> From the Shrine's bell tower came the first deep tones of the carillon calling the hour. I turned, and saw in the distance the domes and columns of the Capitol glimmering in the twilight, bone-colored, ghostly; and behind it still more ghostly buildings, their columned porticoes and marble arches all seeming to melt into the haze of green and violet darkness that descended upon them like sleep.

Style, of course, is a matter of taste and technique. As with all writing, important tools include a good thesaurus and dictionary. A thesaurus can transform even the oldest and most unpalatable of chestnuts. "It was a dark and stormy night" becomes "Somber and tenebrous, the vespertine hour approached." The danger, of course, is that elevated diction easily falls into self-parody. But when well done, it can seduce the reader into believing in—well, in any number of marvelous things:

> Last night I dreamt that I woke to hear some strange, barely audible sound from downstairs—a kind of thin tintinnabulation, like those coloured-glass bird scarers which in my childhood were still sold for hanging up to glitter and tinkle in the garden breeze. I thought I went downstairs to the drawing room. The doors of the china cabinets were standing open, but all the figures were in their places—the Bow Liberty and Matrimony, the Four Seasons of Neale earthenware, the Reinecke girl on her cow; yes, and she herself—the Girl in a Swing. It was from these that the sound came, for they were weeping.

This is from Richard Adams's superb *The Girl in a Swing*, to my mind the best supernatural novel I've ever read.

One of the problems in writing supernatural fiction stems from the fact that "ghost stories" are nearly always better when they are really stories, rather than full-length novels. Many of the classic works of dark fantasy—*The Turn of the Screw*, Charlotte Gilman's "The Yellow Wallpaper," Oliver Onions's "The Beckoning Fair One"—are novellas, a form that suits the supernatural, but which is a hard sell: too short for publishers looking for meaty bestsellers, too long for a magazine market that thrives on the 5,000- to 7,000-word story. It is very difficult to sustain a high level of suspense for several hundred pages. Chapter after chapter of awful doings too often just become awful, with the "cliffhanger" effect ultimately boring the reader.

Characterization is one way of avoiding this pitfall. If your central characters are intriguing, you don't need a constant stream of ghoulish doings to hold a reader's attention. Think of Anne Rice's Lestat, whose melancholy persona has seen him through several sequels. Or the callow student narrator of Donna Tartt's *The Secret History*, a novel which has only a hint of the supernatural about it, but which is more terrifying than any number of haunted houses:

The Secret History is told in the first person, as are *The Girl in a Swing*, Rice's *Vampire Chronicles*, and *Waking the Moon*. In supernatural fiction, it is not enough that the protagonist compel our interest. Readers must also be able to truly identify with him, to experience his growing sense of unease as his familiar world gradually crumbles in the face of some dark intruder, be it spirit or succubus. That is why the first-person narrator is so prevalent in supernatural tales. It is also why most uncanny novels feature individuals whose very normalcy is what sets them apart from others. Like us, they do not believe in ghosts, which makes it all the worse when a ghost actually does appear.

But "normal" does not necessarily mean "dull." Richard Papen, the narrator of *The Secret History*, is drawn into a murderous conspiracy when his college friends seek to evoke Dionysus one drunken winter night. In *The Girl in a Swing*, Alan Desland is a middle-aged bachelor whose most distinguishing characteristic is his extraordinary niceness—until he becomes obsessed with the beautiful Kathe. And in C.S. Lewis's classic *That Hideous Strength*, a peaceful English village is besieged by the forces of darkness.

As with all good fiction, it is important that the central characters are changed by their experiences, whether for good or ill. Lazy writers often use mere physical transformations to effect this change: The heroine becomes a vampire. Or the heroine is prevented from becoming a vampire. Or the heroine is killed. Far more eerie is the plight of the eponymous hero of Peter Ackroyd's terrifying *Hawksmoor*, a police detective drawn into a series of cult murders that took place in London churches two hundred years before:

> Hawksmoor looked for relief from the darkness of wood, stone and metal but he could find none; and the silence of the church had once again descended as he sat down upon a small chair and covered his face. And he allowed it to grow dark.

Nicholas Hawksmoor's unwanted clairvoyance gives him a glimpse of horrors he is unable to forget, and forever alters his perception of the power of good and evil in the world and in his work.

In many ways, the intricacies of plot are less central to supernatural fiction than is pacing (another reason why short stories usually work better than novels). A careful balance must be achieved between scenes of the ordinary and the otherworldly. Usually, a writer alternates the two, with the balance gradually tipping in favor of the unreal: Think of Dracula moving from Transylvania to London, and bringing with him a miasma of palpable evil that slowly infects all around him. In *Waking the Moon*, my heroine's involvement with the supernatural parallels her love affair in the real world. However you choose to do it, don't let the magical elements overwhelm your story completely.

Finally, dare to be different. Does the world really need another vampire novel? How about a lamia instead? Or an evil tree? As always, it's a good idea to be well-read in your chosen genre, so that you don't waste time and ink reinventing Frankenstein's monster. In addition to the works mentioned above, there is a wealth of terrific short supernatural fiction that can teach as well as chill you. *Great Tales of Terror and the Supernatural* (edited by Herbert A. Wise and Phyllis Fraser) is perhaps the indispensable anthology. There are also collections by great writers such as Poe, Robert Aickman, John Collier, Edith Wharton, Isak Dinesen, Sheridan Le Fanu, M.R. James, and many, many others.

Jack Sullivan has written two books that I refer to constantly: *Elegant Nightmares* and *Lost Souls*, classic studies of English ghost stories that can serve as a crash course on how to write elegant horror. These, along with Stephen King's nonfiction *Danse Macabre*, should put you well on your way to creating your own eldritch novel.

Happy haunting!

❋

The most important thing you have to understand is that we lived in a haunted place. A town that over the centuries had survived death by fire, water, wind. . . . The village was founded in 1627 as a far-flung remnant of the old Dutch colony of New Netherland. The oldest houses—stern fieldstone dwellings with steeply pitched roofs and gables—dated from twenty years later, but there were ruins of older houses still, wooden buildings burnt to the ground by the Tankiteke Indians. . . .

. . . [T]he White Hurricane of 1873 left the woods along the Muscanth River as desolate as though they had been struck by a meteor. The forest scarcely had a chance to regenerate when in 1907 it was drowned, the Muscanth dammed to form a reservoir that would provide water for the great city to the south. Most people moved their houses . . . but some refused. Their homes lie there still beneath the green murky waters of Lake Muscanth, alongside rusted-out refrigerators and doomed autos and a few unclaimed corpses.

Through the centuries, high above [the town] stood the strange grand mansion known as Bolerium, its mottled granite walls so covered with moss and lichen they were nearly indistinguishable from the surrounding stones, its turrets and gables and cupolas thrusting from its walls as though carven from the mountain itself. Bolerium seemed not so much separate from

Kamensic as some marvel given birth by the town, phantasm or prodigy or portent. Its whorled-glass windows gazed down upon the lake's deceptively placid dark surface as though dreaming of itself.

Bolerium was the oldest building in Kamensic. Legend had it that when the Dutch settlers arrived, the mansion was already there, torchlight guttering behind its thick panes and shadowy figures moving slowly through its corridors. This was absurd, of course. It would have taken years, decades even, to build such a mammoth structure.

What was known about the house was that its granite blocks were not native to New York State, or even to the New World. During the Victorian era Owen Schelling, founder of Schelling's Market and an amateur geologist, determined that the building material came from the Penwith peninsula, on the westernmost tip of Cornwall. And because of an unusual variation in the stones, he could assign them an exact provenance: the pastel-tinted cliffs of Lamorna Cave, where ancient quarries produced greenstone and the coarse-grained granite that gave birth to that country's tors and neolithic forts and standing stones.

After Schelling's discovery, Bolerium's mysterious stones would periodically draw geologists from universities and museums across the country. They would carefully tap at the mansion's walls and take their slender samples off to the city, where the results were always the same—an unusual mixture of Penwith greenstone and St. Buryan granite. The shaved and splintered rock was examined and dated and filed away, but the mystery remained: there were no records of Bolerium's construction, no ship's manifest detailing how or when or why a million tons of Cornish granite came to New York Harbor, and thence seventy miles inland to a remote hamlet where only hardscrabble farmers lived. . . .

✳

—From the opening pages of Elizabeth Hand's neo-gothic novel, Black Light (HarperCollins, 1999). Copyright © 1999 by Elizabeth Hand.

PART II

THE BUILDING BLOCKS
OF FANTASY STORIES

FIRE, EARTH, WATER, WIND

CHAPTER FOUR

FIRES OF THE HEART:
DEVELOPING FANTASTIC CHARACTERS

CHARACTERS ARE THE BEATING, BURNING HEART of all fiction. Stories revolve around characters, and characters revolve around their desires. What do they want? As Kurt Vonnegut famously said, a story should start with a character who wants something, even if it's just a glass of water. This makes fiction come alive. We all understand wanting something.

Who are the heroes and heroines of fantasy novels? How are they shaped? What drives them? What do they love, hate, aspire to, fear? Not surprisingly, they want what we want: to be loved and respected, to triumph over fears, to do the right thing, to be true to friends and to ourselves. And occasionally, we may wish to be part of something of even greater purpose—a quest for a holy grail, a moment that transcends mere mortality.

These are the fires that blaze in the hearts of characters.

On the first pages of J.R.R. Tolkien's *The Hobbit*, we meet both Bilbo and the great Gandalf.

> All that the unsuspecting Bilbo saw that morning was an old man with a staff. He had a tall pointed blue hat, a long grey cloak, a silver scarf over which his long white beard hung down below his waist, and immense black boots.
>
> "Good morning!" said Bilbo, and he meant it. The sun was shining, and the grass was very green. But Gandalf looked at him from under long bushy eyebrows that stuck out further than the brim of his shady hat.
>
> "What do you mean?" he said. "Do you wish me a good morning, or mean that it is a good morning whether I want it or not; or that you feel good this morning; or that it is a morning to be good on?"

"All of them at once," said Bilbo. . . . Then Bilbo sat down on a seat by his door, crossed his legs, and blew out a beautiful grey ring of smoke that sailed up into the air without breaking and floated away over The Hill.

—*The Hobbit*, 1937, by J.R.R. Tolkien (passages quoted are from the British 4th edition, George Allen & Unwin, 1978)

Within that smoke ring floats the essence of the book: the wispy, ever-expanding ring of adventure and learning that will become the quest of the hobbit. In the next sentence, Tolkien reveals what Gandalf wants: "someone to share in an adventure I am arranging."

A few pages later, Bilbo's "most luxurious hobbit-hole" with its long tunnel-like hall with paneled walls, tiled and carpeted floor, and polished chairs is invaded by a band of visiting dwarves. Though we do not yet know what Gandalf's adventure is, we are discovering much about the modest, contented hobbit. We know what he desires: peace and quiet. He is aghast at the boisterous dwarves who take over his house, freely dispensing his carefully hoarded larder of cider and provisions, and offering to wash up in a carefree way that terrifies the poor furry-toed hobbit.

Chip the glasses and crack the plates!
Blunt the knives and bend the forks!
That's what Bilbo Baggins hates—
Smash the bottles and burn the corks!

Poor hobbit! He just wants to be left alone. And Gandalf? We are brought back to that image of the smoke-ring:

[Thorin, leader of the dwarves] was blowing the most enormous smoke-rings, and wherever he told one to go, it went—up the chimney, or behind the clock on the mantelpiece, or under the table, or round and round the ceiling; but wherever it went it was not quick enough to escape Gandalf. Pop! he sent a smaller smoke-ring from his short clay-pipe straight through each one of Thorin's. Then Gandalf's smoke-ring would go green and come back to hover over the wizard's head. He had a cloud of them about him already, and in the dim light it made him look strange and sorcerous.

The plot is not quite afoot, but something is brewing in the wizard's head underneath the swirling green smoke-rings. We already feel affection for Bilbo, the hobbit; we yearn to see him cope with the dwarves and learn what the master of the smoke-rings has in store. And yet, as readers, we delight in his initial confusion. It is the tinder that sparks the story.

In *The Hobbit*, Tolkien makes use of a classic technique of fantasy. He approaches his story from the point of the only character who doesn't understand what is happening. Bilbo has no idea why dwarf after dwarf is showing up at his hobbit-hole door, each adding to the row of colorful dwarf-capes hanging in his paneled hallway.

This is a surefire way to engage the reader's attention and sympathy. Readers always identify with the character who knows the least about what will happen in a book, for they share this state. They too are trying to understand any puzzling event using the clues provided. Since strange things can occur in a fantasy story, readers enter it with their minds alert and open. A good author takes advantage of that to pique their curiosity, while introducing the story's protagonists.

INTRODUCING CHARACTERS

In the award-winning *Chronicles of Prydain* series by Lloyd Alexander, the princess Eilonwy doesn't want to be treated as a mere girl. Likewise, young Taran desperately wants to be more than an Assistant Pig-Keeper. These desires get them into many scrapes; these same qualities will triumph in the end. The moment they meet face to face, we sense that they will play a big part in each others' lives.

> Eilonwy, as the bewildered Taran saw her for the first time, had, in addition to blue eyes, long hair of reddish gold reaching to her waist, Her face, though smudged, was delicate, elfin, with high cheekbones. Her short, white robe, mud-stained, was girdled with silver links. A crescent moon of silver hung from a fine chain around her neck. She was one or two years younger than he, but fully as tall.

> —*The Book of Three*, 1964, Lloyd Alexander

However, Eilonwy and Taran had met a few pages earlier, mostly through an exchange of dialogue when Eilonwy's golden ball rolls

Thornmallow's real name was Henry. He was a small fellow, thin as a reed, with fair, unmanageable hair the color and shape of dandelion fluff. His eyes were a gooseberry green and hard to read. There was always a smudge or two on his nose as if the nose led him into trouble. But he was actually a quiet boy, shy and obedient to a fault. He had never wanted to be a wizard.
—from the beginning of Wizard's Hall, 1991, by Jane Yolen

into Taran's prison cell. As her blue eyes peer through a slit in the door, we hear that the headstrong girl is not impressed by Taran's hesitant responses.

"Little girl," Taran interrupted, "I don't . . ."

"But I am not a little girl," Eilonwy protested. "Haven't I just been and finished telling you? Are you slow-witted? I'm so sorry for you. It's terrible to be dull and stupid. What's your name?" . . .

"I am Taran of Caer Dallben," Taran said, then wished he had not. . . .

"That's lovely," Eilonwy said gaily. "I'm very glad to meet you. I suppose you're a lord, or a warrior, or a war leader, or a bard, or a monster. Through we haven't had any monsters for a long time."

"I am none of those, said Taran, feeling quite flattered. . . .

"What else is there?"

"I am an Assistant Pig-Keeper," Taran said. He bit his lip as soon as the words were out. . . .

"Now, please, if you don't mind, it's right at your feet."

"I can't pick up your bauble," Taran said, "because my hands are tied."

The blue eyes looked surprised. "Oh? Well, that would account for it. Then I suppose I shall have to come in and get it."

"You can't come in and get it, said Taran wearily. "Don't you see I'm locked up here?"

"Of course I do," said Eilonwy. "What would be the point of having someone in a dungeon if they weren't locked up? Really, Taran of Caer Dallben, you surprise me with some of your remarks. I don't mean to hurt your feelings by asking, but is Assistant Pig-Keeper the kind of work that calls for a great deal of intelligence?"

In the first pages of a story, the reader is like a sponge. Who are these people? What is going on? Very quickly, readers develop a hypothesis about the nature of each character as he or she is introduced. In Susan Cooper's 1973 novel, *The Dark Is Rising*, young Will, exploring a strange world outside his home, arrives at a small village and sees a man.

The man was tall, and wore a dark cloak that fell straight like a robe; his hair, which grew low over his neck, shone with a curious reddish tinge. He patted the horse's neck, murmuring in its ear;

then he seemed to sense the cause of its restlessness, and he turned and saw Will. His arms dropped abruptly. He took a step forward and stood there, waiting.

The brightness went out of the snow and the sky, and the morning darkened a little, as an extra layer of the distant cloudbank swallowed the sun.

—*The Dark Is Rising*, by Susan Cooper

We have been given little of this man's physical description, really only three items: a tall man, a dark cloak, red hair. But other hints are offered. His hair shines with a curious tinge—why "curious"? He whispers to his horse. He steps forward, then stops and waits. Is he being courteous? It's not clear. Then the light dims. Author Susan Cooper, who also works with theater, has used a subtle lighting cue and the faintest of stage movements to introduce us to a man who will not be Will's friend.

In the beginning scene of *Watership Down*, a novel by master storyteller Richard Adams, we meet Hazel the rabbit and quickly sense his confidence:

The first rabbit stopped in a sunny patch and scratched his ear with rapid movements of his hind leg. Although he was a yearling and still below his full weight, he had not the harassed look of most "outskirters"—that is, the rank and file of ordinary rabbits in their first year who . . . get sat on by their elders and live as best they can—often in the open—on the edge of their warren. He looked as though he knew how to take care of himself. There was a shrewd, buoyant air about him as he sat up, looked around and rubbed both front paws over his nose. As soon as he was satisfied that all was well, he laid back his ears and set to work on the grass.

—*Watership Down*, 1974, Richard Adams

We then meet a second rabbit, Fiver:

His companion seemed less at ease. He was small, with wide, staring eyes and a way of raising and turning his head which suggested not so much caution as a kind of ceaseless, nervous tension. His nose moved continually, and when a bumblebee flew humming to a thistle bloom behind him, he jumped and spun around with a start that sent two nearby rabbits scurrying for holes before the nearest, a buck with black-tipped ears, recognized him and returned to feeding.

"Oh, it's only Fiver," said the black-tipped rabbit, "jumping at bluebottles again."

The rabbits of *Watership Down* are described here not by physical description, but by their actions.

Physical description, dialogue, and actions are the tools to use when introducing a main character. With initial introductions, restraint is a good thing. Limiting the information given early on makes each bit of it stronger; it makes the reader eager for what is to come.

MORE QUALITIES UNVEILED

As a story progresses, characters need to come to life. Seeds sown early—behaviors, talents, curious connections, casual revelations—begin to develop deeper meanings. Unlike reality, nothing is accidental in literature. Hidden at first, sprouts soon begin to appear from magic beans planted in the soil, revealing the first tendrils of what will become the towering beanstalk of the story.

In *A Wrinkle in Time* by Madeleine L'Engle, we meet the protagonist Meg, "the snaggle-toothed, the myopic, the clumsy." She thinks herself unattractive and dumb. She, her brother Charles Wallace, and her new friend Calvin are at the center of the story. But the young threesome is echoed by a trio of elder guardians: Mrs. Whatsit, Mrs. Who, and Mrs. Which. Mrs. Whatsit is a frumpy, gray-haired old woman with a voice "like an unoiled grate, but somehow not unpleasant," who lives in an old house back in the woods. In a storm, she appears at the Wallaces' door:

. . . was it the tramp? It seemed small for Meg's idea of a tramp. The age or sex was impossible to tell, for it was completely bundled up in clothes. Several scarves of assorted colors were tied about the head, and a man's felt hat perched atop. A shocking pink stole was knotted about a rough overcoat, and black rubber boots covered the feet.

Appearances can be deceiving. A few chapters later, the children are out in the woods and meet all three ladies. In the golden air, Mrs. Whatsit begins to transform:

"Now don't be frightened, loves," Mrs. Whatsit said. Her plump little body began to shimmer, to quiver, to shift. The wild colors of her clothes became muted, whitened. The pudding-bag shape stretched, lengthened, merged. And suddenly before the children was a creature more beautiful than any Meg had ever imagined, and the beauty lay in far more than the outward description. Outwardly Mrs. Whatsit was surely no longer a Mrs. Whatsit. She was a marble white body with powerful flanks, something like a horse but at the same time completely unlike a horse, for from the magnificently modeled back sprang a nobly formed torso, arms, and a head resembling a man's, but a man with a perfection of dignity and virtue, an exaltation of joy such as Meg had never before seen. . . .

From the shoulders slowly a pair of wings unfolded, wings made of rainbows, of light upon water, of poetry.

—*A Wrinkle in Time* (1962), by Madeleine L'Engle

Transformation is a cornerstone of fantasy. Even more than in ordinary fiction, fantasy characters have an unusual freedom to discover or reveal their true natures. They can transform into intensified versions of themselves, whether that be a Pegasus-like creature or a great hero hidden within an Assistant Pig-Keeper's body.

In some rings of fantasy, transformation is resisted. In the classic vampire story, characters struggle not to give in to their dark desires. They tremble and sweat in their efforts to hold back, although readers know full well what is going on.

In an early scene in *The Vampire Armand* by Anne Rice, one vampire, Armand, sizes up another, David Talbot. The descriptions are lush, redolent with scent, just a step away from sudden violence.

"David Talbot," I said, measuring him coldly with my eyes. . . . "tricked into a vampire as a fiery unstanchable blood invaded his lucky anatomy, sealing his soul up in it as it transformed him into an immortal—a man of dark bronzed skin and dry, lustrous and thick black hair."

"I think you have it right," he said with indulgent politeness.

My skin is loose. It's as though I walk inside it, my muscles rippling beneath a coat. I stop at a coconut tree and spread my claws in wonder. Then I retract them and walk.
A lion's walk. A lion's body. ... I am lion! No insanity, no nightmare, truth. And the hunt starts within the hour.
—Beast, 2000, by Donna Jo Napoli

"A handsome gent," I went on, "the color of caramel, moving with such catlike ease and gilded glances that he makes me think of all things once delectable, and now a potpourri of scent: cinnamon, clove, mild peppers and other spices golden, brown or red, whose fragrances can spike my brain and plunge me into erotic yearnings . . . His skin must smell like cashew nuts and thick almond cream. It does."

He laughed. "I get your point.". . .

He was dressed to kill. With the cleverness of olden times, when men could preen like peacocks, he'd chosen golden sepia and umber colors for his clothes. He was smart and clean and fretted all over with careful bits of pure gold, in a wristband timepiece and buttons and a slender pin for his modern tie, that tailored spill of color men wear in this age, as if to let us grab them all the more easily by its noose. Stupid ornament. Even his shirt of polished cotton was tawny and full of something of the sun and the warmed earth. Even his shoes were brown, glossy as beetles' backs.

—*The Vampire Armand*, by Anne Rice, 1998

Is dark always bad? Is fair hair always good? In this passage, Anne Rice toys with the ambiguous richness of earthy colors, the smells of spices, the glossy-brown of the beetle's back.

INNER FLAWS

The world has held great Heroes,
As history books have showed;
But never a name to go down to fame
Compared with that of Toad!

The clever men at Oxford
Know all that there is to be knowed,
But they none of them know one half as much
As intelligent Mr. Toad! . . .

—"The Further Adventures of Toad," in *The Wind in the Willows*, by Kenneth Grahame, 1908

A key part of any story is the weaknesses of central characters. Though quests may be idealized, people are not. Camelot may be perfect, but Guinevere and Lancelot are flawed. They struggle, slip, and fall.

The appendix of John Steinbeck's book on the Arthurian legends, *The Acts of King Arthur and his Noble Knights*, consists of the author's letters to his literary agent, Elizabeth Otis, and his editor, Chase Horton. In one letter, Steinbeck muses that while the beautiful Guinevere has always been depicted as an idealized symbol of Woman placed on a pedestal, "in fact she must have been a dame." Later on, Steinbeck writes in similar terms about King Arthur, seeking the man behind the legend.

> Alas! . . . Arthur is a dope. It gets so that you want to yell—Not that again! Look out—he's got a gun! the way we used to in the old movies when our beloved hero was blundering stupidly into the villain's lair. Just the same as Arthur. . . . It almost seems that dopiness is required in literature. Only the bad guys can be smart. Could it be that there is a built-in hatred and fear of intelligence . . . so that the heroes must be stupid? Cleverness equates with evil almost invariably. It is a puzzlement, but there it is.

There it is, a summing up of one of the most respected cycles of legends in the world by a great American author, winner of the Nobel Prize for Literature: the Arthurian legend at its core is a story of a dame and a dope.

Much of *The Hobbit* deals with the interaction of types of characters, Tolkien's "races" of Middle-earth: hobbits, dwarves, elves, men, goblins, spiders. Each has its own nature, its deep instinct, which it follows, often blindly. Hobbits, for instance, are unobtrusive, able to creep about stealthily without anyone noticing them—perfect for a thief's role. Though averse to danger, preferring a cozy armchair and afternoon tea, Bilbo reluctantly accepts the thief's role thrust upon him, and is swept into adventures which change him forever.

The dwarves are quarrelsome; they want to reclaim lost gold from their ancestral mountains—a vast treasure now guarded by the dragon Smaug. While good artisans and tough fighters, dwarves are petulant and hot-tempered. In the presence of gold, they lose all reason. They are also not gifted at understanding others. Instead, it is the unassuming hobbit who sees differences and weaknesses and is able to creep in and employ more complex stratagems, while the

Always, if [my characters] came off, they had a seed of something that had moved me—a gesture, a sentence, some little idiosyncrasy.

You can write about nothing, said Tolstoy, unless you love it—not even a tree.

— Eva Ibbotson, from "Hush! Beth is Dying!" in The Writer, February 1974 dwarves are thwarted, stumbling into dangerous situations of their own making.

After the dragon is slain by an archer from a nearby town, the dwarvish leader, Thorin, refuses to share anything with the local townspeople, who end up besieging the stubborn dwarves in the mountain hall. Even Bilbo's attempt at intercession with the help of the great Gandalf fails; only when the dwarves prepare for battle is disaster averted at the last minute by a greater threat from outside forces.

Tolkien, scholar of regional dialects, understood that the desires of different types of characters are shaped not just by individual interests, but also by deep patterns of traditional myths, ethnic grudges, family lore, occupational proclivities. In *The Hobbit*, this richly woven tale of varied groups interacting with each other creates a marvelously textured backdrop for the actions of the characters engaged in the story.

QUIRKS

Quirks seem to offer interest for the reader. But beware: they can lead to silliness and worse, pointlessness. Every character can't be quirky. Quirks are best when they become relevant to the story, when they ultimately "pay off." In *Watership Down*, Fiver's overly sensitive nature quickly becomes very important to the story, as does Hazel's confidence.

When we first meet the dwarves in *The Hobbit*, they are amusing in their rambunctious enthusiasm as they invade Bilbo's hobbit-hole. Eventually, their impetuous nature is their downfall.

Hobbits themselves are generally down-to-earth characters—desirous of comfort, fond of their favorite pipes and buttoned waistcoats, living in well-appointed surroundings. Yet Tolkien notes that Bilbo Baggins had a touch of fairy in him, inherited from his mother. "It had always been said that long ago one or other of the Tooks had married into a fairy family . . . certainly there was still something not entirely hobbitlike about them, and once in a while members of the Took-clan would go and have adventures." Clearly, this unsettling trait will prove to be a factor in the story.

On the other hand, as in the fantasy stories of James Thurber or Carl Sandburg, sometimes the pleasures of language are reason enough to take things to their quirkiest, to combine silliness with pure tenderness:

Around the middle of each corn fairy is a yellow-belly belt. And stuck in this belt is a purple moon shaft hammer. Whenever the wind blows strong and nearly blows the corn down, then the fairies run out and take their yellow-belly belts and nail down nails to keep the corn from blowing down. . . .

Spink and Skabootch ask where the corn fairies get the nails. The answer to Spink and Skabootch is, "Next week you will learn all about where . . . if you will keep your faces washed and your ears washed until next week."

And the next time you stand watching a big cornfield in late summer or early fall, when the wind is running across the green and silver, listen with your littlest and newest ears.

—"How to Tell Corn Fairies When You See 'Em," by Carl Sandburg, in *Rootabaga Stories*, 1922

CASTING AGAINST TYPE

Tolkien's elves stand tall. They are not the elves of his contemporaries, diminutive flitlings with gossamer wings, dancing and cavorting inside the bells of flowers. They are singers of epic songs, craftsmen and artists of the highest order. They are immortal, unless slain in battle. Best of all, in Tolkien's eyes, their sense of imagination is vast.

In the urban fantasy environment of Bordertown, on the other hand (an anthology with contributions from a number of writers), it is not uncommon to see punk elves in chains, pierced ears, and tattoos wandering the streets in gangs looking for trouble. Or you may turn the corner to find a group of rowdy beribboned Morris dancers—on stripped-down Harley motorcycles, wearing antlers on their heads, weaving a drunken Horn Dance down the street.

In *The Tooth Fairy* (1998), by Graham Joyce, malevolent fairy meets modern myth, and the result is unsettling.

The voice came out in a cracked whisper. "Can you see me? . . ."

The intruder—Sam was unable to tell if it was male or female—suddenly cocked its head to one side and smiled. A row of teeth glimmered in the faint moonbeams, a mouthful of blue light. The teeth were perfect, but, unless he was mistaken, they were sharpened to fine dagger points. At full height the intruder stood little

"Not so fast," the Golux said. "Half the places I have been to, never were. I make things up. Half the things I say are there cannot be found. When I was young I told a tale of buried gold, and men from leagues around dug in the woods. I dug myself."

"But why?"

"I thought the tale of treasure might be true."

"You said you made it up."

"I know I did, but . . . I forget things, too."

—Thirteen Clocks, by James Thurber, 1950

more than four feet tall, or at any rate, just a couple of inches taller than Sam. It was difficult to see what the creature was wearing in the dark, but he could identify mustard-and-green striped leggings and heavy, industrial-style boots.

"Yes, I can see you."

"That's bad. Real bad."

The intruder was squinting hard at Sam, as if puzzling what to do next. "And you can hear me. Obviously obviously obviously. Bad." The sharpened teeth gleamed electric-blue again in the moonlight. There was a tiny crackle as the figure placed a finger on the bedpost. Sam felt the crackle ride to the nape of his neck and fan his hair. The intruder was discharging static.

Sam suddenly had an idea who the figure was. "You've come for the tooth, haven't you?"

—*The Tooth Fairy,* by Graham Joyce

In John Gardner's brilliant novel *Grendel,* the monster that will duel with Beowulf is a demented, violent creature. Yet he is intelligent, full of existential fatalism. His bitter anger is that of powerless watcher as he spies on the cunning, also violent men of Hrothgar who are creating a growing kingdom on the Danish shores.

Not, of course, that I fool myself with thoughts that I'm more noble. . . . "Ah, sad one, poor old freak!" I cry, and hug myself, and laugh, letting out salt tears, he he! till I fall down gasping and sobbing. (It's mostly fake.) . . . (It was just here, this shocking green, that once when the moon was tombed in clouds, I tore off sly old Athelgard's head. Here, where the startling tiny jaws of crocuses snap at the late-winter sun like the heads of baby watersnakes, here I killed the old woman with the irongray hair. She tasted of urine and spleen, which made me spit. Sweet mulch for yellow blooms. Such are the tiresome memories of a shadow-shooter, earth-rim-roamer, walker of the world's weird wall.) "Waaah!" I cry, with another quick, nasty face at the sky, mournfully observing the way it is, bitterly remembering the way it was, and idiotically casting tomorrow's nets. "Aargh! Yaww!" I reel, smash trees. . . . "No offense," I say, with a terrible, syncophantish smile, and tip an imaginary hat.

—*Grendel,* 1989, John Gardner

INTERACTION

. . . she comes
In shape no bigger than an agate-stone
On the forefinger of an alderman,
Drawn with a team of little atomies
Athwart men's noses as they lie asleep:
Her wagon-spokes made of long spinners' legs;
The cover, of the wings of grasshoppers;
The traces, of the smallest spider's web;
The collars, of the moonshine's watery beams;
Her whip of cricket's bone; the lash, of film; . . .

And in this state she gallops night by night
Through lover's brains, and then they dream of love;
O'er courtiers' knees, that dream on court'sies straight;
O'er lawyers' fingers, who straight dream on fees;
O'er ladies lips, who straight on kisses dream.

So William Shakespeare describes the nocturnal outings of tiny Queen Mab in *A Midsummer Night's Dream*. Note that he not only depicts her midnight rides, but also tells of the effect she has upon others. Courtiers, lawyers, and ladies dream of their fondest desires in her magical presence.

Good characters not only are interesting in their own right, but also have an effect on others. They learn from each other. They grow to become fast friends. They fall in and out of love. They irritate each other. Sometimes they compete. Always, they react to what others in the story are doing.

Terry Pratchett is a master at this. His *Discworld* series swarms with characters who don't really care much for each other. His novels are friction-powered; characters rub each other the wrong way, constantly prodding and needling. Each of Pratchett's slightly demented characters has a strong opinion about the immense flaws of all the others.

For instance, in Pratchett's 1998 novel *Carpe Jugulum,* the plot centers around a band of stylish vampires who descend on the province of Lancre, in the hinterlands of Discworld. The modern bloodsuckers have embarked on a self-help program to overcome their distaste for garlic, daylight, religious crosses, and so on. Flouting their newfound power, they set up shop in the province, taking over the castle. It appears to be a classic good-versus-evil plot, the vampires against the good Lancrastrians.

But the novel is as much about the friction between characters on the same side who dislike each other heartily. Granny Weatherwax quarrels with the new preacher in town—the insecure Mightily Oats, whose belief in his god, Om, is not quite as strong as his belief in the existence of his pamphlets. He is subject to constant needling from Granny Weatherwax about his inconclusive religious views.

> "It's not a magic amulet, Mistress Weatherwax! Please! A magic amulet is a symbol of primitive and mechanistic superstition, whereas the Turtle of Om is . . . is . . . is . . . well, it's not, do you understand?"
>
> "Oh, right. Thank you for explaining," said Granny.

Confront a wizard with the concept of a bathing suit and he'll start to get nervous. Why does it have to be so skimpy? he'll ask. Where can I put the gold embroidery? How can you have any kind of costume without at least forty useful pockets? . . .
—Terry Pratchett, 1998, The Last Continent

Together, though, they eventually carry the day, bickering their way to victory against the vampires.

For an author, this interaction of characters is difficult to plan; it is more often something that happens as the story progresses.

> I'm always finding out new things about [my characters] throughout the whole story. Despite the fact that I have planned the number of chapters, where certain scenes are going to be set, and where the climax is . . . I don't know *how* events are going to happen and I don't know *what* they are going to mean. . . . [This] really emerges as the characters start interacting. . . .
>
> —Diane Paxson, author of *The White Raven*, 1988, from interview with Raymond H. Thompson, The Camelot Project, July 1989

Characters come alive when they have their own roles to play, their own desires and obsessions. The writer's job is to manage this, like a director of a play, making sure that minor characters don't upstage the major characters. The quality of the imagination involved in creating all characters, major and minor—and the degree to which they interact with each other—helps the story achieve its liveliness.

Orson Scott Card, award-winning writer of speculative-fiction and a respected writing teacher, offers two main rules to follow:

In truth, the secret to all characterization for me is expressible in two maxims: Every character is the hero of his own story. And you don't write characters, you write relationships.

In practice the first maxim means that you must let characters have their own purposes and agendas, not just do what the plot requires.

And the second maxim means that nobody is the same person to everyone—who they are depends in large part on whom they're with.

—Orson Scott Card, interview with Claire E. White, editor of *The Internet Writing Journal* (www.writerswrite.com)

CREATING A HERO

Fantasy literature is often about small protagonists overcoming odds, about Davids in worlds of Goliaths. Classic fantasy presents an underdog hero, an ordinary character drawn into wondrous challenges, with great things at stake.

In Susan Cooper's *The Dark Is Rising*, Will, a teenager, awakens one morning to find his house frozen, his family locked in time, and powerful dark forces appearing that he will have to battle. The odds seem stacked against the young fellow; but he manages to prevail.

J.K. Rowling's Harry Potter and his school friends have to pool their powers to fight playground bullies as well as three-headed monsters, trolls, and dark lords. Likewise the hobbits of Tolkien's tales are diminutive—"small in size," wrote Tolkien, "because it reflects the generally small reach of their imagination—not the small reach of their courage or latent power" (in Humphrey Carpenter's definitive 1977 biography). Tolkien had seen first-hand how ordinary folk drew on vast reserves of heroism when sent into the trenches of World War I. He noted that "we are here, surviving, because of the indomitable courage of quite small people against impossible odds."

It is the ordinary nature of these heroes that causes us to identify with them. As Neil Gaiman said, his protagonist Richard Mayhew in the novel *Neverwhere* had elements of Everyman.

C.S. Lewis wrote an essay all about heroes and Everyman, where he said, "It is very, very important that a hero in a novel not be too odd. How odd events strike odd people is an oddity too much."

> The young mouse took the great sword in both paws. Eyes shining, he gazed at the hard black bound handle with its red pommel stone, the stout crosstree hilt and the magnificent blade. It shone like snowfire.... Once, twice, he tried to swing it above his head. Both times he faltered, failing because of the sword's weight. "Nearly, Father, I can nearly swing it."
> —Brian Jacques, in *Mattimeo*, 1990

[Lewis] pointed out that in *Through the Looking Glass,* Wonderland would not have been anywhere so interesting had Alice not been so dull, so plain. If Alice had been in any way interesting herself, it would have been a much less interesting book.

And I thought, "you've got to try." It seems like a nice position to begin a book from. I wanted a hero who was not a hero. I wanted somebody who was a little bit everybody, someone who was not the kind of person who would make the list if you were putting together a hero roster, but who was going to get by on essentially a good heart and good intentions, which were going to get him into deep trouble, but perhaps get him out again as well.

—Neil Gaiman, interview with Claire E. White, *The Internet Writing Journal* (www.writerswrite.com), March 1999

The hero has a complex dual role to play: to be human and to be larger-than-life. In many ways, Harry Potter and Bilbo the hobbit are like us, their readers. They are shy, quiet, reluctant to take center stage, not seeking fame or heroic stature. Yet they also have special powers, and when called upon, draw on their inner strengths to perform feats of great courage and personal sacrifice.

As Diana Wynne Jones noted:

> The word *agony* also makes part of the word *protagonist.* And it is the same word in origin as *action.* It is as if the facts about heroes are built into our language—if you take action of any kind, you are going to suffer. . . . Agony, which means, in origin, a death-struggle, is a word for both external pain and internal strife (as in "agony of indecision").
>
> . . . The hero is expected to struggle on two fronts, externally with an actual evil, and internally with his/her own doubts and shortcomings. The hero, out there as scapegoat, has to do the suffering for everyone.

—From "Heroes," 1992 (on www.dianawynnejones.com)

While some heroes of fantasy are mighty warriors, even the great ones usually have some human flaw that brings them down to earth. Fantasy heroes are not gods. More often, he or she is just a rather ordinary person, drawn into a great struggle, ever-doubting whether he or she has what it takes to slay the dragon. Small in

"And I—I must send you into the dragon's den again, having barely healed you.... By the gods and hells you have never heard of," Luthe broke out, "do you think I like sending a child to a doom like this, one I know I cannot myself face?"
—The Hero and the Crown, 1984, Robin McKinley

stature, the hero/heroine must struggle to victory on two fronts, within and without.

ULTIMATE DESIRES

In successful fantasy, characters need to want something. What is it they desire? What do they wish to gain, protect, win, discover? Finding this point is the fulcrum of your story. It is Aristotle's point from which the world of a story can be moved. The greater the intensity of their desire, the less effort is needed by you to move the story.

In Gaiman's novel *Neverwhere*, Richard and his fiancée Jessica begin the story with remarkably contrasting desires:

> Richard had been awed by Jessica, who was beautiful, and quite often funny, and was certainly going somewhere. And Jessica saw in Richard an enormous amount of potential, which, properly harnessed by the right woman, would have made him the perfect matrimonial accessory. If only he were a little more focused, she would murmur to herself, and so she gave him books with titles like *Dress for Success* and *A Hundred and Twenty-Five Habits of Successful Men*, and books on how to run a business like a military campaign, and Richard always said thank you, and always intended to read them.
>
> —*Neverwhere*, 1997, Neil Gaiman

Clearly, these desires are incompatible—and also insignificant. Soon, the story plunges Richard into a dark, urban underworld, where he begins to respond to a new set of desires: to survive, to find his way out, to learn more about the mysterious young woman named Door who is being chased by some very fiendish villains.

In the first chapter of the compelling novel *Sirena*, Donna Jo Napoli's young protagonist is a mermaid, one of ten siren sisters who wait for passing ships—to sing and lure them onto the shoals of their Aegean island.

> "Come," Cecelia calls with urgency. "I see the ship."
> We gather quickly—none of us has gone far. We swim around the island to where it rises in a sheer cliff. We go to our favorite singing

Three times every month, Maria bundled up her sleeping baby, then she put on her long wool coat and walked across the fields.... Drawn by desire, she traveled quickly, no matter what the weather might be. On some nights, people thought they saw her, her coat billowing out behind her, running so fast it seemed she was no longer touching the ground.... Whenever they did see Maria in daylight ... they didn't trust what was before them—the pretty face, the cool gray eyes, the black coat, the scent of some flower no one in their town could name.
—Alice Hoffman, Practical Magic, 1995

rock offshore. I climb deftly, using my horizontal tail fin as a foot, and find my place among my sisters.

The men are almost here. My heart pounds. We sing in harmony, in rounds, in unison. We sing chants and melodies.

Come to us, wayfaring sailor. . . .

Our voices weave the invisible net. Our three guardian birds turn their heads to us in approval.

The surface of my entire body stings with anticipation. I am as convinced by our song as the sailors must be. Oh, yes, there is a man on that ship who will be my love. Mine.

—*Sirena*, 1998, by Donna Jo Napoli

According to mythology, a siren can become immortal by winning the love of a human. But young Sirena begins to question her right to shipwreck sailors and risk causing them to die—if not by drowning, then eventually from starvation or thirst—even if they might fall in love with her first. How she struggles with this growing awareness, and then takes action to resolve her conflicting desires for passion and honesty, is the driving force behind this elegant story.

Strong characters need powerful desires. In the course of a good story, these ambitions change and mature. Readers need to understand *why* characters want what they want—and to watch how the characters gradually grow and define their true wishes better as they learn more about themselves. In any event, characters always act more intensely—more courageously, more foolishly, and in far more interesting ways—when they follow their deepest desires.

The presence of magic in fantasy stories should not overwhelm this human drive of desire. What characters want is always far more important to a story than the magic they use to get it.

VILLAINS

We've saved one of the best tasks in character creation for last: the joy of bringing to life a really good villain. If fantasy is about good and evil, just as important as a stalwart hero is a true avatar of evil.

Some villains are pure horror and malice, leaping from the page in a searing image:

> Taran fell back, terrified. Astride the foam-spattered animal rose a monstrous figure. A crimson cloak flamed from his naked shoulders. Crimson stained his gigantic arms. Horror-stricken, Taran saw not the head of a man but the antlered head of a stag.
>
> The Horned King! Taran flung himself against an oak to escape the flying hoofs and the heaving, glistening flanks. Horse and rider swept by. The mask was a human skull; from it, the great antlers rose in cruel curves. The Horned King's eyes blazed behind the gaping sockets of whitened bone.

—*The Book of Three*, 1964, Lloyd Alexander

Other classic villains are half-mad and unpredictable. Any little thing may upset their precarious mental balance and lead to a sudden outbreak of violence.

> Slagar seemed to ignore [Hairbelly, a complaining weasel in Slagar's band] for a moment. Turning to the cart, he whipped out a swirling silk cloak. It was decorated with the same design as his headcover, and the lining was black silk, embellished with gold and silver moon and star symbols. Twirling it expertly, he threw it around his body, leaping nimbly onto a row of pews. There Slagar spread his paws wide in a theatrical gesture.
>
> "I will be Lunar Stellaris, light and shadow, hither and thither like the night breeze, presiding over all. Lord of Mountebanks, now you see me. . . ." He dropped out of sight behind the pews, calling, "And now you don't!"
>
> The audience strained forward to see where he had hidden himself. Slagar was gone from behind the pews.
>
> Suddenly, as if by magic, he reappeared in the midst of his band. Right alongside Hairbelly.
>
> "Haha, Lunar Stellaris, Lord of light and dark. But to those who disobey my word I am Slagar the Cruel, Master of life and death."
>
> Before Hairbelly could blink an eye, Slagar had run him through with his sword.

—*Mattimeo*, 1990, Brian Jacques

We want our children to believe that, inherently, all men are good. But children know that they are not always good; and often, even when they are, they would prefer not to be.
—Bruno Bettelheim, in The Uses of Enchantment: The Meaning and Importance of Fairy Tales, 1976

Still other villains are cold and calculating. These may be the most chilling. Their menace lurks off the page in the minds of the readers, not in any physical presence or volatility.

You can get at greediness and selfishness by making them look ridiculous. The greatest attribute of a human being is kindness, and all the other qualities, like bravery and perseverance, are secondary to that.
—Roald Dahl, from the website, www.puffin.co.uk/Authors

He marched straight to the empty seat at the head of the table and sat in it, as if it was obvious where he would sit. . . . He put out a hand, and [the woman with him] put the little case into it without his needing to look. He slapped the case down on the table and clicked the locks back with a fierce *snap*.

"Good afternoon," he said, in a flat, chilly voice.

"Good afternoon, Mr. Chesney," said nearly every wizard there. . . .

Mr. Chesney had grayish, mouse-colored, lank hair and a bald patch half hidden by the lank hair combed severely across it. His face was small and white and seemed ordinary, until you noticed that his mouth was upside down compared with most people's. It sat in a grim downward curve under his pointed nose and above his small, rock-like chin, like the opening to a man-trap. Once you had noticed that, you noticed that his eyes were like cold gray marbles.

. . . "Someone silence that slave girl with the fiddle, please."

There was a loud twang as one of Shona's strings snapped. Her face went white and then flooded bright red.

. . . "You mean my daughter, Mr. Chesney?" [Derk] asked pleasantly.

"Is she?" said Mr. Chesney. "Then you should control her. I object to noise in a business meeting."

—*Dark Lord of Derkholm*, 1998, Diana Wynne Jones

In general, a reason for the evil foe's nastiness needs to be offered. In old folk tales, the evils of monsters, fairies, and trolls were often attributed to a transgression of tradition: a bowl of porridge had not been left out for the tomte on Christmas, a boggart had been insulted by a member of a household, or someone had accidentally doused a fairy with a pan of washwater tossed out the door without proper warning.

In literary stories, the reasons for evilness need to be more logical and psychologically more complex. These reasons should be carefully woven into the plot and into the expressive nature of the villain.

THE FATAL WEAKNESS

While a hero has a flaw, a villain has a fatal weakness. It may be a tiny chink in the armored scales of a dragon where a sword may enter. It may stem from greed, or feelings of superiority, or a lack of some positive human emotion.

In her humorous novel *Dark Lord of Derkholm,* Diana Wynne Jones plays with this classic twist of fantasy stories. She creates a world visited each year by hordes of tourists in search of fantasy-adventure travel. The tours, following detailed itineraries orchestrated by Mr. Chesney, chase about the countryside in search of the Dark Lord (a local chosen each year to bear the brunt of this role-playing, which also proves, like a lot of tourism, quite destructive). In the preliminary briefing, Mr. Chesney's assistant Mr. Addis hands out the details to local leaders gathered at a huge table.

> He picked up a pink pamphlet. . . . "Please take note that this year's tour is choreographed around the one weakness of the Dark Lord. Each party will pick up clues to the Dark Lord's weak point as it goes around, ending in the retrieval of an object that contains this weakness—this is to be guarded by a dragon in the north—and then going on, after the battle, to kill the Dark Lord. Mr. Dark Lord [the eccentric wizard Derk has been selected this year], I'm sure I can count on you to lay one hundred and twenty-six clues [one for each tourist group scheduled] at each spot marked with an asterisk on the map. And you will, of course, need the same number of objects for the dragon to guard."
> . . . "What kind of objects have you in mind?" [Derk] asked.
> "Any object, at your discretion"—Mr. Addis smiled—"though we tend to prefer something with a romantic bias, such as a goblet or an orb."
>
> —*Dark Lord of Derkholm,* Diana Wynne Jones

Whether it is the snarling Slagar or the ice-cold Mr. Chesney, the bigger they are, the harder they fall—when hit squarely between the eyes by a slingshot pellet from the diminutive David. The more powerful and sinister the fantastic villain, the more satisfying his or her eventual defeat. The evilness of the villain is the measure of the eventual triumph by the hero.

And most writers will admit, great villains are a lot of fun to create and can instantly bring a lagging story to life.

> "Monsters," said Hykrion, winking at Bastian and stroking his huge moustache, "monsters are indispensable if a hero is to be a hero."
>
> At last Bastian understood.
>
> "Listen to me, Hero Hynreck," he said. ". . . The truth is that Princess Oglamar needs your help right now, and that no one else can save her. . . ."
>
> Hero Hynreck pricked up his ears.
>
> ". . . It's true, as you will soon see. Only a few minutes ago Princess Oglamar was seized and kidnapped."
>
> "By whom?"
>
> "By one of the most terrible monsters that have ever existed in Fantastica. The dragon Smerg. She was riding across a clearing in the woods when the monster saw her from the air, swooped down, lifted her off her palfrey's back, and carried her away."
>
> Hynreck jumped up. His eyes flashed, his cheeks were aglow. He clapped his hands for joy. . . . "Tell me, what must I do? Where must I go?"

—*The Neverending Story*, 1979, Michael Ende (English trans. 1983)

CREATING COMPULSION

Interview with Franny Billingsley
by Philip Martin

Franny Billingsley is the author of several acclaimed books for young adults, including Well-Wished and The Folk Keeper. The latter won the Horn Book Award in 2000 as the top novel of the year for young readers. Her writing is praised for its tight, powerful imagery, a style she credits in part to hearing her father sing Scottish ballads to her as she grew up. The language of the ballads, she says, got in her blood, with their melancholy, beautiful images wrapped into a tight narrative structure. Here she talks about the challenges in creating her heroine, Corinna, in The Folk Keeper.

My initial idea was to work with the old selkie [seal-person] legends. I knew my heroine was going to be half-selkie and half-human. But she doesn't know who she is. She looks like a human, but there will be weird things about her she can't explain. And her emotional journey would be toward discovering who she truly is. Is she more human?—will she embrace her life on land? Or is she more of a selkie—will she return to a life in the sea?

In non-fantasy fiction, the question of identify is somewhat abstract. But in fantasy, I could have Corinna wrestle with her identity by giving her an actual sealskin. It could become a real thing, part of the plot. Where is it? Will it fit? Can she take it into the sea?

Of course it's a symbol of who she is. That, to me, is the wonderful thing about fantasy—you can take abstract issues and give them concrete reality.

But when I tried to write that book, it didn't have a lot of oomph. It was really static—sort of boggy. Corinna was pretty passive. I had tried to capture the reader's attention through mystery—having her sit around and dream about the sea and stuff like that. But there was nothing for her to do. There was no action; there was no promise of any action. She would just moon around and look at herself in the mirror and admire the tapestries. But that was about it.

So I tried to mold her into a "spunky" character—with a capital S. And she turned into such a brat. I showed it to my writing group and they said, "God, we can't stand her!" Not that you need to like a character. Characters are more interesting when they are somewhat unlikable. And it gives them room to grow. But this was too contrived. But I persisted and wrote many drafts for two and a half years before I sent it to my editor, Jean Karl [at Atheneum].

And she wrote me back and asked me the key question. She said, the main thing is that we don't know what Corinna really wants.

That was the galvanizing thing for me. I thought, of course! If you give your characters something they really desire, then they're going to go out and do something to try to get it. And that creates narrative energy. Which is what the story had been lacking.

I had just been reading *The Art and Craft of Novel Writing* by Oakley Hall, and he quoted Ray Bradbury as saying something like: "Give your character a compulsion that cuts through the plot like a hawser."

And at the same time I also happened to read an article in *The Writer* magazine by a science-fiction writer who talked about giving her character a job, some kind of fantastical job.

A COMPULSION AND A DANGEROUS JOB

So I decided to give Corinna a job and to make her compelled to do it—even though it would be really a dangerous, creepy sort of job. That's where the idea of the "Folk Keeper" came from.

Most people wouldn't want to be a Folk Keeper. So I gave Corinna a history that explained why she wanted power so much. She'd grown up in a succession of foundling homes and had been essentially marginalized all her life. Being a "Folk Keeper" gave her a certain power. And that was very important to her.

From that point on, Corinna suddenly started to speak in a new way. I always knew what she would say, or what her reaction would be when she encountered something new. It took me a little while to see that it was happening. I was well into the next draft—I write longhand—and when I typed it out, I said, "Oh! Oh! Look at her!" She really had a voice that felt true. She was passionate. She had something she wanted.

I kept some images from earlier drafts, but from then on, it was mostly new writing. Part of what I do is just really hang in there—draft after draft after draft. I don't loose steam when perhaps other people might. I don't settle for publishing it at a too-early stage.

A lot of the challenge is figuring out what is the key thing that is going to make your story work. Often, that key bit of advice comes from somebody outside. My editor helped me get past that point, but it could have been somebody in a writing group.

THE CREATION OF THE "FOLK"

The "Folk" came to me in one of those light-bulb kind of moments.

Where they came from, I don't really know. What I can tell you is that a book that I adored as a kid was a story, *The Princess and the Goblin*, by George MacDonald. It was so spooky and magical—when Curdie goes in the mountains and discovers the goblins.

I felt the same in *The Hobbit* when Bilbo was in the cave with Gollum. I loved those underground, eerie scenes. Another book I adore is called *The Perilous Gard*, by Elisabeth Marie Pope, another version of fairy folk living beneath the ground, stealing away children. And as a kid I had read lots of Scandinavian tales about goblins and trolls. All that stuff was just there, waiting to propel the Folk into being.

I also did a lot of reading in a wonderful book called *The Encyclopedia of Fairies*, by Kate Briggs. It's a wonderful, huge book, mostly about Celtic creatures. You can look up fairies, or trolls, or goblins, or Puck, and get lots of literary and folkloric references.

I didn't model the Folk particularly on any single creature; I modeled them on an amalgam of fairies and trolls and whatnot. For instance, fairies are often averse to cold iron, or salt, or bread. That's where I got the idea of Corinna wearing a necklace of nails, and sprinkling bread around her in a circle—the idea of the Eucharist, the Bread of Life. The Folk can't come near because they're pagan.

And the idea of the Last Word is in there. I was leafing through and saw a reference to an underwater demon. As it comes up and tries to pull a boat down, the fishermen or somebody on the boat can best the demon by spontaneously rhyming rhymes.

So the Folk sort of sprang from everyplace and no place.

At first I tried to describe them. And then I thought—you know, it's going to be so much more powerful not having them really described. Because the thing you don't see is scarier than the thing that you do. I would just limit the reader's imagination.

So I took out all the descriptions that I had started to put in.

And in every review, they mention my simple phrase where I just described the Folk as all "wet mouth and teeth." Everyone picked up on that. At the time, I never knew that was going to be something that made people say . . . "Oooh."

✳

I thought I had all I needed, and more. Delicacies from Cook. . . . Why would these Folk not be content with smoked pheasant and turkey eggs and a tub of milk? I even stirred the milk a long while, blending in the cream. That's how they like it best.

But I opened the Folk Door to the same simmering energy, waiting only for darkness to allow it into the Cellar. I sat myself in double concentric rings of bread and salt. Damp seeped through my breeches. With my fingertips, I snuffed the candle.

Crash! The Door slammed against the wall. A tidal wave of power boiled across cold stone, then sucked itself back at the ring of salt.

The salt couldn't hold then off. I knew that even then, knew it couldn't contain that terrible force. . . . I could perhaps have fled, as many another Folk Keeper would. But in order to keep your place, you have to do your job well, drawing the anger of the Folk upon yourself, diverting it from the livestock and the crops.

There was a rush of power, crossing the salt with screams so shrill they bore into the webbed netting of my bones. Was this what Old Francis had felt, the cramping that doubled my toes to my heels, that pushed my shoulders to my lap? . . . I did not cry out. I poured my screams into silent curses, blasting the Folk with my rage. Me, why me? I, who feed them and stir the milk and sit countless hours on the damp floor!

Foolish girl, Corinna. What are you thinking? The Folk have no hearts; they do not care for kindness.

✳

—From Franny Billingsley's The Folk Keeper, published by Atheneum Books for Young Readers. Copyright © 1999 by Franny Billingsley.

MULTIPLE VOICES & VIEWPOINTS

Interview with Kij Johnson
by Philip Martin

Kij Johnson's 2000 novel, The Fox Woman, led to her receipt of the 2001 Crawford Award from the International Association for the Fantastic in the Arts as the best new fantasy novelist of the year. Based on a 9th-century Japanese fairy tale, The Fox Woman was widely praised for its "musical" language, its "haunting" beauty, and especially for its remarkable presentation of the story through three distinct voices, one for each of the main characters. Here she talks about the challenges in creating these unique voices in her novel of medieval Japan.

(Martin) I wanted to ask you about your novel, *The Fox Woman*, especially about writing in multiple voices and viewpoints. How did you go about that?

(Johnson) I had written a short story version told in just one viewpoint—the fox girl's, Kitsune's. That was fairly easy, because she was a very simple, genuine, straightforward, ingenuous person.

When I decided to expand it into a novel, I became interested in what this story was like for everybody else. Because in some ways, Kitsune is a little juggernaut. She knows what she wants, she's going to get it, and she doesn't care who's hurt in the process. She seeks to avoid pain and maximize her happiness. Even if that hurts other people.

Now, the other two characters, the two people—Shikujo, the wife, and Yoshifuji, her husband—were much more complex. Because life isn't that simple for humans. They compromise all the time. They want happiness desperately. But often they are unwilling to make sacrifices, either of themselves or of other people, to achieve that happiness. Because often one of the things you have to sacrifice is your cherished illusions about yourself. You believe "I'm this sort of a person"—you never question it. And you never understand why you're not happy.

When I was thinking out the novel, I would write long sequences from each of their points of view. I would sit down to say—okay, who is Shikujo? If I'm the woman Shikujo, what am I feeling? Okay, I'm mad, but I can't admit it. I'm hurt, but I can't admit it. I want desperately to be a good wife because that's how I identify myself. If I'm not a good wife, then I don't know what I am.

Or, if I'm Yoshifuji, why am I here, what am I feeling? I'm restless, I'm lonely within my marriage. How can that be? There must be something wrong with the marriage; there's not something wrong with me. He hasn't given up his cherished illusions yet.

So I wrote these long pieces which were much like if you were to take each character to therapy and say, "Tell me about yourself." And for an hour they would just talk. They rambled all over.

But in the course of doing that, because I was writing about what really mattered to them, I tended to find a voice. How they spoke. What they tried to conceal. Because they did try to conceal things. Everybody tries to conceal things all the time. So in therapy, or with very trusted friends, are often the only times that people are willing to get past these places where they're hiding things.

And I just went back again and again. That's a story I rewrote. It didn't write itself so much as it accreted. I would write scenes out of order and then would have to add entire sequences as I went back through all those scenes. And in the rewriting, I was changing the writing—the words and the patterns—to reflect what I now knew about the characters.

(Martin) So what did you achieve by telling the story from three points of view? Why do that? It's definitely harder.

(Johnson) This particular story is such an internal story—plot happens, but there's not really much of it. What's really happening is that we're watching three people come to maturity. And there seemed no way to do that except from their points of view.

For instance, I couldn't have Yoshifuji argue with Shikujo about who he is for most of the story. Because the whole point is that he doesn't learn to argue with Shikujo until he has come to terms with himself.

Yoshifuji, in particular, doesn't have any friends. From outside his point of view, you wouldn't have any idea what's going on for him. And he was a completely unsympathetic character, because he's a jerk from outside. From the inside, though, he is somebody who's just struggling, who's unhappy and is flailing desperately.

I read a story once about wolves gnawing off their paws in traps. Yoshifuji is gnawing, desperately, to get out of what he sees as a trap, without any understanding of what he's doing. If I weren't inside his point of view, I couldn't show that.

Also, the literature of that period was diaries. In Japan in the 11th and 12th centuries, the main two forms of literature which have come down to us are poetry and diaries. And if you want to tell a whole story in diary, you've got to consider: How many words could one person write without her hand falling off? Or would she just write a shorthand version? And how could she tell what other people were thinking?

All this led me to the decision to use multiple viewpoints.

(*Martin*) Were there any special problems?

(*Johnson*) When you're dealing with multiple points of view, you have to be very careful about who tells which parts of the story. And what "doubling up," if any, you're going to permit.

I recently read a new writer's story which had whole scenes which were doubled up. A scene had been told first from Joe's point of view, and then four pages later, you had another four pages from Lucy's point of view. It was the exact same sequence, and you didn't learn anything new. Most of it was just, okay, now I'm seeing it from over here in the room.

What I usually did was just followed whomever a particular scene—or part of a scene—was most relevant to. So sometimes particular characters didn't get to comment about something that they ordinarily would have. For instance, Kitsune comments on the growing friendship between her brother and her husband, but she barely mentions it, although this is her universe, these two men plus her grandfather.

And I wanted to give them distinctive voices. I'd done a lot of thinking about style, and I decided to come up with distinctive voice patterns. How do they speak? Do they speak in complex sentences, or in direct sentences? Do they use lots of Latin words or mostly Anglo-Saxon-based words?

(*Martin*) Anglo-Saxon being more direct?

(*Johnson*) Anglo-Saxon words are those we use in everyday speech. Words like *die. Kill. Eat. Drink. Sleep. Have. Be. Word. Hand.*

The Latin-based words tend to be more distancing. Words like *manual,* as opposed to *by hand.* Or *prevaricate,* rather than *lie.*

They have different implications as well, but mostly, one is a word you would use in everyday language talking to your friends, and one is a word you would only use if you were trying for an elevated or distanced tone, usually in writing. The Latin words often are more indirect. For instance, prevaricate means to preempt the truth. Which is not the same as lie.

※

[from Kitsune's Diary] "Listen!" My grandfather came to his feet, ears pricked forward, toward the fields. "Horses. Oxen. Carts." I had no idea what a horse was. I saw nothing, just the trees and lakes and grasses of the garden stretching to the broken gate. . . . Two huge shaggy hinoki-cedars, their branches bent to the ground, flanked the tumbled gate. We bellied into one of them, and crawled forward to watch. The horse turned out to be pretty much what it sounded like: ox and deer. It smelled like sweat and grass, and was the yellow-orange color of persimmons. . . .

[from Shikujo's Pillow Book] One wrote this [poem] on first seeing the home she left all those years ago: "Is it the garden lost / or merely hidden by the year's thick grasses?" And this question only delays the next: which would one prefer? This should be a simple enough question to answer: I am sure that civilization must always be preferable to barbarity.

[from the Notebook of Kaya No Yoshifuji] This is my gate, my fence, my home: its disorder is my fault. My wife in her cramped carriage, my son's impatient boredom, the loneliness of this uncivilized place, my inability or unwillingness to embrace the delicate life that would have given me a future in the capital. My fault. If I had known I would have to return, I would have tended things better.

※

—From Kij Johnson's The Fox Woman, published by Tor Books. Copyright © 2000 by Kij Johnson.

CHAPTER FIVE

THE EARTH BENEATH MY FEET: DEVELOPING WONDROUS PLACES

I IN THE MOVIE VERSION OF THE WIZARD OF OZ, Dorothy chants the magical phrase, "There's no place like home," and in a twinkling, she wakes up in her bed, surrounding by her worried stepparents. She has returned home from the wondrous land of Oz to the bleak, earth-cracked Kansas plains. But she is delighted to be home.

Place helps explain who we are and why we are different from others. As you create the place in your fantasy story—as you engage in what is known in speculative fiction as "world-building"—pay as close attention to it as you would to a beloved character. If drawn fully enough, the place will bend your characters to it with its great gravitational force, pulling them into a patterned dance around and through its mysterious, magical reaches. It will move your characters to action; it will fuel their passions; it will silence them with reverie. Such is the river in *The Wind in the Willows*, seen by moonrise in this beautiful passage:

> The line of the horizon was clear and hard against the sky, and in one particular quarter it showed black against a silvery climbing phosphorescence that grew and grew. At last, over the rim of the waiting earth the moon lifted with slow majesty till it swung clear of the horizon and rode off, free of moorings; and once more they began to see surfaces—meadows widespread, and quiet gardens, and the river itself from bank to bank, all softly disclosed, all washed clean of mystery and terror, all radiant again as by day. . . .

—Kenneth Grahame, *The Wind in the Willows*

The same magical spell of place is found in *Redwall* series of Brian Jacques, in his descriptions of the great halls, kitchens, and wine cellars of Redwall Abbey; the paths of Mossflower Woods; and the exotic places beyond.

> It was about an hour after dawn when Trimp [a hedgehog] opened her eyes. . . . Feigning sleep, the hedgehog maid peeped out from under her blanket, savouring the day. Downstream looked like a long winding green hall, with alder, bird cherry and weeping willow trees practically forming an arch over the sundappled stream, which was bordered by bright flowering clubrush, sedge and twayblade. Blue and pearly grey, the firesmoke hovered, making gentle swirls between sunshine and shadow in diagonal shafts. Snatches of murmured conversation between early risers were muted in the background, with the sweet odors of smouldering peat and glowing pinebark on the fire. Trimp wished that she could stay like this forever, happy amongst true friends, in tranquil summer woodlands by a stream.

Sacred place is the place where eternity shines through.
—Joseph Campbell

—*The Legend of Luke*, Brian Jacques

Different places have different powers. As Sparrowhawk, a mage in Ursula Le Guin's 1972 book *The Farthest Shore*, from her *Earthsea* trilogy (with roots in Native American concepts of sacred places), tells young Arren:

> "Do you know the saying, *Rules change in the Reaches*? Seamen use it, but it is a wizards' saying, and it means that wizardry itself depends on place. A true spell on Roke may be mere words on Iffish. The language of the Making is not everywhere remembered; here one word, there another. And the weaving of spells is itself interwoven with the earth and the water, the winds and the fall of light of the place where it is cast."

—*The Farthest Shore*, Ursula Le Guin

Even seemingly ordinary places have similar powers. Recall the site of a first kiss, or a visit to a childhood home. Picture climbing back into a favorite crook in a well-known apple tree. Walk into a kitchen that smells like your grandmother's cooking. A sense of familiarity is a powerful force.

We may not always see the same meaning in places. A vast woods will be scary to some, as familiar as a backyard to others. The deep sea is menacing, or freshening. The white heights of a snow-covered mountain peak entice some to climb it; for others it casts a chilling shadow on the land.

Just as characters in fantasy have qualities that reach beyond the ordinary to the archetype, so places in fantasy are a mix of the familiar and the sacred.

"THERE" AND BACK AGAIN

At first glance, *There and Back Again,* the subtitle of Tolkien's book *The Hobbit,* is the epitome of understatement. It seems to reflect something of the homebody nature of the hobbit, of Bilbo's penchant for the ordinary, for simplicity over flowery phrases. The great adventure of going "there," it suggests, means mostly just being away from home. However, as is often true in epic tales, the hero returns home to find that it has changed. Bilbo's own neighbors don't recognize him; they are in the process of selling off his furniture, eager to take over the cozy hobbit-hole they think he has abandoned. Bilbo himself has changed; he is not quite the same hobbit he used to be.

In that marvelous subtitle, Tolkien has summed up the essence of fantasy. He knows that there and back again is the very heart of adventure. To journey through Middle-earth is not just a series of stops on a Caribbean cruise. It is a journey through a mythic place, drawn from the depths of the richest imagination of one of the greatest writers of the 20th century.

In fantasy, a journey often involves travel from place familiar to place unknown. To leave home is perilous. Once outside the small cottage, you enter the dark forest. Beyond is terra incognito, where it is scrawled on the margins on the map: *Dragons be here.* The world out there is a different place, where dangerous beasts attack, wrong turns are made, strange people are encountered.

At the same time, to travel is to encounter lands mysterious and exotic. You must travel to see the palaces of Kublai Khan, or the wonderful treetops of Loth Lorien. On her journeys through Wonderland, Alice encounters the most wonderful creatures who amuse her with dances, songs, and nonsense verse.

There's no "there" there, said Gertrude Stein, infamously, about Oakland, California. In Stein's circle of hip literati and artists, "there-ness" was a prized quality. It described an elevated aspect of place—just as destiny is a special quality of plot, or inner nature is a

"The Silver Shoes," said the Good Witch, "have wonderful powers. And one of the most curious things about them is that they can carry you to any place in the world in three steps.... All you have to do is to knock the heels together three times ..."

"If that is so," said the child joyfully, "I will ask them to carry me back to Kansas at once."

—The Wizard of Oz, 1900, by L. Frank Baum

special aspect of character. This sense of "there-ness" might have been the true meaning of the British climber Mallory's famous answer to the question of why he attempted to climb Mount Everest. "Because it's there," he replied. Perhaps what he really meant was that the high Himalayas had the quintessential "there-ness" of sacred space. Gertrude Stein would have known what he meant.

Perhaps Tolkien did too. *There and Back Again* sums up the essence of fantasy. Fantasy is about going otherwhere. We journey afar and then return—tracing a circular path of discovery.

<table>
<tr>
<td>

Published in 1908, The Wind in the Willows by Kenneth Grahame delighted many readers, though The Times of London sniffed at the antics of Toad and famously reported, "In terms of natural history, the book is insignificant."

</td>
<td>

"Clearly and nearer still," cried the Rat joyously. "Now you must surely hear it! Ah—at last—I see you do!"

Breathless and transfixed the Mole stopped rowing as the liquid run of that glad piping broke on him like a wave, caught him up, and possessed him utterly. He saw the tears on his comrade's cheeks, and bowed his head and understood. For a space they hung there, brushed by the purple loosestrife that fringed the bank. . . . And the light grew steadily stronger, but no birds sang as they were wont to do at the approach of the dawn; and but for the heavenly music all was marvelously still.

On either side of them, as they glided onwards, the rich meadow-grass seemed that morning of a freshness and a green-ness unsurpassable. Never had they noticed the roses so vivid, the willow-herb so riotous, the meadow-sweet so odorous and pervading.

. . . In midmost of the stream, embraced in the weir's shimmer-ing arm-spread, a small island lay anchored, fringed close with willow and silver birch and alder.

—"The Piper at the Gates of Dawn," *The Wind in the Willows*

</td>
</tr>
</table>

INTRODUCING THE PLACE

The primroses were over. Toward the edge of the wood, where the ground became open and sloped down to an old fence and a brambly ditch beyond, only a few fading patches of pale yellow still showed among the dog's mercury and the oak-tree roots. On the other side of the fence, the upper part of the field was full of rabbit holes. In places the grass was gone altogether and everywhere there were clusters of dry droppings, through which nothing but the rag-wort would grow. A hundred yards away, at the bottom of the slope,

ran the brook, no more than three feet wide, half choked with
kingcups, watercress and blue brooklime. The cart track crossed by
a brick culvert and climbed the opposite slope to a five-barred gate
in the thorn hedge. The gate led into the lane.

The May sunset was red in clouds, and there was still half an
hour to twilight. The dry slope was dotted with rabbits . . .

—*Watership Down*, Richard Adams

The opening tone is calm, the pace measured. The rich details
bring us down to the vision of a rabbit: the plants, the edge of the
wood, the oldness of the fence, the brambles of the ditch. We see it
in our mind's eye. The brook is not just any size; it is "no more than
three feet across." The gate has five bars. It's twilight at Nuthanger
Farm, a good place and time, it seems, to be a rabbit.

Yet even in the first short sentence lies unease. A disturbing
decay is creeping closer, though still hidden from us. This is the
initial eroding of goodness that occurs at the beginning of a fantasy
story, or often is underway as the story opens. Sure enough, while
the moment is peaceful, a few pages later the rabbits come across a
strange, dark obelisk: a fresh creosote post planted in the field. A
story is launched.

Part of the secret of Richard Adams' skill in painting this first
scene is revealed in a Note on the copyright page, informing us that
Nuthanger Farm is based on a real place. Likewise, Tolkien's
Middle-earth resembles England in many small particulars. Many
stories of the fantastic are set in very real places, as authors use the
convincing details of an actual landscape to help persuade us of the
"truth" of the fantastic adventures that happen there.

[On "the trick of particularity":]
We believe in Dante's Three Kingdoms. . . . because we have trudged on our own two feet from end to end of it. We are convinced it is there, independently of the poet; if necessary, we could find our way through it without him. We know the landmarks and should recognize them. . . .
—Dorothy Sayers, ". . . And Telling You a Story," in *Essays Presented to Charles Williams*, ed. by C.S. Lewis, 1947

SUBTLE CUES

In the opening pages of Susan Cooper's *The Dark Is Rising*, Will
awakens to find his home transformed from a place of safe comfort
to an inert tableau, frozen in time. His family, motionless, asleep,
will not respond to his calling. He goes outside, where his house is
inexplicably in a dense forest that was not there the day before.

The strange white world lay stroked by silence. No birds sang.
The garden was no longer there, in this forested land. Nor were
the outbuildings nor the old crumbling walls. There lay only a

narrow clearing round the house now, hummocked with unbroken snowdrifts, before the trees began, with a narrow path leading away. . . .

. . . Will came out of the white-arched path into the road, paved smooth with snow and edged everywhere by the great trees, and he looked up between the branches and saw a single black rook flap slowly past, high in the early sky.

Turning to the right, he walked up the narrow road that in his own time was called Huntercombe Lane. . . . Now, it was no more than a track through a forest, great snow-burdened trees enclosing it on both sides. Will moved bright-eyed and watchful through the silence, until he heard a faint noise ahead of him.

He stood still. The sound came again, through the muffling trees: a rhythmically, off-key tapping, like a hammer striking metal. . . .

He trudged on towards the sound of hammering, and soon came to a clearing. There was no village of Huntercombe any more, only this. All his senses sprang to life at once, under a shower of unexpected sounds, sights, smells. He saw two or three low stone buildings thick-roofed with snow; he saw blue wood-smoke rising, and smelt it too, and smelt at the same time a voluptuous scent of new-baked bread that brought the water springing in his mouth. He saw that the nearest of the three buildings was three-walled, open to the track, with a yellow fire burning bright inside like a captive sun. Great showers of sparks were spraying out from an anvil where a man was hammering. Beside the anvil stood a tall black horse, a beautiful gleaming animal. . . .

—*The Dark Is Rising*, Susan Cooper

Besides being a novelist, Cooper has worked in theater and film. Note how carefully she sets the mood. She slows down the scene, painting the silence, the vast forest, the boy's measured movements as he steps through snow down a strange path. The only small break in the stillness—a lonely black rook—magnifies his isolation.

We observe keenly, absorbing details of scenery, colors, background sounds, subtle lighting cues. Like Will, we are watchful. Our breaths are drawn, our senses finely tuned, awaiting something. We then hear the faint ring of the anvil like a monastery bell calling us to a new level of consciousness. We round the corner and inhale the smells: the acrid smoke, the aroma of bread.

While the pace is slow, our imaginations are going full speed. The audience has been given the gift of time: to imagine what this place is. And then the action starts.

THE TWISTED PLACE

Just as in creating characters you consider both heroes and villains, so in writing about place in fantasy you should consider the role of the evil place. It is landscape's version of the villain.

It may be the castle of the Dark Lord.

> The Gerards collectively gasped when they first saw Gnome Mountain, which pleased their ugly captors to no end, for that was indeed the sought-after effect.
>
> The tall peak was massive and hollow, carved with the huge, hideous faces of all the Gnome Kings that had once ruled that miserable kingdom. Windows and stairs had been dug into the very rock, letting an evil, orangey light shine through the glowing openings. At the bottom of the peak was a drawbridge-like entrance.
>
> The Gerards saw all this in reverse, which added to the feeling of dread, as they were tied upside down on poles like trussed-up chickens.
>
> —*Moebius' Arzach*, 2000, by Randy and Jean-Marc Lofficier

Or it may be a dark woods that the characters need to enter, despite their better judgment.

> They found the forest very thick on this side, and it looked dark and gloomy. After the Lion had rested they started along the road of yellow brick, silently wondering, each in his own mind, if ever they would come to the end of the woods and reach the bright sunshine again. To add to their discomfort, they soon heard strange noises in the depths of the forest, and the Lion whispered to them that it was in this part of the country that the Kalidahs lived.
>
> "What are the Kalidahs?" asked the girl.
>
> "They are monstrous beasts with bodies like bears and heads like tigers," replied the Lion. . . .
>
> —*The Wizard of Oz*, 1900, L. Frank Baum

Caves in fantasy all seem to be airy, well-lit places full of perfect marble staircases and veins of pure gold....When a story takes me into a cave like that, I ask myself: Where is the mud? Where is the darkness? Where is cool, slightly clammy air? Where are the loose rocks on the floor, and the smell, and the bats?
—Roger MacBride Allen, in "The Standard Deviations of Writing," from www.sfwa.org/writing

The dark place may be close at hand—like the cellar in Billingsley's *The Folk Keeper*. It may be a whole invisible world, like the goblin tunnels hidden underground not far from the home of the princess in *The Princess and the Goblin*, by George MacDonald. In myth and fairy tale, caves and underground worlds are the realms of dragons, goblins, evil spirits, and the dead.

Other evil places are bleak expanses of desert, marshes, or mountains, like the dreadful reaches of Mordor in Tolkien's *The Lord of the Rings*.

The solitary, steep hill called Corona Heights was black as pitch and very silent, like the heart of the unknown. It looked steadily downward and northeast away at the nervous, bright lights of downtown San Francisco as if it were a great predatory beast of night....
On every side of Corona Heights the street and house lights ... hemmed it in apprehensively, as if it were indeed a dangerous animal.
—The opening to
Our Lady of Darkness,
by Fritz Lieber, 1978

> They came to a cleft between two dark crags, and passing
> through found themselves on the very edge of the last fence of
> Mordor. Below them, at the bottom of a fall of some fifteen hun-
> dred feet, lay the inner plain stretching away into a formless
> gloom. . . . There smokes trailed on the ground and lurked in hol-
> lows, and fumes leaked from fissures in the earth.
>
> Still far away, forty miles at least, they saw Mount Doom, its feet
> founded in ashen ruin, its huge cone rising to a great height,
> where its reeking head was swathed in cloud. Its fires were now
> dimmed, and it stood in smouldering slumber, as threatening and
> dangerous as a sleeping beast.
>
> —*The Return of the King*, 1955, J.R.R. Tolkien

In gothic fiction, the desolate place is completely wrapped around the story. In Mervyn Peake's brilliant *Gormanghast* trilogy, the sprawling, decaying wreck is home and prison to the young Lord of the immense castle. The decadence of the place reflects the bizarre characters encountered within its dark cobwebbed recesses.

> Gormanghast, that is, the main massing of the original stone,
> taken by itself would have displayed a certain ponderous architec-
> tural quality were it possible to have ignored the circumfusion of
> those mean dwellings that swarmed like an epidemic around its
> outer walls. . . . Over their irregular roofs would fall throughout
> the seasons, the shadows of time-eaten buttresses, of broken and
> lofty turrets, and, most enormous of all, the shadow of the Tower
> of Flints. This tower, patched unevenly with black ivy, arose like a
> mutilated finger from among the fists of knuckled masonry and

pointed blasphemously at heaven. At night the owls made of it an echoing throat; by day it stood voiceless and cast its long shadow.

—*Titus Groan*, Mervyn Peake

The sprawling place has come alive, gesturing rudely to the heavens, casting its long shadow across the pages that follow. The place is an active character; the characters bound to its gloomy confines.

Unlike characters, places usually can't act directly. The writer has to create influences, effects, miasmas, that are reflected in what the characters see, feel, and fear in its presence. Mysterious lighting and sound cues help draw in the reader's attention, creating the suspicion that something is about to happen. Sometimes the heightening of tension is effected by the absence of the familiar: the interior of an empty house, the stillness of a dark desolate woods.

And occasionally, the place might just reach out with its long, snaky fingers and make its own presence known.

> I turned and saw a face. It looked like melted candlewax, the color of bacon fat, except for the blobby red nose. The eyes were round as a doll's eyes, and they watched us from a hole in a hollow tree with a no-color hatred. . . . There was a smell, too, I remember, all around us, like a refrigerator that really needs cleaning out.
> —from Tamsin, 1999, by Peter S. Beagle

A voice came over the loudspeaker, that formal, disembodied male voice that warned, "Mind the Gap." It was intended to keep unwary passengers from stepping into the space between the [subway] train and the platform. Richard, like most Londoners, barely heard it anymore—it was like aural wallpaper. But suddenly, Hunter's hand was on his arm. "Mind the Gap" . . . .

"What?" said Richard.

"I *said*," said Hunter, "mind the—"

And then it erupted over the side of the platform. It was diaphanous, dreamlike, a ghost-thing, the color of black smoke, and it welled up like silk under water, and, moving astonishingly fast while still seeming to drift almost in slow motion, it wrapped itself tightly around Richard's ankle. It stung, even through the fabric of his Levi's. The thing pulled him toward the edge of the platform, and he staggered.

He realized, as if from a distance, that Hunter had pulled out her staff and was smacking the tentacle of smoke with it, hard, repeatedly.

There was a faraway screaming noise, thin and mindless, like an idiot child deprived of its toy. The smoke-tentacle let go of Richard's ankle and slid back over the edge of the platform, and it was gone. Hunter took Richard by the scruff of the neck and pulled him toward the back wall, where Richard slumped against it. . . .

The color had been sucked from his jeans wherever the thing had touched him, making them look as if they'd been ineptly bleached. He pulled up the trouser leg: tiny purple welts were coming up on the skin of his ankle and calf. "What . . .?" he tried to say, but nothing came out. . . .

. . . "Mind the Gap," boomed the recorded voice again.

— *Neverwhere*, 1997, Neil Gaiman

INTO THE FAUN'S PARLOR

by Jane Yolen

Jane Yolen has been called the Hans Christian Andersen of America. She is the acclaimed author of more than 200 books for children, young adults, and adults, including Wizard's Hall, The Devil's Arithmetic, and The Wild Hunt. Her many awards include the World Fantasy Award, the Christopher Medal, and the Mythopoeic Society's Aslan Award. She has also written a number of works on folklore, storytelling, and fiction. A frequent contributor to The Writer magazine, this article is drawn from her classic book, Writing Books for Children, 1983.

The piling up of corroborating details helps inspire the reader's belief in a fantastical world. If you read carefully, you will see that fantasy authors have such a visual sense of their world that it is impossible not to see it through their eyes. . . .

This is a description from *Alice in Wonderland*, as Alice is falling down the rabbit hole.

> Either the well was very deep, or she fell very slowly, for she had plenty of time as she went down to look about her, and to wonder what was going to happen next. First, she tried to look down and make out what she was coming to, but it was too dark to see anything; then she looked at the sides of the well, and noticed that they were filled with cupboards and bookshelves: here and there she saw maps and pictures hung upon pegs. She took down a jar from one of the shelves as she passed: it was labelled "Orange Marmalade," but to her great disappointment it was empty; she did not like to drop the jar for fear of killing somebody, so managed to put it into one of the cupboards as she fell past it.

And this is from the first of the Narnia books (C.S. Lewis), *The Lion, the Witch and the Wardrobe*, a description of Mr. Tumnus' parlor. Mr. Tumnus happens to be a faun, and he has invited young Lucy to tea:

> Lucy thought she had never been in a nicer place. It was a little, dry, clean cave of reddish stone with a carpet on the floor and two little chairs ("one for me and one for a friend," said Mr. Tumnus) and a table and a dresser and a mantelpiece over the fire and above that a picture of an old Faun with a grey beard. In one corner there was a door which Lucy thought must lead to Mr. Tumnus' bedroom, and on one wall was a shelf full of books. Lucy looked at these while he was setting out the tea things. They had titles like *The Life and Letters of Silenus* or *Nymphs and Their Ways* or *Men, Monks, and Gamekeepers: A Study in Popular Legend* or *Is Man a Myth?*

And this last is a description of the wizard's warren under the fountain, from my book *The Wizard of Washington Square*:

> The Wizard sat in a large velvet-cushioned oak chair in front of a tremendous table. The table was as long as a large door and had nine sturdy legs, each ending in a claw. One claw clutched a wooden ball and, at odd moments, it would suddenly roll the ball to another leg. Then that claw would snatch the ball and stand very proudly on it. In this way, every few minutes the table would take on a slightly different tilt. Each time the game began again, all the beakers and bowls and pitchers and jars on top of the table—for the table was littered with glassware and crockery—would jangle and clank. But surprisingly, nothing was ever broken.

These details of place are precise. The jar of marmalade from the long, dark tunnel cupboard; the book titles that would surely be on any genteel faun's bookshelf; the crockery set a-rattling on the table's surface. Nothing is fuzzy or wishy-washy or only partially visualized. There is no doubt that the authors have been there. They believe. The readers, therefore, left believing too.

If, as Henry James says about the novel, its supreme virtue is its "solidity of specification," that must be twice as true about a work of fantasy. For in a work of everyday fiction, if you say "apartment" or "ranch house" or meadow," there are immediate sympathetic vibrations set up in a reader. The reader will know from experience—

either direct or indirect—what an apartment or ranch house or meadow looks like. Any description the author gives will be merely secondary information. But if you say "tunnel cupboard" or "faun's parlor" or "wizard's warren," it will mean absolutely nothing to a reader without a verbal visit that includes very specific details.

It all has to be done very solidly, and it has to be very real. Lloyd Alexander, in talking about his own work in the Prydain books, wrote: "What appears gossamer is underneath as solid as prestressed concrete."

Perhaps it will help you, before you even begin a fantasy novel, to write out a travelogue of your world. Take yourself for a trip to its most famous points of interest. Or pretend you are writing an article for an encyclopedia that will include customs, laws, historical background, flora and fauna, and the Gross National Product.

It will help you develop that "solidity of specification" which James so prized. Even if you never use half the material you have gathered for your mythical land, it will help you construct it for the reader.

Remember, too, what you don't put down can be as important as what you do. Lao-Tse in his *Tao Te Ching* wrote that in a vessel of clay, it is the emptiness inside that makes it useful.

And Wang Wei, a great Chinese poet-painter, said: "The ultimate concern of the artist is not to paint mountains and clouds and trees but the air between them."

So it is, also, with writing.

·※·

Just then he heard the nearby sound of water over stone. Following the sound he came to a small river winding between willows. There was a large grey rock half in and half out of the water and he sat upon it to rest. It was smooth and cool; he liked the feel of it. When he leaned over to look into the water, he was startled by a silvery flash.

Fish, his conscious mind told him. But as he continued staring at its sinuous movement, he became mesmerized, and suddenly he found himself in the water, swimming by the fish's side. Overhead, light filtered through the river's ceiling in a shower of golden shards.

The boy swam nose to tail with the trout, following it into deeper and deeper waters where the sunlight could not penetrate. Yet, oddly, he could still see clearly in the blue-green of the river morning.

He did not question that he could breathe under the water; indeed it seemed as natural to him as breathing air.

Little tendrils of plants, like the touch of soft fingers, brushed by him. Smaller fish darted at the edges of his sight. Then nose to tail, he and the trout traveled even further down into the depths of the darkening pool.

The trout was thick along its back and covered with a shimmer of silver marked with black spots and crosses, like a shield. As it swam, it browsed on tiny shrimp, a moveable feast. Then, suddenly, it turned and stared at him with one bold eye.

"Do not rise to the lure, lad," it said in a voice surprisingly chesty and deep. Bubbles fizzed from its mouth like punctuation. Then it was gone in a flurry of waves, so fast the boy could not follow. He blinked, and once more found himself sitting upon the rock, completely dry.

❊

—From Jane Yolen's novel, Merlin (book 3 of her Young Merlin trilogy), published by Harcourt Brace. Copyright © 1997 by Jane Yolen.

DISCOVERING EARTHSEA

Interview with Ursula K. Le Guin
by Philip Martin

Ursula K. Le Guin is one of the premier writers of fiction today. Her work crosses into many genres, including fantasy, science fiction, general fiction, and essays on narrative and culture. Her fantasy work is best known for the influential Earthsea series, tales of an ocean archipelago rich in magic and folklore. To her initial trilogy—A Wizard of Earthsea (1968), The Tombs of Atuan (1971), and The Farthest Shore (1972)—she added a fourth book, Tehanu (1990), with a feminist perspective on her creation. While Tehanu was subtitled "The Last Book of Earthsea," Le Guin was drawn back again a decade later, releasing a collection of stories, Tales from Earthsea (2000), followed by a novel, The Other Wind (2001). Her books are imbued with a quiet strength rooted in the ritual power of language and a connection to place.

(Martin) Your stories seem to reflect a strong sense of place. What can you tell me about that?

(Le Guin) A lot of my stories really start with the discovery of a place— and who lives there. That's how *The Tombs of Atuan* began. I took a three-day trip, my first trip, into the Oregon high desert. I'd never seen country like that or anything remotely like it in my life. And I came back knowing that I had to write a book about it. And the place then sort of gave me the people.

I respond intensely to the mood of a place. After all, place has something to do with community often—and therefore with people really understanding each other.

One of the first things I did when I wrote the very first story about Earthsea, I drew a map of this place with all these islands. And that was the beginning. And you know an awful lot of kids draw maps of imaginary places. And some grownups go right on doing it.

Look at Tolkien. He drew very careful maps all his life.

This is a way of somehow exploring a part of yourself, I guess.

To me, Earthsea is one of the landscapes I see, when I look wherever it is you look when you're writing a story. So it must be partly a map of me. But it feels more as if I just went there, rather than it was me. It's more like I was a traveler in that country, finding out things and observing.

(*Martin*) What drew you back to that world, years after writing *Tehanu*, which you called at the time the "last book" of Earthsea?

(*Le Guin*) When I finished *Tehanu*, I thought I'd come to the end of the story. And I had in many ways. But I did leave a big unanswered question at the end of the book: who is the child Therru—who or what is she? The dragon has called her "daughter." What does that mean?

So there were a lot of questions hanging. At the time I thought, that's alright, you don't have to answer all the questions at the end of a book.

But as time went on, I kept thinking about Earthsea. And I found myself going back in its history to find out some questions that puzzled me. Like why aren't women allowed to be mages—why can they only be witches, and despised for it?

And I began getting answers. In other words, I began getting stories.

Those became the collection *Tales from Earthsea*. And the last story, "Dragonfly," leads right into the new novel, *The Other Wind*.

Once again I'll use the landscape metaphor—it's like exploring a country. You've been over this mountain range, but there's another one. You want to go see what that one looks like. And to discover the country in between.

(*Martin*) How do you go about it? Things start in your imagination somehow. Then they become some kind of story. And then you start to link these together. . . .

(*Le Guin*) I have never fully understood the processes of making a story. For me, a lot of the linkage takes place subconsciously. You see where the story's going in a general way, but you don't know exactly how you're going there. You might not be all that sure of exactly where you're going. But you have some sort of general map in mind.

So I just plunge in and find out what is going on.

Of course, the place needs to be coherent. That's a touchstone word in fantasy. The fantasy world, no matter how large or how small, has to be internally coherent. It can't contradict itself. It can contradict the real world, happily! But it has to follow its own rules.

And then soon, the characters begin to lead you. You have to find out what they say and what they do, and let them do it. You can't push them around. You can't be in total control or else you'll lose that input from your own unconscious—which comes through the characters.

A lot of the connections in all my work remain mysterious to me. Sometimes I see them explained by an intelligent, sensitive critic, and I say, "Oh, wow, is that what I was doing?" I think that's a very common experience for writers. But our business really is not that; we aren't critics. We're storytellers. Our business is just to get the story right. The intellectual connections are such that we don't have to make them if we've made the emotional ones.

(Martin) I hear you mention the word "true" in the sense of stories being true. Do you mean true to their own fantasy—or do you mean true in a larger sense?

(Le Guin) Stories need to be "true" in the senses of being consistent and coherent—true to themselves. And if you start a moral question or an emotional problem—you need to follow it through. Not just slap an easy answer on to it. In other words, stories need to be morally and emotionally true to human experience. Even if the stories are extremely fantastic.

For instance, it seems to be important to me to keep my wizards and witches grounded in ordinary life—things like gathering eggs or sweeping the floor—just the real gritty, plain things that people have to do to make a living in most places, most times. I couldn't give you a simple answer why that's important to me, but it has been right from the start.

Ged, you know, starts out as a goat-herd in a poor little village. So the whole wizardry of Earthsea—all the beauty and glory of the magic they can do—grows out of this very gritty, ordinary ground. It just makes it real to me, I guess.

(Martin) Your story, "The Bones of the Earth," is literally about mud.

(*Le Guin*) Yes, there's a lot about mud in that story. The mage Dulse has to walk right into the mud, and eventually he has to go right into the ground. So that one takes you back down to the ground.

(*Martin*) It has a beautiful image at the end where Dulse's student, Ogion, lies down on the ground and weeps for Dulse. And he makes a little more mud.

(*Le Guin*) Yes, yes. Now you see, he just did that, I didn't think that up. I swear I didn't. He just did it.

When the story's carrying you, it's like riding a horse or a ship or something. It takes you where you need to go. And that is such a wonderful feeling.

(*Martin*) Jane Yolen says she writes books to find out what happens.

(*Le Guin*) Tolkien said he wrote the whole Lord of the Rings because nobody else would. It's a wonderful reason. You write a book that you want to read.

(*Martin*) Was your writing influenced at all by J.R.R. Tolkien, by his tales of "there and back again"?

(*Le Guin*) I was born in 1929, and Tolkien hadn't been published when I was a kid. I didn't read him until the '50s, so I was well in my thirties. And—oh, man! I was bowled over. I was glad that I hadn't read him as a child because he probably would have had such an overwhelming influence on me. I had already begun finding my own voice, so he didn't just blow me out of the water the way he might have done.

That phrase, "there and back again," does really describe Tolkien's writing, which is highly rhythmical. It's like a pendulum beat. It's moving. It's a walking beat. There and then back—that's a marvelous phrase about his own work.

But I've always felt that Tolkien's journeys are really spirals. You do end up back home. But of course home is different from what it was. Yes, you come back, but it's not just a closed circle, but sort of a spiral. You're coming back on a different level, to a somewhat changed place.

In one of my books, somebody says the important thing about life is coming home, as long as you understand that home isn't a place you ever saw before!

It's a little bit like Heracleitus saying you cannot step twice into the same river.

For instance, in *The Lord of the Rings*, when they get home, things have spiraled down badly in the Shire. And it takes a lot of hard work to restore it to anything like what is was.

(*Martin*) For a story like "The Bones of the Earth," do you contemplate specific themes or images—like mud, for instance—before you start?

(*Le Guin*) No, those themes and motifs just begin to show up in the story. Often they are the part that comes without my even noticing them. Until somewhere along in the story, I'm looking ahead, or I'm casting back and revising a little and I say, "hey, look at that—look at that mud. That belongs here!" It's mostly in revision, I think, that those repeated motifs, in the musical sense, get heightened and brought out a little.

(*Martin*) In that story, the mage talks about standing on the island of Gont and imagining the deep, physical roots of the island. And he suddenly realizes that the islands of Earthsea are all connected, far under the water. Which is a very striking image for the writing of Earthsea, because you've got a series of stories with a lot of deep connections.

(*Le Guin*) Yes. The sea is what connects the islands—and the sea is what separates them. Both.

(*Martin*) As you continue these stories, do you feel a sense of obligation to your readers?

(*Le Guin*) Responsibility might be the word. Over the years, I have gotten a good deal of feedback on the Earthsea books. People really do want to know what happened after *Tehanu*—is Therru going to be the next archmage? Things like that. In fantasy, the readers—children and adults—want to know things. And they are not shy about asking what they want to know.

That is one nice thing about writing science fiction and fantasy. You have these active, verbal people reading you who are very likely to write you a letter. People responding to what you wrote—telling you what they think about what you said.

In writing the Earthsea stories, the encouragement of readers is wonderful—to know that people love the stories, that they read their own lives into the stories in different ways, and they find them nourishing. And they tell me about it.

So many writers get so little feedback. But in genre fiction, people aren't afraid to do it. We who write in these genres are not set apart in peoples' minds by academic barriers. There is a real community of people who love fantasy and science fiction. They tend to write each other, and they also write their authors.

Particularly for a young writer, to get this kind of feedback can be incredibly encouraging and decisive.

When I teach writing workshops, I often focus on fantasy and science fiction, where a new writer has some real hope of getting published. And there is a community which can be very useful to a young writer. You meet other writers and you meet your readers. Maybe just electronically or by letter, but also face to face.

And I think this is healthy for artists.

❄

Dulse wandered a bit before he found what he took to be the Dark Pond. It was small, half mud and reeds, with one vague, boggy path to the water, and no tracks on that but goat hoofs. The water was dark, though it lay out under the bright sky and far above the peat soils. Dulse followed the goat tracks, growling when his foot slipped in the mud and he wrenched his ankle to keep from falling. At the brink of the water he stood still. He stooped to rub his ankle. He listened.

It was absolutely still.

No wind. No birdcall. No distant lowing or bleating or call of voice. As if all the island had gone still. Not a fly buzzed.

He looked at the dark water. It reflected nothing.

Reluctant, he stepped forward, barefoot and bare-legged. . . . Reeds brushed his legs. The mud was soft and sucking under his feet, full of tangling reed-roots. He made no noise as he moved slowly out into the pool, and the circles of ripples from his movement were slight and small. It was shallow for a long way. Then his cautious foot felt no bottom, and he paused.

The water shivered. He felt it first on his thighs, a lapping like the tickling touch of fur; then he saw it, the trembling of the surface all over the pond.

❄

—From Ursula K. Le Guin's story, "The Bones of the Earth," in her book Tales from Earthsea, published by Harcourt. Copyright © 2001 by Ursula K. Le Guin.

CHAPTER SIX

WATER FROM DEEP WELLS:
THE PATTERNS OF FANTASY

As FISH SWIM IN WATER but do not see it, so people swim in a world of language. We talk, we listen, we reply. Language is a way in which we exchange factual information.

It is also more than that. Language is the ancient means we use to lubricate the exchange of that mysterious matter we call myth, or in its fictional form, fantasy. In fantasy, whether we fall under the spells of Shakespeare, Lord Dunsany, Tolkien, or Thurber, language is a silvery river, a swell of tides in the moonlight.

How much of that slippery medium, the matter of old wives' tales and storytellers' fantasies, can be considered true? Whether its message is "true" or not depends on how you define truth. Truth, says Madeleine L'Engle, is that which goes beyond facts. In a famous exchange between good friends C.S. Lewis and J.R.R. Tolkien as they strolled together in Oxford one evening, Lewis made the bold statement that "myths are lies, even through lies breathed through silver."

Tolkien disagreed. Through fantasy's liquid patterns, Tolkien knew, we can share old truths, wondrous beyond the point of fact. Ancient heroes can emerge as newborns left on a doorstep with a note. Brave knights ride forth into timeless woods. Dragons are slain and reborn. All this happens through the flow of language, the *aqua vitae*, the "water of life" of fantasy.

He ate, and filled his water-bottle, and travelled all day eastwards, and at evening the mountains of faery came floating into view, the colour of pale forget-me-nots. . . . And then, as he pushed through a hedge into a field untended, there suddenly close before him in the field was, as his father had told, the frontier of twilight. It stretched across the fields in front of him, blue

133

and dense as water; and things seen through it seemed misshapen
and shining.

—*The King of Elfland's Daughter*, 1924, Lord Dunsany

THE POWER OF NAMES

Fantasy celebrates the magical power of words—the advantage of
knowing the names of things. Harry Potter's nemesis, Lord Voldemort, is referred to as "he-who-must-not-be-named" by those who
fear him. Likewise, in *She*, H. Rider Haggard's novel of a lost civilization, the tribesmen call the jungle goddess "She-who-must-be-
obeyed" (a name later recalled in fiction by the beleaguered
barrister, Rumpole, to refer to his wife). To name a thing out loud
is to connect to it, to call forth its presence.

Great names are earned in battle or by other deeds. True names
are often hidden. Other names are revealed in visions or dreams.
To know a name is to wield power over it.

> [Robert E. Howard] …
> may have been wiser …
> when he borrowed names
> from history rather than
> coining them himself.
> Here are a few typical
> gems … Thak, Thaug,
> Thog, Yog, Yara, Yogah,
> Zang, Zogar, Sag.
> —Imaginary Worlds:
> The Art of Fantasy, 1973,
> by Lin Carter

Even for a being twelve feet tall, he appeared gnarled with muscles, like an oak come to life. He was dressed in a heavy leather
jerkin and leggings, and carried no weapons. A short beard, as stiff
as iron, jutted from his face. And his eyes were small, deep-set and
enthusiastic. From under his brows, massed over his sockets like
the wall of a fortress, his glances flashed piercingly, like gleams
from his cavernous thoughts. . . .

"Hail, Rocksister," he said in a soft, bubbling tenor voice which
sounded too light and gentle to come from his bemuscled throat,
"What is your need? . . ."

. . . Atiaran asked, "What is your name?"

"That is another long story," the Giant returned, and repeated,
"What is your need?"

But Atiaran insisted dully, "Your name."

Again a gleam sprang from under the Giant's massive brows.
"There is power in names. I do not wish to be invoked by any but
friends."

—*Lord Foul's Bane*, 1977, Stephen R. Donaldson

In *The Hobbit*, the small, stalwart Bilbo creeps into the den of the dragon, who appears to be asleep. Bilbo is invisible, but when he turns to go, the dragon senses his presence:

> "You have nice manners for a thief and a liar," said the dragon. "You seem familiar with my name, but I don't seem to remember smelling you before. Who are you and where do you come from, may I ask?"
> "You may indeed! I come from under the hill, and under the hills and over the hills my paths led. And through the air. I am he that walks unseen."
> "So I can well believe," said Smaug, "but that is hardly your usual name."

—*The Hobbit*, J.R.R. Tolkien

The dragon, puzzled but intrigued, probes further, while the hobbit deflects the creature by offering names like Ringwinner and Barrel-rider, based on adventures earlier in the story. Tolkien notes that "this is the way to talk with dragons, if you don't want to reveal your proper name (which is wise) and also don't want to infuriate them by a flat refusal (which is also very wise)."

Tolkien, like many others, drew on the imagery and cadences of old Norse legend, on rural folklore, on literary tales, on oral poetry like *Beowulf*.

Seamus Heaney is another writer who fell under the spell of *Beowulf*'s poetry. In his new translation, Heaney wraps his gracious and gritty Irish-bred tongue around the classic hero's tale. In the following passage, Beowulf and his men have just arrived on the Danish shores and walk from the cove to the hall of Hrothgar.

> It was a paved track, a path that kept them
> in marching order. Their mail-shirts glinted,
> hard and hand-linked; the high-gloss iron
> of their armour rang. So they duly arrived
> in their grim war-graith and gear at the hall,
> and, weary from the sea, stacked wide shields
> of the toughest hardwood against the wall,
> then collapsed on the benches; battle-dress
> and weapons clashed. They collected their spears

When he spoke the dragon's name it was as if he held the huge being on a fine, thin leash, tightening it on his throat. He could feel the ancient malice and experience of men in the dragon's gaze that rested on him, he could see the steel talons each as long as a man's forearm, and the stone-hard hide, and the withering fire that lurked in the dragon's throat; and yet always the leash tightened, tightened.
—Ursula K. Le Guin, in A Wizard of Earthsea

in a seafarers' stook, a stand of greyish
tapering ash. And the troops themselves
were as good as their weapons.

—*Beowulf*, transl. by Seamus Heaney, 2000

The words echo the clank of armor, the toughness of the warriors. All prose should be so vivid that we see the men by their
weapons. Heaney wrote in his preface, "It is one thing to find lexical
meanings for the words and to have some feel for how the metre
might go, but it is quite another thing to find the tuning fork that
will give you the note and pitch for the overall music of the work."

To his students at Oxford, J.R.R. Tolkien taught the epic poem
not as a fragment of dim legend, but as the imaginative work of a
poet. To Tolkien, *Beowulf* was not just a scrap of Baltic history, but a
living art—a true story made real again each time in the telling.

THE STORYTELLER'S ART

Storytelling is an art that, like Pinocchio's nose, swells with imagination. Tales when told expand like a genie from an uncorked
bottle, and shrink as quickly to nothingness when the story is done.
The traditional tellers of fantastic stories are transients—traveling
peddlers, hired men, nursemaids, and minstrels who pass through,
tell their tales, then move on to the next audience as it pleases them.

> "Beyond that," [Mr. Elimas] went on, "I earn a bit telling sto-
> ries round the inns. Right now I've got a set of seven, all nicely
> thought-out, all with an element of truth in them. However much
> you put into a story out of your own head ... there are always four
> or five threads of truth in it too, things that you might have carried
> in your memory without realizing it."
> "Well, that's for sure," said my master who happened to hear
> this. "And this very evening you could give us the gist of one of
> your stories."
> "Certainly, sir," said the Musselman . . . "and I could start on it
> right away if the lad would be so kind as to bring me another cup of
> coffee."
> I ran off at once to fetch it, and we all sat down in the broad
> shade of the fig-tree—Merlin in his rocking chair, the Musselman

on the ground as is their custom, me with legs astride the big branch.

—*Merlin and Company* (1955), by Alvaro Cunqueiro

The storyteller selects what details to reveal, and which parts to embellish.

"Those, then," said Mr. Elimas, "are the first three tales, and I generally tell them the first night at the inn. Naturally I dress them up a bit, giving details about people: saying that some character was lame, or had made a second marriage with a deaf woman who had money, or had a lawsuit going on about the water supply, things like that. And I add bits about the towns, their size, how many squares and streets they have, what the fairs are like, what the local fashions are. Stories, you know, like women, like dishes, need some decoration."

—*Merlin and Company*, Alvaro Cunqueiro

Each and every part of a story has its role, from Once Upon a Time to Happily Ever After.

"No, I don't like talking about myself," said the earthenware pot. "Let's have an evening's entertainment. I'll begin. I shall describe something everyone has experienced: that'll be something we can all enter into with pleasure, and it will be very amusing. 'Near the Baltic, by the Danish beeches—'"
"That's a good beginning!" said all the plates together. "It's going to be the kind of story I like!"
"Yes, I spent my youth there in a very quiet family. The furniture was polished, the floor washed, and clean curtains put up every fortnight."
"What an interesting way you have of telling a story!" said the broom. . . .
And the pot went on telling her story, and the end was just as good as the beginning.

—"The Flying Trunk," by Hans Christian Andersen, transl. by L.W. Kingsland, in *Hans Andersen's Fairy Tales: A Selection* (Univ. of Washington Press, 1959)

Thy trivial harp will never please / Or fill my craving ear;
Its chords should ring as blows the breeze,
Free, peremptory, clear.
No jingling serenader's art,
Nor tinkle of piano strings,
Can make the wild blood start / In its mystic springs.
The kingly bard
Must smite the chords rudely and hard . . .
—From "Merlin I," by Ralph Waldo Emerson

When you tell a story, you want your audience perched on the edge of their seats. What you don't want is this:

> . . . I followed the direction of his eye, and saw that a very old and white-bearded man, clothed in a flowing black gown, had risen and was standing at the table upon unsteady legs. . . .
>
> "Marry, we shall have it again," sighed the boy, "that same old weary tale that he hath told a thousand times in the same words. . . ."
>
> "Who is it?"
>
> "Merlin, the mighty liar and magician, perdition singe him for the weariness he worketh with his one tale. . . . He telleth it always in the third person. . . ."
>
> The boy nestled himself upon my shoulder and pretended to go to sleep. The old man began his tale; and presently the lad was asleep in reality; so were also the dogs, and the court, the lackeys, and the files of men-at-arms. The droning voice droned on; a soft snoring arose on all sides and supported it like a deep and subdued accompaniment of wind instruments. Some heads were bowed upon folded arms, some lay back with open mouths that issued unconscious music; the flies buzzed and bit, unmolested, the rats swarmed softly out from a hundred holes, and pattered about, and made themselves at home everywhere; and one of them sat up like a squirrel on the king's head and held a bit of cheese in its hands and nibbled it, and dribbled the crumbs in the king's face with naïve and impudent irreverence. It was a tranquil scene, and restful to the jaded eye and the jaded spirit.

—*A Connecticut Yankee in King Arthur's Court* (1889), Mark Twain

RICHNESS AND REPETITION

While the language of fantasy is rich, it is also repetitious. Freshness and originality are useful, but stronger magic lies in the traditions of the well-told tale. Good stories enchant time and again. As C.S. Lewis noted, great literature is meant to be reread. In a second or third reading, the small surprises of the plot disappear; we know what will happen. Great literature, however, achieves another kind of surprise, what Lewis calls "a certain ideal surprisingness." This is the pure magic of story itself, the golden elixir of language so rich we are surprised each time we hear it.

The power of repetition is seen in the delight children take in having the same story read to them time and again without a single word changed. How many adults have tried to abbreviate a bedtime story only to have the child protest, "No! Read it the way it's supposed to be." Each time we see it coming, yet take delight at that moment of revelation—when the wolf disguised in Grandmother's clothing bares wolfish teeth and cries, "The better to eat you with, my dear!"

The wonder of story itself is surprise enough—"free," says Lewis, "from the shock of actual surprise." To waste a good story on a first-time reading, he felt, is "like wasting great wine on a ravenous natural thirst."

Everyone who has enjoyed multiple readings of *The Lord of the Rings* knows this wine, as do those who have drunk more than once of the flowing language of *The Wind in the Willows*, or Carl Sandburg's *Rootabaga Stories*, or the stories of Lord Dunsany:

> The witch approached it and pared its edges with a sword that she drew from her thigh. Then she sat down beside it on the earth and sang to it while it cooled. Not like the runes that enraged the flames was the song she sang to the sword: she whose curses had blasted the fire till it shrivelled big logs of oak crooned now a melody like a wind in summer blowing from wild wood gardens that no man tended, down valleys loved once by children, now lost to them but for dreams, a song of such memories as lurk and hide along the edges of oblivion, now flashing from beautiful years of glimpse of some golden moment, now passing swiftly out of remembrance again, to go back to the shades of oblivion, and leaving on the mind those faintest traces of little shining feet which when dimly perceived by us are called regrets.

—*The King of Elfland's Daughter* (1924), by Lord Dunsany

Repetition is an important element of traditional stories. In the structure of fantasy, many stories use the "rule of three." The pattern is found most often in fairy tales like The Three Bears or The Three Wishes. The first event is the set-up, the second confirms the pattern, and the third does something new and unexpected. In Billy Goats Gruff, the smallest goat meets the troll under the bridge, the middle goat repeats the encounter and establishes the pattern in our

Perhaps this book should come with a warning.... It is the real thing. It's a rich red wine, which may come as a shock if all one has had so far has been cola.
—Neil Gaiman, in his introduction to The King of Elfland's Daughter, 1924, by Lord Dunsany (Del Rey edition, 1999)

minds—and the third and biggest goat surprises us and resolves the situation by butting the troll to high heaven.

Beowulf undertakes three great battles with three monsters: Grendel, Grendel's monstrous mother in her underwater lair, and the dragon in the king's barrow who inflicts the mortal wound.

As an extension of the rule of three, the concept of the circle holds a special place in traditional tales. The hero returns home and the cycle starts again. The Worm Ouroubus encircles the earth holding its own tail in its mouth; the beginning *is* the end. Death follows birth follows death. In fantasy, great powers are not created, they are reborn. In Robert Jordan's fantasy series, the *Wheel of Time*, his hero Rand al'Thor reluctantly faces his role as a reborn hero. He has one foot in what happened ages ago, one foot in the new pattern emerging as Rand and his friends struggle with the forces of dark and light. Jordan's *Wheel of Time* series has often been compared to Tolkien's expansive vision of Middle-earth.

In Native American lore, the four directions of the compass indicate the circular wholeness of the world.

> Giving anything form gives you a confidence in the universe…that it has form.
> —Robert Frost

MAGIC

Magic is the language of transformation. There a split vote amongst creators of magicians about how dangerous it is for the user. Some shape their magicians to be absent-minded, prone to misconjuring, and sorely in need of malpractice insurance. Mice or small owl's nests in the beard proliferate; general confusion reigns.

> The Shouter twins were still quarreling when they got to the depot, but they stopped when they saw, standing on the pavement beside the bus, a small brown coffee table.
>
> "It's her again," said Nancy.
>
> "Silly old crone," said Nora. . . .
>
> They glared at the squat, round table, which seemed to be swaying a little from side to side. …
>
> The coffee table was in fact a very old witch called Mother Bloodwort. . . . [who] had been a formidable witch of the old school, bringing people out in boils, putting the evil eye on butchers who sold her gristly chops, and casting spells on babies in perambulators so that their own mothers didn't know them.

But now she was old. Her memory was gone, and like many old people she got fancies. One of her fancies was to turn herself into a coffee table. There was no point in her being a coffee table: Mother Bloodwort did not drink coffee, which was far too expensive, and since she lived alone there was no one who might have wanted to put a cup and saucer down on her. But she was a cranky old witch and every so often she remembered the spell that changed her from a white-haired, whiskery old woman into a low, oak table with carved legs and a glass top, and then there was no stopping her.

What she did *not* often remember was how to turn herself back again.

—*Which Witch?*, Eva Ibbotson, 1979

Others create magicians more dreadful. Stephen King is a master of this end of the spectrum.

The magic in that country was so thick and tenacious that it settled over the land like chalk-dust and over floors and shelves like slightly sticky plaster-dust. (House-cleaners in that country earned unusually good wages.)
—Spindle's End, by Robin McKinley, 2000

Flagg, one of the greatest magicians who ever lived, knew all the poisons that we know—arsenic; strychnine; the curare, which steals inward, paralyzing all the muscles and the heart last; nicotine; belladonna; nightshade; toadstool. He knew the poison venoms of a hundred snakes and spiders. . . . Flagg did not know just dozens of poisons but dozens of dozens, each worse that the last. They were all neatly ranked on the shelves of an inner room where no servant ever went. They were in beakers, in phials, in little envelopes. Each deadly item was neatly marked. This was Flagg's chapel of screams-in-waiting—agony's antechamber, foyer of fevers, dressing room for death. Flagg visited it often when he felt out of sorts and wanted to cheer himself up. In this devil's marketplace waited all those things that humans, who are made of flesh and are so weak, dread: hammering headaches, screaming stomach cramps, detonations of diarrhea, vomiting, collapsing blood vessels, paralysis of the heart, exploding eyeballs, swelling, blackening tongues, madness.

But the worst poison of all Flagg kept separate from even these. . . .

Inside the packet was a small quantity of green sand. Pretty, you would have said, but nothing spectacular. Nothing to write home to Mother about. Yet this green sand was one of the deadliest poisons in all the worlds . . . because a single breath of the fumes which came from the desert of Grehn would cause death.

Not instant death. That was not the way the poison worked. For a day or two—perhaps even three—the person who breathed the poison fumes (or even worse, swallowed the grains of sand) would feel fine—perhaps even better than ever before in his life. Then, suddenly, his lungs would grow red-hot, his skin would begin to shrivel like the body of a mummy. Then he would drop dead, often with his hair on fire. . . .

This was Dragon Sand, and there was no antidote, no cure. What fun.

—*The Eyes of the Dragon*, Stephen King

This is Stephen King at his finest: the asides ("Nothing to write home to Mother about"); the delightfully horrific possibilities ("exploding eyeballs"); the macabre lists of poisons; the perverse effect of the poison ("for a day or two, the person would feel better than ever . . ."); the tongue-in-cheek summary ("What fun.").

Above all, magicians must live by rules. Chants and incantations must be performed correctly, or risk disaster. Like the Sorcerer's Apprentice, a magician needs to know not only how to invoke a bit of magic, but how to control it. Consistency is the watchword.

Just as important as the powers of magic are its limitations. A plot is destroyed by an all-powerful magic; the wand is waved and all problems solved. Where is the narrative tension in that? As Fraser Sherman wrote in *The Writer*:

A story in which magic can do literally anything would be unworkable—but how do you set limits on the impossible?

Here are some ways to rein in magic:

—There are no strong wizards. If all magic can do is light a candle or clean the laundry, it won't upset your story much.

—Magic works only under specific circumstances. If wizards can cast spells only through their Wands of Power, smashing the wands makes them powerless.

—A magic talisman (a ring, a sacred necklace, an ancient sword) neutralizes magic; as long as a character possesses it, he's safe from enemy magic.

—The magician has a weakness. *The Lord of the Rings* hinges on Sauron's having placed most of his power in the Magic One Ring; when Frodo destroys the ring, Sauron can't survive.

—The magician has personal reasons for holding off; He wants to destroy his hated enemy face-to-face, or to wait until they've unearthed the lost treasure he seeks.

—"We're Off To See the Wizards," Fraser Sherman, in *The Writer*

What will your rules be? Perhaps magic loses its potency with distance from a source, or in the presence of other counter-charms, or if used for the wrong purposes. It might take great attention to details memorized in long studies of arcane books of magic. In the Harry Potter books, young Harry must spend many years learning Defense Against the Dark Arts; the trick is knowing the right spell to use at the right time. Or it might take the opposite: a complete clearing of the mind. In Philip Pullman's *The Golden Compass*, the young Lyra must carefully put her mind at rest before she asks a question of the magical device.

Often, the use of magic transforms the user—if not the entire world. As Ged's mentor, the Master Hand, tells the fledgling mage in *A Wizard of Earthsea* by Ursula Le Guin:

> "You must not change one thing, one pebble, one grain of sand, until you know what good and evil will follow on that act. The world is in balance, in Equilibrium. A wizard's power of Changing and of Summoning can shake the balance of the world. It is dangerous, that power. It is most perilous. It must follow knowledge and serve need. To light a candle is to cast a shadow. . . ."

—*A Wizard of Earthsea*, Ursula Le Guin

By the end of the third book of Earthsea, Ged has learned the hard way the meaning of the phrase: "To light a candle is to cast a shadow." All is connected, in magic and in fantasy.

In the Harry Potter books, Harry's nemesis, Lord Voldemort, has terrific powers, but they are limited. Lord Voldemort has to plan his moves carefully, to recruit minions to help him carry out evil deeds, to strike at just the right time. And he is steadily thwarted. That delightful pattern of move and counter-move is entertaining for readers as they try to guess what may happen. What prevents the Dark Lord from triumphing over the smaller, apparently less-powerful hero? Usually, until the final resolution when greater forces

The world a writer creates may have as its laws that the inhabitants are nothing but a pack of cards, that animals converse intelligently while messing about in boats, or that a magic ring can make its bearer invisible at the long, slow cost of his soul. But once these laws are set down, the writer cannot, on a whim, set them aside. They must work in the fantasy world as surely as gravity works in ours.
—Jane Yolen, in Writing Books for Children, 1983

come into play, the balance between good and evil is kept in check simply by the rules of magic.

DUELS & RIDDLES

And at the far end of the chamber stood a man dressed in white, with a red sword girt at his side, and she knew him at once, for she had seen his face often enough in her mirror.
—The Hero and the Crown, 1984, by Robin McKinley

In fantasy, well-worn conventions include the tip-toed descent into the dragon's lair, the rescuing of the damsel under a spell, the ordinary object that is revealed to have magical powers at a crucial point, the cloak of invisibility, the spell that freezes all, the boastful ogre, the duel between the hero and the Dark Lord.

> Will was instantly a furious Old One, so furious that he did not pause to think what he should do. . . . He stretched out his right hand with its fingers spread stiff towards his family, and saw them instantly caught into a stop in time, frozen out of all movement. . . .
>
> "How dare you come in here!" he shouted at the Rider. The two of them stood facing one another across the room, the only living and moving objects there; no human moved, the hands of the clock on the mantelpiece did not move, and though the flames of the fire flickered, they did not consume the logs that they burned.
>
> "How dare you! At Christmas, on Christmas morning! Get out!" . . .
>
> The Rider said softly, "Contain yourself." In the Old Speech, his accent was suddenly much more marked. He smiled at Will without a flicker of change in his cold blue eyes. "I can cross your threshold, my friend, and pass your berried holly, because I have been invited. . . ."
>
> —*The Dark Is Rising*, Susan Cooper

This entire book by Cooper describes a tautly drawn duel between the forces of good and evil. All takes place within twelve days, from Midwinter Day to Christmas, a time when traditionally the cycle of the year was believed to hang in the balance, when age-old custom required that certain steps be taken to beat back the forces of the dark that were at their greatest strength in the midwinter solstice.

The riddle is a cross between a game and a duel, a challenge between poser and solver. Riddles play a special role in fantasy, because they combine the duel with the power of hidden names for

things. Solving the puzzle can unlock valuable secrets, as does a
series of riddles in the *Pearls of Lutra* (1996) in the *Redwall* series.

> I shed my second tear, into the cup of cheer,
> But look not into any cup, the answer's written here!
> My first is in blood and also in battle,
> My second in acorn, oak and apple,
> My third and fourth are both the same,
> In the center of sorrow and twice in refrain,
> My fifth starts eternity ending here,
> My last is the first of last . . . Oh dear!
> If I told you the answer then you would know,
> 'Twas made in the winter of deepest snow.

—*Pearls of Lutra*, by Brian Jacques

In the first Harry Potter book, young Harry encounters the
mirror of Erised, in which he sees what he desires, reflected. His
knowledge of that plays into the book's closing battle with Lord
Voldemort, who lacks an understanding of the puzzle of the mirror.

Confrontations can be played with creatively or conventionally.
Avoid, however, the crime of the stereotype, which is basically a
convention gone bad. Diana Wynne Jones' humorous *Tough Guide to
Fantasyland* deals mercilessly with stereotypes, the trite and tired,
from Adept to Zombie. Here, for instance, is a tongue-in-cheek
checklist of options for one of the standard encounters in fantasy:
the "Small Ambiguous Confrontation":

> You meet . . . the Unpleasant Stranger. You are cheated by a
> Ferryman or River Travelers. You have a run-in with Dwarves,
> Gnomes, and Desert Nomads. You try to get money from a Coun-
> cil. You meet a Ghost/Elemental. You are captured by Marsh
> Dwellers and have Language problems. You come upon a Nunnery
> and talk to the survivor [of a recent attack]. . . .

—*The Tough Guide to Fantasyland* (1996), Diana Wynne Jones

Some forms of fantasy literature—gothic novels, for instance—
thrive on stereotypes. Conventions are part of the craft. Even then,
avoid the worst of them, and seek the fresh use of language whenever
possible.

PREMONITIONS & PROPHECIES

In general fiction, foreshadowing refers to the writer's trick of sowing small hints into the furrows of a plot to emerge later. But in fantasy literature there is a more powerful tool: the premonition or prophecy. These are ominous, sometime blood-chilling portents of triumph or disaster ahead. They are direct glimpses of the future, although seen in a mirror, darkly.

Readers and the characters themselves are likely to ponder the meaning. Will Birnam Wood come to the castle? Unlikely, we think, but our next thought is . . . how? How can a man not be born of woman and if so, how will he overthrow Macbeth?

Sometimes the portent is simply an odd natural occurrence: the shape of a dragon in clouds or a brilliant sunset. Other portents are known as forerunners of evil—such as the animals running in panic through the forest in Lloyd Alexander's *The Book of Three*, literally fore-runners of the soon-to-appear Horned King.

In fantasy, there is never a doubt that the prophecies will come true. The only question is how.

Often, the simplest suggestive device is just a sudden shiver experienced by a character, the sense of someone "walking on your grave." This small hint is quickly communicated to readers, and the story goes on. But it is a clear signal that evil has begun to act, and that our hero will soon come face to face with it.

Premonitions are powerful bits of information. They combine in Hitchcockian fashion the twin elements of advance knowledge and suspense. We see the shadow coming, but cannot turn away.

> Elphaba was sitting under the dock with the looking glass that Turtle Heart had made. She held it in two hands, and started at it with one eye closed. She peered, she squinted; her open eye was distant and hollow.
>
> Reflection from the starlight off the water, thought Frex, hoped Frex, but he knew the bright vacant eye was not lit by starlight.
>
> "Horrors," murmured Elphaba.
>
> Turtle Heart tumbled to his knees. "She sees him coming," he said thickly, "she sees him to come, he is to come from the air; is arriving. A balloon from the sky, the color of a bubble of blood; a huge crimson globe, a ruby globe; he falls from the sky. The Regent is fallen. The House of Ozma is fallen. The Clock was right. A minute to judgment.". . .

"Horrors," she said again, looking without binocular vision, staring at the glass in which her parents and Nanny could make out nothing but darkness. "Horrors."

—*Wicked: The Life and Times of the Wicked Witch of the West*, 1995, by Gregory Maguire

Readers familiar with the story of Oz will recognize that the "bubble of blood, the ruby globe," indicates the arrival of the Wizard, fallen from the sky when his red balloon crashes. How can we not read on to discover what horrors await?

SIGNS & SYMBOLS

When the Dark comes rising, six shall turn it back,
Three from the circle, three from the track;
Wood, bronze, iron; water, fire, stone;
Five will return, and one go alone.

—*The Dark Is Rising*, by Susan Cooper

Signs equal significance. As Christian scholar Peter Kreeft wrote in a 1991 essay, "Darkness at Noon: The Eclipse of 'The Permanent Things'": "The reason Lewis and Chesterton and Williams and Tolkien fascinate us so much is fundamentally that they still live in a medieval world, a world chock full of built-in, God-designed significance. . . . For them, everything means something beyond itself. Everything is not only a thing, but a sign, full of significance."

Elemental objects of wood, bronze, and so on play a great role in fantasy. Swords, goblets, rings, crowns and such are tangible things and also symbols of metaphysical powers. Finding these objects in a story and discovering their importance are often key plot points.

Fantasy stories are meaningful, but usually not allegories. Allegories are direct coded symbols of something else; once you know the code, you replace "x" with "y," and you then perceive the hidden meaning. The stories of C.S. Lewis, for instance, are not allegories; although rooted in Christian beliefs, the Narnia tales are fully imagined stories in their own right. Aslan, the lion-king of Narnia, Lewis said, has traits in common with the Christian God, but is not synonymous with God. Aslan, said Lewis, was only what God might be like if He chose to appear as a lion in Narnia.

His work was like that of his friend Tolkien's, whose great romantic fantasy, Lewis noted, *The Lord of the Rings*, "is like a flower whose smell reminds you of something you can't quite place."

Elemental symbols, then, are not there in fantasy to represent something else. They are complex metaphors that suggest a range of ideas. When writers select ancient symbols like wood or water, earth or fire, stone or steel—they are recreating these qualities in a fresh, new way. These symbols are powerful not because they are ancient, but because these basic qualities are still meaningful and vital: the fluidity of water, the hardness of stone, the flux of fire.

HUMOR AND PARODY

Humor is often close to the surface in fantasy literature. Since fantasy looks in new ways at the human condition, it easily touches on predicaments and surprises that verge on the ridiculous. Like humor, fantasy often involves the exaggeration of otherwise normal qualities to absurd proportions.

Peter S. Beagle is one of the great modern fantasists, bringing modern settings and sensibilities into the field. His 1995 story, "Professor Gottesman and the Indian Rhinoceros," is a wonderful tale that plays with the basis of rational convictions. The story is launched when the professor visits a local zoo and meets a rhinoceros that speaks to him. They exchange views on unicorns; the rhinoceros insists he is one, while the Professor takes the only slightly more rational view that the beast is nothing more than a talking rhinoceros. Soon after, the rhinoceros appears in the Professor's apartment, lounging on the sofa. The two continue their debate as their friendship grows.

> He found himself, despite himself, gradually warming toward the rhinoceros, Still formal, he asked, "May I perhaps offer you a drink. Some coffee or tea?"
>
> "Tea would be very nice," the rhinoceros answered, "if you should happen to have a bucket." Professor Gottesman did not, and the rhinoceros told him not to worry about it. It settled back down before the fire, and the Professor drew up a rocking chair. The rhinoceros said, "I must admit, I do wish I could hear you speak on the scholastic philosophers. That's really my period, after all."

"I will be giving such a course next year," the Professor said, a little shyly. "It is to be a series of lectures on medieval Christian thought, beginning with St. Augustine and the Neoplatonists and ending with William of Occam. Possibly you could attend some of those talks?"

The rhinoceros's obvious pleasure at the invitation touched Professor Gottesman surprisingly deeply. . . . He was beginning to wonder whether there might be a way to permit the rhinoceros to sample the cream sherry he kept aside for company, when the creature added, with a wheezy chuckle, "Of course, Augustine and the rest never did quite come to terms with such pagan survivals as unicorns. The best they could do was to associate us with the Virgin Mary; and to suggest that our horns somehow represented the unity of Christ and his church. Bernard of Trèves even went so far as to identify Christ directly with the unicorn, but it was never a comfortable union. Spiral peg in square hole, so to speak."

—In *Modern Classics of Fantasy*, ed. by Gardner Dozois, 1977

Parody of the fantasy genre itself is a fond pursuit for many writers. Since the field is so accustomed to recycling its own age-old myths and themes, it makes an easy target.

"And the only thing that can break this spell is a kiss from a princess."

The princess thought for a moment about whether sexual harassment could take place between species, but her heart went out to the frog for his predicament. She bent down and kissed the frog on the forehead. Instantly the frog grew and changed. And there, standing in the water where the frog had been, was a man in a golf shirt and loud plaid pants—middle-aged, vertically challenged, and losing a little bit of hair on top.

The princess was taken aback. "I'm sorry if this sounds a little classist," she stammered, "but . . . what I mean to say is . . . don't sorcerers usually cast their spells on *princes*?"

—*Politically Correct Bedtime Stories*, James Finney Garner, 1994

Some of "The Top 100 Things I'd Do if I Ever Became an Evil Overlord":
1. My ventilation ducts will be too small to crawl through.
2. My noble half-brother whose throne I usurped will be killed, not kept anonymously imprisoned in a forgotten cell of my dungeon.
3. I will not gloat over my enemies' predicament before killing them.
4. I will dress in bright and cheery colors and so throw my enemies into confusion.
—Peter Anspach, 1997, from his website, www.eviloverlord.com

PURE IMAGINATION

With his combination of humor and inventive language, Michael Ende first rocketed to fame in 1979 with *The Neverending Story*, in which a boy, Bastian, finds a magical book in a bookseller's shop. The volume, bound in copper-colored silk, has a cover illustration of two snakes eating each other's tail. Beginning to read, the boy enters the land of Fantastica and becomes directly embroiled in its adventures. Ultimately the story becomes a symbol of fantasy itself, with its power to absorb and enchant.

Another book by Ende, *The Night of Wishes* (1989, English translation 1992), begins with equally brilliant imagination.

> Nothing was stirring within the Villa Nightmare—except for the flickering shadow of the fire, its green flames burning in the hearth and casting an eerie glow over the sorcerer's laboratory.
>
> The works of the pendulum clock above the mantelpiece rattled to life. It was a cuckoo clock of sorts, except that its elaborate mechanism consisted of a sore thumb being struck by a hammer.
>
> "Ouch!" it said. "Ouch!—Ouch!—Ouch!—Ouch!"
>
> So it was five o'clock. . . .

Michael Ende's writing is a candy-store counter of apparitions, a modern European combination of Heironymus Bosch, Dr. Seuss, and Carlos Castenada. Anyone who wishes to write fantastical scenes should read his books.

Fantasy's traditions are, for some, like a glass of pure water drawn from a deep well. For others, fantasy's language fills an entire ocean. The patterns are infinite: the streaks of sunset splashed across a distant horizon, the endless waves, the twisted flotsam cast high by storms, the tidal pools swarming with sea-life, the strange monsters found far beneath the waves.

The liquid magic of fantasy's language runs through and around every story. Whether we draw from the deepest wells or from the open ocean, we have not dug these wells nor filled the seas with our own hands. Yet the ancient patterns are there, waiting for us to recognize their invisible tides, tugging on our imagination.

THE ART OF THE STORYTELLER

Interview with Peter S. Beagle
by Philip Martin

Peter Beagle has been praised for his "opulence of imagination and mastery of style"; his work stands with the best of Tolkien and C.S. Lewis. His light-hearted novel, The Last Unicorn (1968), first earned him this stature, sustained by subsequent works, including A Fine and Private Place and The Innkeeper's Song. His lyrical style is that of the storyteller, offering compelling stories full of engaging characters whose voices ring true. In this interview, he talks about the writing of Tamsin (1999), a novel of ghostly apparitions set in New York and rural England.

I can remember, a long time ago, when we were in the same writing class, Ken Kesey asking me: If you couldn't be a writer, what would you be?

And I said more or less without hesitation, I'd be one of those old guys who sat in the marketplace, cross-legged, telling stories. And at a certain point in the story, he stops, holds out his hand and says, "If you want to hear what happens to the princess and the genie—you'll have to drop a few coins in here."

There's a good bit of the performer in me. I don't use the word "artist" a lot. I think of myself first as a storyteller, and entertainer, and perhaps artist. But my first job is to tell a story.

I'm very aware that as a fantasist, you have to be a full-time realist. I'm asking you to believe something essentially impossible. And to do that I have to make the background—the world my story is happening in—as bedrock real as possible.

I recall something Isaac Asimov said to me once, when we were working together on a project. We spoke on the phone about some plot twist that I had put in and I asked, "Isaac, would you say this is scientifically feasible?" And he said, "Absolutely not. Now, what we have to do is make it plausible."

And of course, that's it. I work in my books very hard to make the essentially impossible . . . plausible.

I'm not really a minimalist, but I consider myself a Count Basie-ist. Count Basie said late in life: "It has taken me fifty years to learn what not to play." That I understand. Sometimes I'll put something in and look at it later and think, there's nothing wrong with that, it's nicely written. But if you don't need it, it's got to go.

When I write, I tell the story. I will literally walk around the room talking dialogue and description to myself. I'm going for rhythm, without being too obvious about it. I love to read aloud. And I love to memorize poetry, as I did when I was a child.

It's funny, but I'm often considered a Tolkien expert. I get letters now and then in Elvish, which of course I can't read. I'm not really a Tolkien scholar, but I read him when I was in college in the late '50s. And I loved the books. I wrote an early article on Tolkien for *Holiday* magazine and then was asked to write the Foreword that's still included the Tolkien paperbacks.

But I don't consider Tolkien a major influence on me. Not as much as T.H. White and Robert Nathan. And Lord Dunsany and James Thurber, and a wonderful Irish writer, James Stevens.

But what Tolkien illustrates best is the depth of passion a writer needs to have with his world and his characters. As a writer, you often find yourself talking about your characters—what they did that day—as if they were live children or something. Just as an actor psyches himself up into believing a character he's playing, I really have to believe that the people I'm writing about are real, have their own wills, and I can't simply manipulate them.

So many writers, young writers especially, but also published writers, think that fantasy is easy. All you have to do is rip off some elves, goblins, and a few other things from Tolkien and spend about ten minutes making up imaginary words and another ten minutes working up a rough idea of the country and a little local history and bingo, you're in business. You're a fantasist.

It's not at all like that. What made Tolkien unique is that he spent fifty years building his world, and he built it from the inside out. Nobody else did it as thoroughly as he did. In the field of fantasy, the man was a mountain.

ON WRITING TAMSIN

You can write an outline for a book, and it's important to do that. But it doesn't explain where certain characters come from. It's like Dickens as a young writer who just got a contract to serialize a novel in a London paper, which is a great thing and will feed his growing family—except that he doesn't *have* a novel. And he just says in his biographical writings, "Then I thought of Mr. Pickwick." He doesn't say how he thought of Mr. Pickwick. It just happened. And that is how it works sometimes.

For me it's always been something like possession—like what happens to actors when they're working their way into a part. I was lucky with Jenny, because I heard her voice very clearly. It was rather like being locked on a radar beam. It didn't tell me what to do, but if I got off the beam, if I wrote something that wasn't Jenny's voice, or tried to make the character do something Jenny wouldn't do, I knew right away.

This is not always the case. You can get through a whole book, then realize that you forced certain characters to do things they never would do. But in *Tamsin*, I didn't have that problem.

It didn't matter that Jenny was a girl. I remember being 13. I wanted to be invisible too. I had to watch out to make sure I wasn't putting too much in. I wanted to allow for the fact that Jenny at times whines and bitches, and she's aware that she is. There's a lot of self-knowledge. And she's trying very hard to write an honest book.

One way I can tell if I've done it right is that when I finish, I miss the characters. And I really miss Jenny. I enjoyed my time of being Jenny.

Before, I'd always either written about an area I knew pretty well or I'd simply make up an imaginary world. But I'd never been to Dorset, where most of *Tamsin* takes place. And you can only get so much out of Thomas Harding, even if you read all his books. I did go to Dorset after the first draft was done. What pleases me is that I knew a few people in Dorset who say that it's accurate—that it doesn't read as though it were written by an American making it up.

I'd been reading a book by Robert Graves, called *Wife to Mr. Milton*, set more or less in Tamsin's period. And in the back, Graves included a glossary of late 17th-century slang phrases and catch words. Then I came across a book published in 1876 of Dorset dialect. There I found an embarrassment of riches, a lot of phrases for the local people. But I didn't want to overdo it. I put some phrases in and then took them out again, because it just sounded like I had gotten ahold of a book of Dorset dialect.

As for Tamsin's appearance, I deliberately delayed it—partly because I felt that was right for the book. Before Tamsin appeared, I knew I had to establish Jenny's situation beyond any question, her physical reality. I knew I had to make the house and Dorset real and show Jenny's growing awareness of this new place.

But also, I was scared. I didn't know, after all the build-up, how not to have the story climax when the ghost does show up. But the moment Tamsin showed up, there she was. Even then, I didn't know what her secret was. Tamsin didn't remember, and neither did I. I really didn't. I just had to trust that I would know when the time came.

When I'm really working, it's kind of like just tightening the focus on a microscope of some sort. Just screwing down this lens as closely and tightly as I can. Eventually, things come into view that were always there; they just weren't in focus yet.

But I always have an overall plan. Without a detailed plan, ideally chapter by chapter, I find myself thinking "Is that enough? Am I putting in too much time on this, when I should be getting to that? What's the right proportion here?" That's always the concern—getting the proportions right, and the rhythm of the story.

I always feel I can get it eventually, because if there's one thing I know, it's how to rewrite. I don't have any shame in turning around and saying "Well, that didn't work—and it's a good thing nobody saw it. Let's try it another way." But I still feel I waste a lot of time leaning on my elbow and thinking to myself, "alright sucker, now what?"

I used to get hung up over a paragraph for weeks because something was wrong. I couldn't just skip it and come back and fix it later on. That was one thing scriptwriting taught me. Movie work is so modular—you can snap scenes out here and snap them back in somewhere else. From that I learned—alright, skip this, pick up here. You know what's missing. You'll come back and put that in.

But as baseball players say, when you hit the ball right, when you hit on the sweet spot of the bat—everything gets into it, your wrists, your shoulders. You can feel the shock through your whole body and you know it's going out before you've taken a few steps away from home plate.

There are days like that with the English language, too.

DRAWING ON MYTH & LEGEND

Interview with Susan Cooper
by Raymond H. Thompson

Susan Cooper is the renowned author of The Dark Is Rising series, five books published in the 1960s and '70s, featuring young characters in modern England and Wales drawn into dramatic conflicts between dark and light forces. One of the books, The Grey King, won the prestigious Newbery Medal in 1976. More recently, her novel of a boy thrown back in time to Shakespeare's day, King of Shadows, was an Honor Book for the 2000 Horn Book Awards. Here, in an excerpted portion of an interview with Arthurian scholar Prof. Raymond Thompson, Cooper talks about the relationship of the ancient patterns of Arthurian legend and her mythic series.

(Thompson) What attracted you to the Arthurian legend as an ingredient in your series *The Dark Is Rising*?

(Cooper) It never occurred to me that I was writing about the Arthurian legend as such. I was just writing a series of fantasies which drew on everything I'd ever read, lived through, and absorbed. I wrote *Over Sea, Under Stone* when I was a very young journalist [in England]. A publishing company had a competition for a family adventure story, and I thought I would go in for this. So the book started off as an adventure story. Very early on, however, this character called Merriman turned up, and the book turned itself into a fantasy.

Once I was writing fantasy . . . I just felt like I'd come home. You don't say to yourself, I am writing fantasy. . . . You just tell the story. Or you're really living in it and reporting on what you find. Of course what you find comes out of your own subconscious.

(Thompson) What is the relationship between Arthur and Herne the Hunter in your series?

(Cooper) One of the things I tend to believe, largely as a result of reading Robert Graves [*White Goddess*], is that there is a blurring of identity between an awful lot of figures. The mythic territory of the totally mythical Herne and the possibly-once-real Arthur can cross and overlap, and this happens with the figures in my story.

Nothing is precise in myth. When you're using myth you can be precise for the purposes of your book, but you do it at your own peril. The mythic elements are all intended to be slightly out of focus, like an impressionistic painting, and if you try to sharpen the focus you will lose something. You will lose the magic.

(Thompson) Why did you decide to make Bran the son of Arthur?

(Cooper) It was not a rational decision. I start a book knowing it's a road. You know the beginning, you know who's going with you on the road, you know roughly where they're going, but you don't know anything at all (at least I don't) about what's going to happen on the way. You find out as you go along.

When I write a novel, I have two things. I have the manuscript as it comes out very slowly, from the typewriter or on the page. And at the same time I keep a notebook. It's full of random scraps from all over the place, and they often turn up in the book: quotations, images, historical allusions, etc. But in it I also talk back to myself.

I'm sure if I looked back at the notebook for *The Grey King*, I would find at some point a realization that Bran is going to be the son of Arthur. Just as there was a point at which Merriman turned out to be Merlin. Your head does things before it tells you it's doing them.

(Thompson) When did you recognize that Merriman was Merlin?

(Cooper) At the end of *Over Sea, Under Stone* one of the characters, a small boy named Barney, says, "Merry Lyon . . . Merlion . . . Merlin." It was only when I reached that point in the writing that I realized who he was.

[But] he's my character, not the Merlin of tradition. Merriman is an Old One in my books, a figure of the Light that opposes the Dark, which is my rather obvious classification of good and evil. He doesn't have the ambiguous dark qualities or Merlin in Arthurian legend. The sinister side of Merriman Lyon, and indeed all the Old Ones, is that absolute good, like absolute evil, is fanatical. As one of my characters points out, there is no room for human ambiguity. Absolute good is like a blinding light, which can be very cruel, and to that extent Merriman is not a sympathetic character.

(*Thompson*) Do you have specific locations in mind for your settings, or are they an amalgamation?

(*Cooper*) Oh, very specific. *Over Sea, Under Stone* and *Greenwitch* are both set in Trewissick, based on a village in Cornwall called Mevagissey. We used to go there when I was a child. *The Dark is Rising* is set in the part of Buckinghamshire where I grew up. Every stick is real. It doesn't look that way now, a lot of it, but some of it does. The little church is still exactly the same. Huntercombe is based on the village of Dorney and the Great Hall is Dorney Court.

The Welsh setting in *The Grey King* and *Silver on the Tree* is around Aberdyfi, the village where my grandmother was born and where my parents lived. My aunt, who still lives there, occasionally has people knocking on the door and saying, is this the certain point from that book.

(*Thompson*) Did you check details of the topography after you had started writing?

(*Cooper*) I had two ordnance survey maps pinned up in my study inside a cupboard door, so that if I wanted to check them I went to the cupboard. Also, I used to go home every year. I can remember going out of the door from my parents' house when I was visiting Aberdyfi, to remind myself what it was like to go across the dunes and down to the sea in the very early morning. The images that I encountered on the way went into *Silver on the Tree*, where a character called Jane does just that.

An awful lot of detail comes out of your memory, however. You don't know it's there until you start writing about it. In that same book, Will and Bran are on a mountaintop on one side of the River Dyfi, and there appears a magical arching bridge which takes them down into a timeless place called the Lost Land. When I was writing that passage, I had them on the mountaintop, and I didn't know what happened next.

Then I remembered the last time I was home being up on that particular mountain, looking out across the estuary of the River Dyfi. Ever since I was a child I had known the legend about the drowned country, and I could almost see it.

As I recalled that moment I thought, that's what they do! They go down there, over a bridge! It's lovely when that happens. It's not a rational decision. You can't control it. You say, oh, I see!

(*Thompson*) Did you find that what you had written in the earlier books [in the series] committed you to directions that you subsequently regretted, or wished you had more freedom to change?

(*Cooper*) No. It was wonderful. It was like writing a symphony, in which each movement is different and yet they all link together. An early book leads to something in a later book. When I wrote the first book, of course, I didn't envision a series. But later, when I first had the idea of writing the whole sequence, I drew up a plan on a piece of paper. I had little notes written down: the four times of the year—focused on the solstices, Beltane, and such festivals—I had places, and very roughly, the characters who were in each book.

There were things I had to remember from early books that had to be either resolved or referred to in later books. *Silver on the Tree* suffered from being the last book where I was tying up all the ends. My head was going off in all directions. There was even more in it, but I took some out. Of course, when you're dealing with the substance of myth, which is the fight between good and evil, I suppose, you have to provide the ultimate, terrific, enormous climax. It's almost impossible.

(*Thompson*) Did the elements you had drawn from Arthurian legend contribute significantly to that feeling of congestion?

(*Cooper*) I had to move away from it because it seems to me that the Arthurian legend is parallel to the Christian story of the leader who dies for our salvation. Whereas what my books were trying to say is that nobody else can save us. We have to save ourselves.

Silver on the Tree contains a reference to a poem that I remember my mother reciting to me. It's about Drake being in his hammock, which recalls the local legend in Devon that Sir Francis Drake will come back to rescue England. Similarly, Arthur will come back, and Christ.

I didn't want to use that idea. The Arthur that I was using goes to Avalon, and saving the world is up to the people in it.

Prof. Raymond H. Thompson's interviews with modern Arthurian authors, including the full text of this one, can be found on the website for The Camelot Project, at www.lib.rochester.edu/camelot/CPHOME.stm.

CHAPTER SEVEN

THE WINDS OF CHANGE: THE POWER OF PLOT & PURPOSE

To some degree, we can all create clever characters, places, and patterns of language. But can we combine these three elements into a compelling story? Putting these together to form a successful narrative is the role of a fourth element: the plot.

An author need not focus on plot first. Stories often originate elsewhere, with an engaging character, an intriguing place, a traditional pattern of a tale. Often, plot is the last thing to happen.

But plot is pivotal. Plot is what brings a story alive. If a reader enters a story, and that story moves forward, a magic world is brought to life. If the reader's curiosity is fully engaged, he or she will stay up late into the night to read "just one more chapter," and then another, and another. Readers read, as George R.R. Martin says, to find out what happens. If they don't care—worse, if they do care but nothing happens—you will lose them. "What happens next" is the matter of plot.

If we think of story as a boat, bobbing on the high seas of fantasy, then plot is the wind that must fill the sails. When there is enough wind, the story moves forward, propelling ship and cargo on a journey from here to there.

Without wind or sail, your story just sits there, becalmed. This does not mean that every moment in a plot needs to be action-packed, beating around Cape Horn in a wild gale. Sometimes a ship needs to rest in harbor, sitting serenely in the moonlight.

But ultimately plot is the motive power that sets everything in motion. Those who would travel across fantasy's vast ocean need to know all the seafarer's skills: to use a compass, to chart a course, to steer by the stars.

A story needs to go somewhere. It's what *story* does.

THE HERO'S JOURNEY

A plot is often charted as a line of rising tension. After a slow rise comes an escalating series of small jagged peaks, growing in magnitude as each event is approached, experienced, and then resolved. After each incident, the action drops slightly into a valley until the next event is approached, each greater than the last. After the highest peak, the line plummets and the story ends. This line represents the flow of the dramatic story.

In fantasy fiction, there is an age-old version of the "rising action" plot called the Hero's Journey. Defined by scholar Joseph Campbell based on his studies of ancient tales around the world, the Hero's Journey is similar to standard plots found in general fiction, but it uses special devices dear to fantasy. Though formulaic, it is rooted in deeply-seated archetypes and patterns that have proven successful in creating good stories for many centuries.

In the Hero's Journey, after we first meet the hero in the ordinary world, at some point the hero crosses a threshold from the ordinary world to the magical—and the quest is underway. A series of trials of increasing challenge is presented. In some stories, the hero succeeds at each task. In others, early failure leads to despair, but the plucky hero continues nonetheless.

To assist the hero, helpers are met who lend support or contribute key bits of knowledge. Some of these may join the quest as companions. Companions often have odd natures, and may even seem to be a hindrance. Often a wise mentor is met who provides both philosophical and practical guidance to the hero.

The ongoing trials are faced, one by one. This leads to what seems to be a final challenge, but soon after, it is realized that one more great test needs to be faced before the evil powers are conquered completely. The hero must return one more time to the deepest level of the underworld, to the most remote castle of the evil lord, there to engage in the ultimate confrontation.

The final trial is a great battle, a showdown, an impossible task with little hope of success. The hero, however, is victorious, often with the help of the special skills of companions, the advice of the mentor, and a realization of the hero's own inner strengths.

Victorious, the hero is able to return home, sometimes as a hero, sometimes unrecognized. There is often an aftermath scene, when people at home are re-encountered, outstanding matters are resolved, rewards are distributed, knowledge shared.

Many fantasy stories fit into this scheme. For instance, in *The Silver Chair* by C.S. Lewis, young Jill, persecuted at boarding school by bullies, escapes through a magic door into another world. She meets a wise, powerful lion, Aslan, who presents the task: to rescue a prince of Narnia, who has been kidnapped.

> "I lay on you this command, that you seek this lost prince until either you have found him and brought him to his father's house, or else died in the attempt. . . ."
>
> "How, please?" said Jill.
>
> ". . . These are the signs by which I will guide you in your quest. First; as soon as the Boy Eustace sets foot in Narnia, he will meet an old and dear friend. He must greet that friend at once; if he does, you will both have good help. Second; you must journey out of Narnia to the north till you come to the ruined city of the giants. Third; you shall find a writing on a stone in that ruined city, and you must do what the writing tells you. Fourth; you will know the lost prince (if you find him) by this, that he will be the first person you have met in your travels who will ask you to do something in my name, in the name of Aslan."

—*The Silver Chair*, 1953, C.S. Lewis

So when the storyteller by the hearth starts out: "Once upon a time, a long way from here, lived a king who had three sons," that story will be telling us that things change; that events have consequences; that choices are to be made; that the king does not live forever.
—Ursula Le Guin, "Some Thoughts on Narrative," in Dancing On the Edge of the World, 1989

Is this a formula? Surely! But it is also very satisfying. We enjoy following Jill and Eustace on their quest. It is more pleasurable because it has been so clearly defined. The formulaic plot is refreshed by the endearing characters of the two children and the companion who joins them: Puddleglum, the pessimistic "marsh-wiggle."

As the story progress, Lewis plays with our expectations. Things are not always what they seem. Like many heroes, the children are not perfect; they make mistakes. Yet they succeed in their task—and return home to see the school bullies banished.

BEGINNINGS

Stories that get published have a strong plot, usually one that moves out quickly from the start. When in doubt, start with action. Start in the middle of a scene. Let the story move quickly. Draw readers in immediately. Later, you can fill in background details and broaden the scope of the story.

Not all stories start with clever beginnings on the first page. Some start slowly; as the curtain rises, all appears at peace. Yet even on those first pages, we sense that something is imminent. By the end of the first chapter, the plot usually needs to be afoot.

In John Steinbeck's Arthurian saga, *The Acts of King Arthur and His Noble Knights*, the story takes off like a knight in a jousting tournament. Within the first three pages, King Uther has met the wife of the Duke of Cornwall and has fallen madly in love with her. The Duke and his wife have fled to Tintagel, their castle. Love-lorn, Uther declares war, lays siege, and failing to take the castle, calls Merlin to his chambers.

Merlin knows what the king desires, and the magician wants something in return:

> "Sir, I know every corner of your heart and mind. And if you will swear by your anointed kingship to grant me my wish, you shall have what I know your heart desires."
>
> And so great was Uther's eagerness that he swore by the four Evangelists to keep his promise.
>
> Then Merlin said, "This is my desire. The first time you make love to Igraine she will conceive a child by you. When that child is born it must be given to me to do with as I wish. But I promise that this will be to your honor and to the child's advantage. Do you agree?"
>
> "It shall be as you wish," said the king.
>
> "Then rise and make yourself ready," Merlin said. "This very night you will lie with Igraine in the castle of Tintagel by the sea."

> —*The Acts of King Arthur and His Noble Knights*, John Steinbeck

No delays there. Thus is launched one of the greatest sagas in the Western canon, the story of Merlin, Uther's son Arthur (born of that magical deception), and Camelot—a story that ends in tragedy when Arthur is betrayed by his beautiful wife Guinevere and trusted friend, Lancelot.

Likewise in Stephen King's book, *The Eyes of the Dragon*, the author wastes no time filling the sails with a strong wind. By the end of page one, we know that the old king of Delain, Roland the Good, is sickly and will die soon. Everyone assumes the heir will be his eldest son, Peter. But we also learn at the bottom of the first page:

This is the tale of the wonders that befell on the evening of the eleventh of December, when they did what they were told not to do.
—"The Ice Dragon, or Do as You Are Told," by E. Nesbit, in The Book of Dragons, 1900

And one man thought and planned and brooded on something else: how to make sure that Roland's younger son, Thomas, should be crowned King instead. This man was Flagg, the King's magician.

—*The Eyes of the Dragon*, Stephen King

In the first two pages of *The Wizard of Oz*, we meet Dorothy and her stepparents, Aunt Em and Uncle Henry. By page three, a cyclone is spotted. By page four, the house with Dorothy and Toto in it is aloft.

A basic rule of thumb: even for stories that do not swirl with such gale-force power, in the first scene we should meet the main character. We should sense soon that this character has some desire, urge, or drive. And we should get at least a whiff of an impending action, problem, or event.

CROSSING THE THRESHOLD

Here is an excerpt from the front-flap of Andre Norton's book, *Scent of Magic* (1998):

> Norton's latest creation is a faraway dukedom rich in intoxicating aromas: powerful fragrances carried on gentle breezes, some with the capacity to enchant and befuddle, some capable even of toppling great leaders from their thrones. A scullery maid—an orphaned child—possesses an uncanny ability to sense and understand the magical odors that pervade her world. . . .
>
> But there is a malevolence lurking within the castle's walls, inspiring brazen treacheries and usurpations, and a foul abduction as unthinkable as it is unexpected. . . . And a young girl finds the heightened sense that has been her fortune now drawing her down into a maelstrom of evil. Now a great quest is in Willadene's future: a journey to a place of darkness. . . . For the extraordinary power that has molded her destiny is propelling her toward shocking self-knowledge and an impossible rescue in a realm of shadows. . . .

Andre Norton has built her award-winning career spanning more than 50 years on stories with strong plots and likable characters. The plot of *Scent of Magic* covers the bases. Norton has devised a unique version of magic based on scents. On the opening pages, she introduces a young orphan with remarkable powers, though not yet

The ideal opening, then, will instantly beguile and interest; it will be direct and concise; it will make promises which later are made good; it will plummet you into the story in the author's wake.
—Eva Ibbotson, in The Writer, "In the Beginning . . ." August 1971

fully recognized. Around her swirls a struggle for power. A precipitating event occurs—a kidnapping—and the Hero's Journey begins. The young scullery-maid, Willadene, leaves the castle on a rescue quest leading into a dark realm.

Crossing a threshold, characters commit themselves to a new world, a place very different from the one they know best. As writer Jane Yolen recalled a passage in one of her favorite works by George MacDonald, *The Golden Key*:

> The Old Man of the Earth stooped over the floor of the cave, raised a huge stone from it, and left it leaning. It disclosed a great hole that went plumb-down.
> "That is the way," he said.
> "But there are no stairs."
> "You must throw yourself in. There is no other way."

There is a kind of net that is as old as Methuselah, as soft as a cobweb and as full of holes, yet it had retained its strength to this day. When a demon wearies of chasing after yesterdays or of going round in circle on a windmill, he can install himself inside a mirror. There he waits like a spider in its web, and the fly is certain to be caught.
—Opening of "The Mirror," by Isaac Bashevis Singer, in Gimpel the Fool, 1953

Often this occurs right at the beginning of a story. The characters pass from the ordinary world into a fantasy realm, as when four children realize that the back of the wardrobe is open and they step through into Narnia. Alice plunges down the rabbit hole or passes through the looking glass.

At the beginning of each Harry Potter book, the boy goes to the train station to step through an invisible portal which puts him on the magical Platform 9¾, where he can catch the express that will take him to Hogwarts to begin the new school year.

In the first *Earthsea* book, young Ged comes to the isle of Roke to attend wizard school. He is not sure where it is, but wandering the streets, soon spies a "mean little door," with an old man as doorkeeper. He invites Ged to enter, but the boy cannot. Each time he steps through it, he finds himself back outside on the street. Only when Ged speaks his own name out loud (a risky affair in Earthsea) can he come inside. As he looks back, he sees that the doorway:

> . . . was not plain wood as he had thought, but ivory without joint or seam; it was cut, as he knew later, from a tooth of the Great Dragon. The door that the old man closed behind him was of polished horn, through which the daylight shone dimly, and on its inner face was carved the Thousand-Leaved Tree.

> —*A Wizard of Earthsea* (1968), by Ursula Le Guin

A threshold has been crossed; a magical journey is underway.

MAGICAL JOURNEYS

Used by storytellers from Homer to today's fantasists, a journey is both a metaphor and a practical device. Journeys suggest discovery; they deliver a ready-made sense of motion and destination.

> "And how shall we start?" said Scrubb.
>
> "Well," said the Marsh-wiggle very slowly, "all the others who ever went to look for Prince Rilian started from the same fountain. . . . And as none of them ever came back, we can't exactly say how they got on."
>
> "We've got to start by finding a ruined city or giants," said Jill. "Aslan said so."
>
> "Got to start by finding it, have we?" answered Puddleglum. "Not allowed start by looking for it, I suppose?"

—*The Silver Chair*, by C.S. Lewis

In many stories, the author creates multiple storylines and then interweaves them. In *The Lord of the Rings*, Tolkien manages to orchestrate the progress of multiple groups traveling across Middle-earth, each with its own limited view of what is happening. In his insightful book on Tolkien's work, *J.R.R. Tolkien: Author of the Century* (2001), Tom Shippey calls this technique "interlacing"; he notes that the main effect is not only surprise and suspense, but that it helps "to create a profound sense of reality, of that being *the way things are*. There is a pattern in Tolkien's story, but his characters can never see it (naturally, because they are in it)." This leads to puzzlement, supposition, curiosity on the part of the characters—and interest for the reader trying to piece together key observances.

Other stories, like *The Odyssey*, take a main character and follow him or her from beginning to end. We get on the ship with Ulysses and his crew and stick with them through a series of fabulous adventures as they wend their way home. In Neil Gaiman's story of London's underground, *Neverwhere*, we follow Richard through the labyrinth as he meets a cast of odd and dangerous denizens of the subterranean world. In such stories, the journey *is* the plot.

Often, the physical journey parallels another: the inner journey of maturation. Fantasy has special things to say about growing up.

To a story-teller a journey is a marvelous device. It provides a strong thread on which a multitude of things that he has in mind may be strung....
—J.R.R. Tolkien, in The Letters of J.R.R. Tolkien, ed. by Humphrey Carpenter, 1981

This is why it is so popular with small children as fairy tales with mock-adult dilemmas, with young adults as coming-of-age stories, and with adults as stories recalling their own crossing of that threshold—from innocence to awareness.

> Then something began to hurt Mowgli inside him, as he had never been hurt in his life before, and he caught his breath and sobbed, and the tears ran down his face.
> "What is it? What is it?" he said. "I do not wish to leave the Jungle, and I do now know what this is. Am I dying, Bagheera?"
> "No, Little Brother. Those are only tears such as men use," said Bagheera. "Now I know that thou art a man, and a man's cub no longer."

> —"Mowgli's Brothers," by Rudyard Kipling

To go on fantasy's journey is to be changed. In *The Hobbit*, Bilbo arrives at the mountain and finds himself creeping down a long tunnel toward the snoozing dragon Smaug. Midway, he realizes he is not the same comfy-armchair hobbit who left home many adventures ago. He pauses to reflect that he hasn't had a white handkerchief for a long time, then pulls out his knife from its sheath and continues his stealthy creep. He has changed.

Fairy-tale transformation is growth's journey, only on a magical scale. In Hans Christian Andersen's bittersweet tale "The Little Mermaid," a young mermaid saves the life of a teenaged prince. She falls in love with him—and with the promise that getting a mortal to fall in love with her will give her an immortal soul. So the young mermaid lets a vicious sea-witch cut apart her tail, turning it into two legs. The price she must pay, however, is that every step she takes feels like treading on "pointed tools"; her feet bleed incessantly. And she has to give her lovely voice to the witch, leaving her mute.

The young mermaid abandons her sisters to become a graceful companion to the prince. She sleeps outside his door on a velvet cushion, and dances gracefully for him, although her feet pain her terribly. She dresses like a man to go riding with him through the "scented forest" and climbs mountains with him. But he does not respond to her love; he forsakes her to marry another.

On the wedding night, the nuptial party goes out to spend the night upon a ship in the harbor, accompanied by the mermaid in her human form.

The little mermaid could not help thinking of the first time she had dived up to the surface of the sea and had seen the same splendour and rejoicing, and she whirled in the dance with the rest, swerving as a swallow swerves when it is pursued, and they all applauded her in admiration . . . . Sharp knives seemed to cut into her delicate feet, but she did not feel it, for the pain in her heart cut yet more sharply.

The ship grew still and quiet; only the helmsman stood by the wheel. The little mermaid laid her white arms upon the rail and looked towards the east for the first red of morning—the first ray of the sun, she knew, would kill her.

—"The Little Mermaid," by Hans Christian Andersen, 1836, transl. by L.W. Kingsland, in *Hans Andersen's Fairy Tales: A Selection* (Univ. of Washington Press, 1959)

In Philip Pullman's trilogy, *His Dark Materials*, transformation is the coin of the realm. All is in flux for children, adults, angels, witches, armored bears. Holes are being opened between parallel realms. The stuff of life, Dust, is changing its patterns, being sucked away into a mysterious void. In the midst of this turmoil, Pullman draws three intersecting plot lines: the story of Lyra, a fierce, self-protective girl; Will, a more cautious, worrisome boy; and Mary, a scientist studying the odd behavior of quantum particles. As Will and Lyra mature into adulthood, the universe is unraveling. Vast forces meet head-on in this brilliant tale of invisible forces made visible through fantasy's unique spyglass.

Whether the author employs the general "rising action" plot or the more structured Hero's Journey, the plot must come to a climax. The journey, growth, transformation, or conflict must culminate in a resolution. Whether the story ends happily or in sorrow, the story's destination must be reached. What happened?

He tightened his grip on his sword, peered into the mists ahead. He charged alone through the fog, and somehow he knew that was how it was meant to be.

Suddenly, Ba'alzamon was before him in the mists, throwing his arms wide.

Red reared wildly, hurling Rand from his saddle. . . . When he climbed to his feet, his horse was gone, but Ba'alzamon was still there, striding toward him with a long, black-charred staff in his hands. They were alone . . .

—*The Great Hunt*, by Robert Jordan, 1990

The two white horses snorted snowy mist in the cool green glade that led down to the harbor. A fair wind stood for Yarrow and, looking far to sea, the Princess Saralinda thought she saw, as people often think they see, on clear and windless days, the distant shining shores of Ever After. Your guess is quite as good as mine (there are a lot of things that shine) but I have always thought that she did, and I will always think so.

—The Thirteen Clocks, by James Thurber

In the end, kingdoms are won or lost, evil threats averted, damsels rescued. Characters have grown, lessons have been learned, values reaffirmed. Whether the canvas is immense, as in thick 700-page books by Robert Jordan or George R.R. Martin, or small like the slimmest storybook for young readers, fantasy tales need to arrive at an ending that fulfills the plot's promise.

THREE QUESTIONS

When you can answer these three questions, you have a story with a good, solid plot.

1. What happens? What devices will keep your story moving ahead briskly? The promise of plot is that *something* will happen; the wind of plot must create forward motion. The author must keep the reader turning pages, employing all manner of twists, conflicts, discoveries, encounters, impediments, suspense, and surprises.

2. Where does it go? Plot also promises that this motion (and commotion) will lead *somewhere*; a destination will be reached. From the beginning when characters are introduced, to the end when desires and destinies are fulfilled, plot moves a story to that finish. A storyline is not straight, but it is connected and intentional.

3. Why do we care? Plot's ultimate promise is that the journey has a purpose that *satisfies*; we care how the story ends. This does not always mean a happy ending or one that makes us feel comfortable. As Ursula Le Guin has says, a story need not answer every question a reader may have. But it should not sidestep central issues it has raised. There is nothing more disappointing than a wonderfully written book that dodges or dies at the end.

ABOUT THEME

C.S. Lewis described plot using a different metaphor than a wind filling a sail. Plot, Lewis said in his essay "On Stories" (in *Essays Presented to Charles Williams*, 1947), is a net. A story is "a series of events: but it must be understood that this series—the plot, as we call it—is only really a net whereby to catch something else." Lewis's image suggests as well the act of letting some small things escape, while seeking to catch something bigger.

That "something else," said Lewis, is the "real theme." Plot's purpose, he suggested, is to catch the theme—like a bird in the net—if only for a few moments in the story. "The bird has escaped us. But at least it was entangled in the net. We saw it close and enjoyed the plumage." A poor story is one that catches nothing, or worse, catches too much.

John Steinbeck, as he was doing research in England on his Arthurian story, commented on the work involved in erecting great stone circles. "I am surrounded by the works of heroes right back to man's first entrance. I don't know how the monoliths were set up in the circles without tools but there was something more involved than petty thievery and schoolboy laziness and the anguish of overfed ladies on the psycho couch. Someone moved a whole lot of earth around for something beyond 'making a buck.'"

This same thing could be said for fantasy itself. Why did an author bother to "move a whole lot of dirt around"? Not just to make a buck, although professional writers pride themselves on that as well. But there are easier ways to make a living. Writers, for the most part, write because they care about something. Their job is to make sure the reader cares, too.

Speculative-fiction author and teacher James Gunn has said that the job of the author is "the management of the reader's enjoyment." He uses the word enjoyment; people read voluntarily and a story needs to entice them to do this. They also read to experience more than they could on their own.

They reach the end of a book with visions of things never before imagined; yet they have also seen a mirror of themselves. They have seen their own values challenged or embraced, parodied or venerated. They have met new characters about whom they care deeply, like friends, be they furry-toed hobbits or suave vampires or honey-seeking bears.

There is no other way, agrees Jane Yolen. She remembered her own experience as a child:

> If you call forth the reaction to your work that E.B. White once did from me, you will have succeeded. My father came home one day from work to find my mother and me dissolved in tears. "My God," he shouted, fearing the worst had happened to my baby brother. "What is it, what has happened?" "Oh, Daddy," I cried,

In modern mainstream fiction, if you discuss good and evil, you're castigated for being judgmental or old-fashioned.... That has been transmogrified into a belief that anything goes ... there is no real morality, no right, no wrong—it's simply what produces the Platonic definition of evil: "a temporary disadvantage for the one perceiving evil."
In fantasy [however], we can talk about right and wrong, and good and evil, and do it with a straight face.
—Robert Jordan, in interview in Locus Magazine, 2000

"Charlotte is dead." "Charlotte? Charlotte? I don't know any Charlotte," he said, puzzled. It took several minutes of misunderstanding before we could make it snufflingly clear that a spider in a book called *Charlotte's Web* had died. We had been reading it together. My father, though, was quite right. He did not know any Charlotte. But my mother and I knew Charlotte. We both knew her well. And we had been with her when she died.

—Jane Yolen, in *Writing Books for Children*

THE INVISIBLE THREAD

When you choose one way out of many, all the ways you don't take are snuffed out like candles, as if they'd never existed. At the moment all Will's choices existed at once. But to keep them all in existence meant doing nothing. He had to choose, after all.
—From The Amber Spyglass, 2000, by Philip Pullman

In George MacDonald's novel *The Princess and the Goblin*, the princess meets an old woman spinning thread in a tower in a castle. The woman is the girl's great-grandmother. She gives the princess a ring. To it, the old woman attaches an invisible thread.

The wise old woman explains that wherever the princess goes, the thread will be there to guide the girl back to that room in times of need. The child is perplexed; she cannot see the thread, nor the ball to which it is attached. But the thread is there.

In the same way, the thread of your narrative needs to be there, whether or not your reader can see or touch it. Everything from the beginning of your story to the end is tied together. Writing stories is believing in that invisible thread, understanding how readers will follow that same thread to guide them through your story.

A thread. A net. A wind in a sail. Take your pick. The point is that plot is important. An author needs to discover what Ursula Le Guin said was a story: choices, consequences, changes. In her essay, "Some Thoughts on Narrative," in *Dancing at the Edge of the World* (1989), Le Guin said that narrative ultimately is "a survival skill."

> Only imagination can get us out of the bind of the eternal present, inventing or hypothesizing or pretending or discovering a way that reason can then follow into the infinity of options, a clue through the labyrinths of choice, a golden string. . . .

She is talking about the fantastic adventure we call story.

ON PLOT & PURPOSE

SEEKING THE HEART OF THE FANTASTIC

Interview with Midori Snyder
by Philip Martin

Midori Snyder has published numerous fantasy novels for adults and for young adult readers, including the Oran Trilogy (New Moon, Sadar's Keep, and Beldan's Fire) and a fantasy set in the 19th-century American West, The Flight of Michael McBride. A recent project took her to Italy to research and write her award-winning novel, The Innamorati, praised as a complex and sensual tale, based on Roman mythology and the theater of the Commedia dell'Arte.

Too many people in the genre, I think, just use the fantastic as a vehicle—sort of deus ex machina. The hero can't be a hero without the magic sword. Or the hero is in a locked room, and needs matches, and they appear magically. They use magic as transportation or as fantastic articles that we strap on to our human form.

But I'm not interested in that. I'm interested in stories where human beings have to confront the fantastic. It's tense, it's disagreeable. And it forces change. I think that's when fantasy is important: when the fantastic is a concrete image, but represents some abstract struggle that the hero or the heroine character is going through.

So at least the way I use it, it's like the traditional fairy tale. We start with this human world that we're familiar with, but conflicts occur that drive us away. And "out there," in that fantastic place, whether the forest or the maze, we confront the fantastic. And we then have a parallel and metaphorical confrontation of the same struggles that before were "here"—but now they're "there."

And in that new, fantastic place, it becomes possible for the protagonist to wrestle from the fantastic what they need in order to change fully.

That's when the fantastic is interesting. That's when it's really vital in a story.

And it's also a lot more fun to write as a writer. It's more powerful than just coming up with magic swords, and horses with eight legs to move heroes along.

My theme as a workshop leader at Wiscon [a speculative-fiction conference for writers held annually in Madison, Wisconsin] a few years ago was balance; learning how to balance the fantastic with the realistic elements.

One story I read had a real problem with that. The fantastic was too large. And the real issue, a father/daughter issue, was too small. But that was the real issue the author wanted to write about. In the workshop discussion, we helped him see that. And the moment he heard it, he knew what to do. And the revised story is getting published.

One woman was locked into writing clever ideas, clever concepts, but not knowing then how to use them in a story. She rewrote the same story four or five times. Each time she brought it to me, and I'd say, well, what does it mean here when your character does this? Can you answer that?

She kept going back and revising. Finally she came and said, "Okay—the story has only one idea. I'm afraid it's too simple."

"Oh," I said, "those are the *best!*" Those are the best stories, if you know what it's about and it touches you emotionally. And the story was gorgeous.

After all, love is "only" one idea. But it's a good idea.

In fantasy, if the emotional content is there, readers will fill in with their own experience. If it's "true"—if it's a human condition, if it's a recognizable emotion—people automatically put in their own history, their memory of those moments in their own lives.

Skellig, by David Almond, is that kind of novel. There's never any explanation of what that strange creature in the garage really is. It really is an image—a very evocative, powerful image—of pure mystery.

It's them. It's not them. It's extraordinary; it's banal.

It eats Chinese take-out. It's wonderful.

It's linked to Blake's poetry.

And there's never any explanation of what it is.

It's elusive.

It's brilliant.

One theme that has interested me especially in young-adult literature is that children assume they know the story of their family. They firmly believe they know who their parents are, and they believe they know who they themselves are. And parents assume the same about their children.

What's fascinating to me that neither of those groups really knows as much as they think they do. Lots of stories for young adults deal with encountering that moment of their own change—when they realize that nothing is secure. And yet there often is a family history and lineage, in part unknown to them. Sometimes a discovery there can help them go forward.

In a novel of mine, *Hannah's Garden* (2001), I wanted to write about a girl who discovers something about herself, about her mother, and about her family. Something she already knew in the bone, but didn't yet know consciously.

So I constructed a story, set in Wisconsin, about a girl who lives with her mother. They have a grandfather who lives up north who is a mad painter. He's eccentric and really quite mad.

The young girl is a very fine violinist. And a series of events occurs: she meets a fiddler at a music session in Milwaukee who has a fiddle with the head of a woman. And she meets a guy on a motorcycle who's very frightening and yet is very attractive.

And at the same time they get a phone call that the grandfather's in the hospital. They have to go north, into the world of her grandfather, which is falling apart. The girl has to confront things she doesn't understand—about her family, about the land and the house. And this fiddler she met keeps showing up.

Then she finds the journal of her great-grandmother. There are images of wild hares everywhere, and she sees the young fiddler in a collection of old photographs. How can that be? He would have to be over a hundred years old.

Slowly, as the story unwinds, it turns out that her lineage is connected to forest tricksters, changelings, shape-shifters. She gradually realizes these things about herself and about her mother, who didn't want to stay on the farm because to commit to the fantastic is to go mad. And the girl has to deal with the approaching death of her grandfather.

While I was planning this story, my own father became very sick. I wrote the first chapter. And then I went and sat with him for a week, and then he died in the hospital. It was terrible; I was in Columbus, Ohio, and in the midst of this shattering grief.

But as I left the hospital and went back to our horrible motel room, in a state of shock, somehow, in the back of my head, I wrote the ending of *Hannah's Garden*. I reconfigured my father's death into the last scene, which is a transformation of the old man into the fantastic forest.

It's emotionally difficult, but if you begin with those most intense moments in fantasy, and let them become metaphorical and fantastic, then the writing opens up. You reveal the heart of the story. For others—and for yourself.

When you do that, the reader out there doesn't need to know every detail about my personal family history, or my father's death. They only have to know emotionally, through the tale that I construct, that same moment of recognition and surprise—when death is transformed into something else.

There's that moment of, "Oh, my god, now I understand something better." But it's never been realized until that fantastic image pulls something into focus. Although I'm often surprised at the way in which people respond to my writing. Sometimes people's interpretations are astonishing.

It means you reached them on some level.

That's what I often tell my writing students: You've got the beginning of a story. You've got a very competent narrative. Now, go back and crack it open.

You've got the skeleton. Now, add the flesh. Add the heart.

❊

She grabbed him by the bosom of his shirt, her eyes boring into the shallow well of his breast. Now I will sing for you! she thought angrily, drunk with the dust of the masks' magic.

Sound boiled in her throat, filled the cavern of her mouth, pressed against her teeth. She tilted back her head and released one long note in a thin stream of blue light. . . . the flowing sound scraped the hard crust of loneliness from her skin like the sea tearing the mussels from the rocks. . . . Her song coiled in the ears, blinded the eyes, filled the nostrils. It crashed over mortals like sea spray, drowning them in their own tears.

❊

—From Midori Snyder's novel, The Innamorati, published by Tor Books. Copyright © 1998 by Midori Snyder.

CONSIDERING WICKED

by Gregory Maguire

Gregory Maguire's novel, Wicked: The Life and Times of the Wicked Witch of the West, takes a fresh look at a central theme of fantasy: the matter of evil. With references to the 1939 film and original 1900 novel, The Wizard of Oz, Maguire weaves a fascinating tale of a young girl, green in skin color, growing up in a land dominated by a tyrant. At the core of his novel is the question: what happens when there are differing ideas on truth? Do those who disagree automatically become evil?

This is an important issue for authors of fantasy fiction. The thoughtful work of Philip Pullman comes to mind; his brilliant trilogy, His Dark Materials, offers a complex reinterpretation of themes of good and evil. Other fantasy writers have challenged icons, as in Marion Zimmer Bradley's feminist novel, The Mists of Avalon, which reconsiders the implicit goodness in Arthur's conquest of pagan Britain.

While the classic goodness of authors like J.R.R. Tolkien and J.K. Rowling is part of their appeal, fantasy also allows authors to explore the world from the viewpoint of the "Other": those who fall outside of social norms or who have decided to question authority.

I was born in the 1950s, a decade that was for most Americans genuinely more benign than those it followed and preceded. So when did I, as a child, learn the idea that there is a shapeless thing that sometimes molds itself into an avatar of malice? The first television screening of *The Wizard of Oz* on November 3, 1956.

Thirteen million people watched it. In December 1959 the MGM film was rebroadcast at an earlier hour, and the number of viewers jumped by the millions. Thereafter the film was shown annually from 1960 to 1980; in 1980 it made the leap to videocassette.

Let's face it. For those of us from a rather strict upbringing, the annual TV broadcasts of *The Wizard of Oz* marked our national celebration of terror. I daresay for a certain segment of the population, one of the most horrific of psychic metamorphoses takes place in the Witch's crystal ball, when Auntie Em, crying out for Dorothy, transmogrifies into the leering, mocking face of the Wicked Witch of the West. Let us avoid other traumatic memories such as the flying monkeys, or there'll be puddles on the floor.

Of course kids today are more jaded. One of my godchildren, aged 7, watched the film without obvious terror, and merely remarked at the end, "Somebody oughta get that dog a leash."

In the book by L. Frank Baum called *The Wonderful Wizard of Oz* (1900), the Wicked Witch of the West has a relatively small part. The old hag does not show up in Munchkinland immediately following Dorothy's unfortunate crash landing on top of her sister. She is referred to only occasionally. Though Dorothy and friends do pass through a field of poppies and fall into a state of altered consciousness, it is not the Witch's doing. She does not skywrite "Surrender Dorothy" with her jet-propelled magic broom. No, the early references to the Witch are all by Glinda and by the Wizard. And Dorothy trusts implicitly what they say.

If we look at the two pages in the book in which the assignment to kill the Wicked Witch is handed out by the Wizard, we see the incitement to murder is unmistakable. Hollywood softened this up by having the Wizard say, "Bring me the broom of the Witch—" but in the original the direction is much more clear and cold-blooded.

"You have no right to expect me to send you back to Kansas unless you do something for me in return. In this country everyone must pay for everything he gets. If you wish me to use my magic power to send you home again you must do something for me first. Help me and I will help you."

"What must I do?" asked the girl.

"Kill the wicked Witch of the West," answered Oz.

. . . The little girl began to weep. . . . "I never killed anything, willingly," she sobbed, "and even if I wanted to, how could I kill the Wicked Witch? If you, who are Great and Terrible, cannot kill her yourself, how do you expect me to do it?"

"I do not know," said the Head, "but that is my answer, and until the Wicked Witch dies you will not see your Uncle and Aunt again. Remember that the Witch is Wicked—tremendously Wicked—and ought to be killed. Now go, and do not ask to see me again until you have done your task."

Though Dorothy initially says, "There is no hope for me . . . for Oz will not send me home until I have killed the Wicked Witch of the West; and that I can never do," a few pages later she dries her eyes and says, "I suppose we must try it. . ." She is buying into the argument that the ends justify the means, though she has no personal experience of the Witch's evil.

In the book, the Wicked Witch of the West doesn't make an appearance until page 140—only 15 pages before she makes her splashy exit. She is described as such:

> "Now the Wicked Witch of the West had but one eye, yet that was
> as powerful as a telescope, and could see everywhere. So, as she sat
> in the door of her castle, she happened to look around and saw
> Dorothy lying asleep, with her friends all about her. They were a
> long distance off, but the Wicked Witch was angry to find them
> in her country, so she blew upon a silver whistle that hung around
> her neck."

The end in the book is scripted differently as well—and much more clumsily—than the movie revision of it.

> Now the Wicked Witch had a great longing to have for her own
> the Silver Shoes which the girl always wore. . . The wicked creature
> was very cunning, and she finally thought of a trick that would give
> her what she wanted. She placed a bar of iron in the middle of the
> kitchen floor, and then by her magic arts made the iron invisible to
> human eyes. So that when Dorothy walked across the floor she
> stumbled over the bar, not being able to see it, and fell at full
> length. She was not much hurt, but in her fall one of the Silver
> Shoes came off, and before she could reach it the Witch had
> snatched it away and put in on her own skinny foot.
> . . . The little girl, seeing she had lost one of her pretty shoes,
> grew angry, and said to the Witch, "Give me back my shoe! . . . You
> have no right to take my shoe from me."
> "I shall keep it, just the same," said the Witch, laughing at her,
> "and some day I shall get the other one from you, too."

This made Dorothy so very angry that she picked up the bucket of water that stood near and dashed it over the Witch, wetting her from head to foot.

Instantly the wicked woman gave a loud cry of fear; and then, as Dorothy looked at her in wonder, the Witch began to shrink and fall away. "See what you have done!" she screamed. "In a minute I shall melt away."

"I'm very sorry, indeed," said Dorothy, who was truly frightened to see the Witch actually melting away like brown sugar before her very eyes.

"Didn't you know water would be the end of me?" asked the Witch, in a wailing, despairing voice.

"Of course not," answered Dorothy; "how should I?"

"Well, in a few minutes I shall be all melted, and you will have the castle to yourself. I have been wicked in my day, but I never thought a little girl like you would ever be able to melt me and end my wicked deeds. Look out—here I go!"

With these words the Witch fell down in a brown, melted, shapeless mass and began to spread over the clean boards of the kitchen floor. Seeing that she had really melted away to nothing, Dorothy drew another bucket of water and threw it over the mess. She then swept it all out the door."

Let us think for a minute what L. Frank Baum has done with this character.

In the introduction of his book, he wrote—in April of 1900—"The time has come for a series of newer 'wonder tales' in which the stereotyped genie, dwarf and fairy are eliminated, together with all the horrible and blood-curdling incident devised by their authors to point a fearsome moral to each tale. . . . Having this thought in mind, the story of 'The Wonderful Wizard of Oz' was written solely to pleasure children of today. It aspires to be a modern fairy tale, in which the wonderment and joy are retained and the heart-aches and nightmares are left out."

It is true that the Cowardly Lion, the Scarecrow, and the Tin Woodman have served an American appetite for fantastic characters far more vigorously than Puck or Titania or Rumpelstiltskin could any longer do.

But his inventiveness seized up when it came to writing about evil. The Wicked Witch of the West, with her single eye and her winged monkeys, lives in a castle and treats Dorothy with the cruelty and abandon of the best of her Northern European forebears. The witch in Hansel and Gretel is perhaps the cousin she most closely resembles.

L. Frank Baum could invent new ways of being good, and interesting. But the chiefest way of being bad he had to borrow. And for good reason. The Witch had to be a stereotype so that she could be recognized and hated and feared without the time it takes to characterize her and know her. The word "wicked" is her single most significant tag. That is really all we need to know in order to approve of Dorothy's actions. (For Dorothy threw the water at the Witch deliberately. She may not have known the Witch was allergic, but it was still an act of malice and impatience.)

In the MGM film, the Witch—immortalized by Margaret Hamilton—is famously on screen for only 12½ minutes of the film. But what a 12½ minutes it is. Dorothy kills the Witch by an accident, not born of rage but of charity—in trying to save the Scarecrow, she melts the Witch. And the Witch says, "Ohhh! You cursed brat! Look what you've done! I'm melting! Melting! Oh, what a world! What a world! Who would have thought a good little girl like you could destroy my beautiful wickedness? Ohhh! Look out! Look out! I'm going. Ohhh—Ohhhhhhhhh!"

The Witch in the film is significantly different from Baum's creation in other ways. For one thing, technicolor having just been invented, the Witch is green. (Baum never mentions her skin color.) And when else in American culture have we seen color and moral stature equated?—hmmm.

Yet, though she threatens Dorothy and her friends, and does, in the end, set fire to the Scarecrow, she is never guilty of the crime the Wizard commits. She never lies. She is never devious. She is merely threatening—until Dorothy and cohorts approach to steal her broom.

Which brings us to the Wicked Witch of the West in my novel, *Wicked*. She is green. She is born that way, a condition that greatly distresses her parents. The Witch is given a respectable old name—Elphaba—which I created by pronouncing the sounds of the initials of L. Frank Baum—L. F. B.—Elphaba. The name is meant to carry freights of suggested meaning in its wake, with words such as fable, fabulous, alphabet, and elfin.

To explore the roots of "evil" in a character, I tried to tell the story of Elphaba from the very beginning; her childhood, her relationship with her parents and siblings; her college years, in which she roomed with a ditzy socialite named Glinda; her years as a political terrorist, falling in love with a mountain princeling from the West; her eventual search for forgiveness for the death of her lover.

While readers will take away their own impressions, I hope their understanding will include the essential ideas about evil and character that, in the end, I finally did decide to pursue in her character.

One idea is that it is the nature of evil to be secret. If we could know its nature, we would not fear it. Perhaps evil is really best defined as: That whose nature we find it impossible to know. And we are scared of what we do not know. I will add that we are always more able to imagine evil—devils are more popular than saints, and always have been, though angels have been making something of a comeback in recent years. Evil is always more interesting to imagine than good.

The second thought about evil is this. We may have differing opinions about the nature of evil. Perhaps evil is a creation of God designed to help us be worthy of redemption or to prove us unworthy. Perhaps evil is an aberration of the nature of God, in a flawed universe in which God is not as all-powerful as we had once hoped. Perhaps the universe is God-less, and so evil is an attribute of human behavior alone. Perhaps evil is merely a human interpretation of a violence that is a natural part of our biological being.

But I think it is always true, in every instance we can name, that the evil act as perpetrated by a human being is the act of a human being who is filled with self-hatred. Someone said once, "Self-esteem can not be given, it can only be earned." But we can help create the proper growing climate in which one another can earn, and can learn, self-esteem.

As a children's book author I lead creative writing seminars, seeing some ten thousand schoolchildren each spring on an annual teaching tour. Many students prepare stories for me, or hunker down to scribble and worry over something even as I address them. In the 15 years since I started doing this I've noticed a sea change.

The incidence of children writing about violence is on the rise.

Oh, it's always been fashionable, and at all ages. From the writing of kids I've learned all about Freddie Krueger and the Terminator and Cujo and Hannibal the Cannibal. I don't call this cause for alarm, or not usually. Childhood is the period of apprenticeship in which you attempt to master the resources that will overcome the impossible odds. And we all know that in the end children don't succeed—we don't, either. Death comes to all.

But the stories I saw last year are different. The villains are no longer the monsters with clicking razor-blade fingers, or the slime-bag oozing from the deep. The monsters are pictured as ordinary folk. Parents, plumbers, teachers, neighbors, even babysitters. This is scary enough to me—but I could deal with it if the story kept its traditional pattern—where a developed narrative resounds with a purpose, or moral. In the fairy tales, the French ones anyway, a moral was often tacked on in couplets just to be sure the point was clear. In horror stories, when the horror is demonic, the unspoken assumption is that the universe also includes the power of good, the side of the angels.

But the difference today is this: Children write about death—about horrid, grotesque slayings—as if death were an object of art, worthy of being praised for its own value alone. Children isolate death in frozen frame, they begin their fictions where terror begins—the creaking floorboard, the rattling doorknob—and end it when the victim is dead. All these deaths occur in a vacuum.

So I have begun to append a new rule when I go into schools and children are going to write for themselves and for each other and for me. I don't have many rules, but this is becoming a firm one. It's called Honor Your Readers. Even in comedy or horror writing. The equation or syllogism of it says, "If blood, then grief."

I won't forbid children to write about psychotic serial murderers. But the story may not end with the victim gasping his or her last. I require there be at least one paragraph of reaction. I require context. The victim can't be vilely murdered unless the writer is willing to imply the life from which the victim emerged, and to witness the consternation and grief in that circle when the death is recognized and felt.

No more anonymous victims. No more freezing the frame at the juiciest point. If you want me to care that he or she is dead, I tell my students, you must make me care that he or she was alive first. Death is not like a painting of flowers, occurring out of space and time for the sake of its own beauty. Death is inextricably related to life, and doesn't work aesthetically unless the life is evoked too.

In other words, I want the moral of the story. I want my students to accept that there is a moral even if they can't point it out.

I want to wean myself off the habit of gaping at death on the TV news and in the pages of magazines as if it were the spring fashions or celebrity gossip. In their writing—and in my own—I want to resist the glut of visual stimulation about death, isolating it from its natural contexts of life, community, and even hopes of transcendence beyond. I want to help my writing students develop a renewed reverence of the context of death—which, for lack of a better term, we call life.

I chose to write about the Wicked Witch of the West because I wanted to know the context of her death. When she cried, "What a world, what a world," what was she saying? Perhaps it was not all irony, despair, rage. Perhaps she was looking on the face of all that was great and terrible as she died.

At any rate, in my novel, *Wicked*, we learn something about her context, so we may never again merely laugh at her death.

❄

Elphaba stood facing the fire. . . . The Munchkinlander was in her nightgown, a drab sack without benefit of lace edging or piping. The green face above the wheat-gray fabric seemed almost to glow, and the glorious long straight black hair fell right over where breasts should be if she would ever reveal any evidence that she possessed them. Elphaba looked like something more than life but not quite Life. . . . There was an expectancy but no intuition, was that it?—like a child who has never remembered having a dream being told to have sweet dreams.

"Oh, put on the damn hat, really," said Galinda. . . .

. . . "Is there a looking glass?" . . .

"Well then," decided Galinda, "can you find an angle without hiding the firelight, and look at your reflection in the dark window?"

They both gazed at the green and flowery spectre [of the hat] reflected in the watery old glass, surrounded by the blackness, driven through with the wild rain beyond. A maplefruit leaf, shaped like a star with blunted points, or like a heart grown lopsided, suddenly whirled out of the night and plastered itself on the reflection in the glass, gleaming red and reflecting the firelight, just where the heart would be . . . .

❄

—From the novel Wicked: The Life and Times of the Wicked Witch of the West, published by ReganBooks. Copyright © 1995 Gregory Maguire.

PART III

TECHNIQUES
OF WRITING FANTASY

FANTASY WRITERS ON THEIR CRAFT

CHAPTER EIGHT

GENERATING IDEAS

ESTABLISHED WRITERS OF IMAGINATIVE FICTION find the question, "Where do you get your ideas?" annoying, for two reasons. First, it is so commonly asked by audiences of all ages. Second, it is so hard to answer, since it goes right to the heart of their craft.

In *Dancing at the Edge of the World* (1989), a collection of essays on writing, narrative, and culture, Ursula Le Guin gives a no-nonsense warning about the misconceptions that lurk in that seemingly innocent question.

Whenever I talk with an audience after a reading or lecture, somebody asks me, "Where do you get your ideas from?" . . . .

The reason why it is unanswerable is, I think, that it involves at least two false notions, myths, about how fiction is written.

First myth: There is a secret to being a writer. If you can just learn the secret, you will instantly be a writer; and the secret might be where the ides come from.

Second myth: Stories start from ideas; the origin of a story is an idea.

I will dispose of the first myth as quickly as possible. The "secret" is skill. If you haven't learned how to do something, the people who have may seem to be magicians, possessors of mysterious secrets. In a fairly simple art, such as making pie crust, there are certain teachable "secrets" of method that lead almost infallibly to good results; but in any complex art, such as house-keeping, piano-playing, clothes-making, or story-writing, there are so many techniques, skills, choices of method, so many variables, so many "secrets," some teachable and some not, that you can learn them only by methodical, repeated, long-continued practice—in other words, by work.

. . . Some of the secretiveness of many artists about their techniques, recipes, etc., may be taken as a warning to the unskilled: What works for me isn't going to work for you unless you've worked for it.

So much for secrets. How about ideas?

The more I think about the word "idea," the less idea I have what it means. Writers do say things like "That gives me an idea" or "I got the idea for that story when I had food poisoning in a motel in New Jersey." I think this is a kind of shorthand use of "idea" to stand for the complicated, obscure, un-understood process of the conception and formation of what is going to be a story when it gets written down. The process may not involve ideas in the sense of intelligible thoughts; it may well not even involve words. It may be a matter of mood, resonances, mental glimpses, voices, emotions, visions, dreams, anything. It is different in every writer, and in many of us it is different every time.

—From "Where Do You Get Your Ideas From?" (1987)

British fantasist Diana Wynne Jones feels much the same about that pesky question.

My very favourite form of it was asked by a twelve-year-old: *Where do you get your ideas, or do you think of them for yourself?*

Very shrewdly put, because some part of an idea, if it is going to start a book developing, has to relate to something outside me, even if I don't exactly get it from this outside thing. It has to be a creative mix of interior and exterior notions. The best ideas conflate three or more things, rather in the way dreams do, or the minds of very small children.

A very good example is a baroque muddle of my own when, at the age of five, I was evacuated to the Lake District early in World War II. I was told I was there because the Germans were about to invade. Almost in the same breath, I was warned not to drink the water from the washbasin because it came from the lake and was full of typhoid germs. I assumed that *germs* was short for *Germans*. Looking warily at the washbasin, I saw it was considerably labelled *Twyford*, clearly warning people against germ warfare. Night after night, I had a half-waking nightmare in which Germans (who had fair, floating hair and were clad in sort of cheesecloth Anglo-Saxon

I suppose I start out a story even before it actually becomes a story. I try to understand my own feelings and what I want to express about life at the moment; I look to see what emotions are in the back of my mind. . . . If I understand those things, then I start imagining the kind of story that will best express them.
—Lloyd Alexander, in Scholastic, Inc. interview (posted at http://teacher.scholastic.com/authorsandbooks)

tunics) came racing across the surface of the lake to come up through the plughole of this washbasin and give us all Twyford.

This has all the elements of something needed to start a book off, the magical prohibition, the supernatural villains, the beleaguered good people and, for good measure, the quite incommunicable fears children have. I prefer my ideas to have this last element if possible. . . .

—From "The Profession of Science Fiction: Answers to Some Questions," in *Foundation* (Summer 1997)

Robin McKinley, author of the Newbery Award-winning novel, *The Hero and the Crown*, describes her image of running into ideas, almost literally: "My stories happen to me; I bump into them like pieces of furniture; and they are clear and plain to me—like pieces of furniture."

Although every story does not start with an "idea" that's as clear and plain as an armchair, some do. And those ideas, tangible or ghostly, come from somewhere. Author Harlan Ellison claims, tongue in cheek, that all story ideas come from a post-office box in Schenectady, or Poughkeepsie—for a fee.

ON LEAF MOLD AND COMPOST HEAPS

One writes such a story out of the leaf-mould of the mind.

—J.R.R. Tolkien, in *J.R.R. Tolkien: A Biography*, 1977, by Humphrey Carpenter

Poet Gary Snyder called this unconscious source of ideas a compost heap, much the same idea as leaf-mould—perhaps more accurate, as a compost heap is human-made, and should be turned on occasion with a garden fork to help the process along. In either case, the source of ideas is jumbled and of uncertain origins. It is nutrient-rich with the broken-down matter of the past. All previous work and every real-life episode is drawn into the writer's compost heap.

The Hobbit, for instance, according to the astute Carpenter, includes fragments of a youthful Alpine trek in 1911, the goblins of George MacDonald's books, and an episode from Beowulf in which

Wonder is so central to creative behavior that D.H. Lawrence elevated it to the status of a sixth sense.
—Gabriele Rico, in *Writing the Natural Way*, 2000

a cup is stolen from a sleeping barrow-dragon. For the battle scenes, Tolkien must have drawn on memories of his service as a signalman during the First World War, where he saw first-hand the horrors of the trenches. Tolkien also was a lover of nature, especially venerable trees, and would create a whole race of trees, the Ents, and a leader Treebeard—whose booming voice, he admitted, was reminiscent of that of his friend, C.S. Lewis.

From his 1911 Alpine trek, Tolkien brought home a postcard. He saved it, eventually placing it in an envelope that he marked as the origins of Gandalf, the great wizard of Middle-earth. That postcard showed a painting of the spirit of the mountain: an old man with flowing beard, broad-brimmed hat and long cloak, sitting on a rock under a pine.

Every intriguing item or curiosity is a starting point. The writer is always asking not "What does that mean?" but "What *could* it mean?"—if transferred to another context. Like rich compost, the origins of an idea are less important then the nature of the new growth that springs from it in the writer's garden.

From the leaf-mold of the writer's imagination come fantastic ideas—at all hours of the day and night. The clever writer knows to jot them all down as soon as possible. Anne Rice admits that she has risen on occasion late at night to write down a half-dreamed idea on her room's wallpaper, so she could remember it in the morning.

When Tolkien started *The Lord of the Rings*, he did not know where the story would go. He only knew that the magic ring carried over from his prior story, *The Hobbit*, would play a role. So he started by writing the first chapter, a feast. Afterwards, he started a trio of Bilbo's descendants out on a new journey, not really knowing where or why. In the initial draft their names were Bingo, Odo, and Frodo. Only while writing the early scenes did Tolkien conceive in a blaze of inspiration the true power of the ring—that of three magical rings, it was the mightiest, the one that ruled the others. This became the means to bring all the forces of Middle-earth to bear on that journey of Bingo, Odo, and Frodo. Later, the trio became a duo—Frodo, now with his faithful servant, Sam Gamgee.

If Tolkien had not started writing and sent his threesome off on an unexplained journey, *The Lord of the Rings* might not have taken shape. The first idea became the next idea, and so on. The act of writing is its own story generator; a story underway creates its own surprises.

TAPPING THE RIGHT SIDE OF THE BRAIN

Many inventive writers use of a method of writing which taps into the creative right side of the brain—the nonanalytical, instinctive side. This method is described well by Dorothea Brande in her powerful 1934 book on writing, *Becoming a Writer*.

> So if you are to have the full benefit of the richness of the unconscious you must learn to write . . . when the unconscious is in the ascendant.
>
> The best way to do this is to rise half an hour, or a full hour, earlier than you customarily rise. Just as soon as you can—and without talking, without reading the morning's paper, without picking up the book you laid aside the night before—begin to write. Write anything that comes into your head: last night's dream, if you are able to remember it; the activities of the day before; a conversation, real or imaginary; an examination of conscience. Write any sort of early morning reverie, rapidly and uncritically. The excellence or ultimate worth of what you write is of no importance yet. . . .
>
> —*Becoming a Writer*, Dorothea Brande

When I'm really writing, I'm listening. . . . It takes us places we have no idea where we're going. Surprises always follow.
—Madeleine L'Engle, interview with Maria Ruiz Scaperlanda, in St. Anthony Messenger, June 2000

In his book about the writing process, *Zen in the Art of Writing*, Ray Bradbury tells how he used this same process in his early twenties. He found he could get his creative juices flowing by sitting down immediately upon awakening to write down a word or several words. "I would then take arms against the word, or for it," he said, "and bring on an assortment of characters to weigh the word and show me its meaning. . . ." As he wrote his meditations on these words, after a few pages, a crystalizing idea or character would emerge, interesting enough to reshape into a story.

Bradbury recalled that his routine was to write his first draft of a story on Monday morning. Then he would write a successive draft each day of the week, finishing on Saturday, when he immediately put the final (sixth) draft in the mail to a prospective publisher. In this way, he produced a story a week for ten years or more. These short writings established his career and were pulled together into some of his most famous works: *The Martian Chronicles*, *The Illustrated Man*, *Dandelion Wine*, *Something Wicked This Way Comes*, and other collections of his delightfully inventive prose.

In *Writing the Natural Way*, Gabriele Rico presents a related technique called clustering. This technique begins with placing one or more key words in the middle of a blank page. Then, by associating freely with any of those central words, strings of new words are created, each word suggesting the next, radiating outwards in clusters of association. Eventually the page is filled with words, a spider's web of far-flung words, ideas, and tenuous connections.

In a follow-up stage of the exercise, the writer looks back into the web of words. What kind of a story might be drawn from these clusters of words? Are there possible meanings—real or imaginary? Often the key idea will appear off in the margin, in an unexpected cluster of words, as spun strands of associations begin to weave their own images.

While every attempt at this exercise may not create a great story, you will be surprised at how effectively this technique can tap into the powers of imagination that lurk in the nonrational hemisphere of your brain. And it often takes only one brilliant, unexpected association to suggest a great story.

THE WRITER'S NOTEBOOK

A writer needs a place to keep random, unorganized ideas. A notebook is the perfect place.

For fantasy writers, the ideal notebook would be a large volume, big enough to cover a small table, leather-bound with florid golden clasps and hinges and cryptic symbols inscribed on the cover. A slight haze would surround it, perhaps a whiff of unknown spices. When opened, a strange pressed fern-leaf would fall out and transform magically into a wonderfully feathered bird that would fly to a nearby perch and look over the writer's shoulder as he or she peered into the book, taking a long quill in hand. . . .

However, these are hard to find at the office-supply store, so an ordinary loose-leaf or spiral-bound notebook will have to do.

In a 1981 essay on the writing of her fantasy stories, Susan Cooper says:

> A writer's notebooks are perhaps the best illustration (better in some ways than the books themselves) of the way his mind works. Some consist of detailed blueprints for books or plays, set out with mathematical precision; some are filled with discursive examinations of character, building up backgrounds which may never

"Screwball? Why do they call you that?"

"I talk to myself sometimes."

"What kind of things do you say?"

"I think up stories. I invent names and words that don't exist. That kind of thing."

"And you say these things to yourself? Why?"

"Well, nobody else would be interested."

—The Neverending Story, 1979, by Michael Ende (English transl. 1983) appear in the story but which show the writer getting to know the people he has made. My own notes are mostly cryptic and random, full of images, scattered with quotations and ideas which often seem totally irrelevant to the book in hand—though they weren't at the time. Rereading them, I have always again the feel of what it is like to write fantasy. . . .

[some of her selected journal entries follow:]

If you wear agrimony, you may see witches. And if you look into their eyes, you see no reflection of yourself. The scarlet pimpernel is a charm against them.

Names of fields in Hitcham: Great and Lower Cogmarthon; Upper and Lower Brissels; Homer Corner; Hogg Hill.

The sword comes from the drowned land.

The opening of doors. Wakening of things sleeping. Revealing of old things forgotten.

Don't forget: "The mountains are singing, and the Lady comes."

Bird Rock. The birds remember. It is their door.

Sandpipers run, and scoot off into the air, in pairs and little flocks. One leads Will somewhere.

In Welsh, "glas" can mean green as well as blue, silver, greyish-white and slate-colored. The Welsh word for "grass" is "glas-wellt" (lit. green straw).

A sailor tattooed with a star between thumb and forefinger.

When does the Tree grow? Well—now, I suppose. Or outside time.

—From "Escaping into Ourselves," in *Dreams and Wishes: Essays on Writing for Children* (1996), by Susan Cooper

He loved to collect things. When he was young it was birds' eggs and chocolate wrappers. As an adult he collected wine and paintings. However, he also collected ideas. He had a small exercise book in which he wrote down words that he liked the sound of. His mind was twitchy, like his fingers, which were always moving, as though he wished he could wrap them around a pencil and keep writing.
—Ophelia Dahl, about her father, author Roald Dahl (from the website, www.puffin.co.uk/Authors)

Ideas are everywhere. As Joan Aiken described in *The Writer* (May 1968), in an essay titled "Thought on Plots":

> Once you are in the way of noting down ideas for plots, they spring up everywhere: half-seen street signs, overheard remarks, dreams, news items. I used to find the personal ad columns very fertile sources. Sometimes, as an exercise, I set myself the task of combining two or three into a short story. Consider these: "Agile bagpiper with waterproof kilt wanted for party." "Who would invite advertiser to haunted house? (Promise not to interfere with ghost's activities.)" "For sale: circular staircase." "Model rhinoceros wanted." "Would exchange gentleman's library for Jersey herd." These are all genuine items from the *London Times*. . . .

Both Aiken and Ray Bradbury also use another technique: writing down intriguing titles for stories, and then imagining stories to fit. Bradbury is fond, he admits in his book *Zen in the Art of Writing*, of "starter" titles that are provocative nouns: The Lake. The Night. The Crickets. The Ravine. The Attic.

Aiken notes that it takes two ideas, "colliding," to spark a story.

> I shall always remember H.E. Bates, that master of the short story form, saying that besides inspiration and a lot of sheer hard labor, a story requires, for its germination, at least two separate ideas which, fusing together, begin to work and ferment and presently produce a plot. This tallies with my own experience. . . .

—From "Thoughts on Plots," Joan Aiken, in *The Writer*, May 1968

Aiken suggests three things that all writers should do: 1) Keep a small notebook with you at all times. 2) Write something everyday. 3) Keep everything you write.

Your notebooks of ideas will come in handy someday, perhaps in unexpected ways.

CHAPTER NINE

PLANNING & PREPARATION

WHETHER IDEAS ARE WRITTEN DOWN in a notebook or just left to steam in the mental compost pile, most writers should prepare in a more organized fashion before the actual writing begins.

How carefully should a writer organize a story before starting? The bigger the story, the more preparation is needed. For a longer work, John Gardner says in his book, *On Becoming a Novelist* (1983), that it doesn't matter whether you use a bulging notebook or great sheets of paper taped to the walls. He does recommend that a writer, especially a beginner, create a written plan. It helps to ensure that key problems are considered before they are encountered deep into a story—with no easy way out.

Philip Pullman does his writing in a well-equipped shed out in his garden. It has two comfortable chairs, a computer, a guitar, a saxophone, and a six-foot-tall Rat of Sumatra—a stuffed prop that was used in his play, *Sherlock Holmes and the Limehouse Horror*. He likes to plot his novels by using lots of Post-it notes. He writes brief plot points on these and then arranges and rearranges them to his liking on a big piece of paper hung on the wall, with space for 60 or more such notes.

This approach to visual "storyboarding" is a method often used by screenplay writers to work out just the right order for scenes. For many writers, the sheer physical act of moving around tangible pieces of paper is an important part of the creative process. Index cards also work well; they can be shuffled, laid out on a table, or pinned to a corkboard (and offer a little more space than Post-its to make notes about scenes).

Using a storyboard approach, themes can be traced through your story. Colored marks allow you to trace the flow of subplots, or characters, through the course of the story.

FOUR KINDS OF WRITERS

Author Diana Wynne Jones agrees that each writer is different and needs to find what works best for him or her. She sums up four main approaches to planning a story:

1. Those who *do* make a careful plan.

These are the rarest. Even writers who write detective stories often only have jotted notes about what order the clues come out in. You do a careful plan if it makes you feel safe. Otherwise try one of the other ways.

2. Careful realistic writers.

These writers have little cards written out with descriptions and past histories of all the people they might want in the story, and the same for all the places. This is quite a good way to work, because the story often falls into place in your head while you are discovering the things on the cards. But it takes a long time, though it can be fun. You will often find you have far more information on the cards than you will ever get into the story . . . so *don't* try to get it all in. You will drown your story.

3. Back-to-front and inside-out writers.

These writers start by writing Chapter Eleven and then Chapter Twenty. Sometimes they have no idea what the story is and have to put the chapters away until they see what the story is that they fit into. A writer called Joyce Carey had a whole chest of drawers filled with chapters out of books that he never got round to finishing. When he did write a book, it always started this way, with a chapter from the middle. I sometimes work this way, but I warn you, it takes a very clear head to sort it out in the end. It *is* a good way to get started, however.

4. My way.

If you're the kind of person who gets stuck writing a story, try this. When I start writing a book, I know the beginning and what probably happens in the end, plus a tiny but extremely bright picture of something going on in the middle. Often this tiny picture is so different from the beginning that I get really excited trying to think how they got from the start to there. This is the way to get a story moving, because I can't wait to find out. And by not planning it any more than that I leave space for the story to go in unexpected ways.

—From "Hints About Writing a Story," Diana Wynne Jones, from www.dianawynnejones.com

Terry Brooks, author of the bestselling *Shannara* series, is one of those authors who creates a carefully detailed outline. He confesses that he also likes to line up all his pencils in a row; having things in order helps him feel comfortable in his writing space. Each writer need to develop soothing, comfortable routines. There are many distractions to writing; habits help to overcome these.

The more complicated a story is, the more essential an outline becomes. Some authors create a complex array of maps, character dossiers, and plot outlines. For other writers, all they need are brief sentences, with a word or two on characters involved, key actions, and themes being developed.

Garth Nix, author of *Sabriel* (1995) and *Lireal* (2001), popular books for young-adult readers, creates a simple outline. Just a note for each chapter helps him break the work down into manageable chunks, none of which is overwhelming.

> Basic to the way I write is an emotional outline. I script books to emotions that I want to deal with. I think to myself, "This chapter has been really light and carefree, and I'm doing that because I want the next chapter to be very dark."
> —Terry Goodkind, author of the Sword of Truth series, interview with Amazon.com

I'm often asked by would-be writers how I can write a full-length novel which takes a year or more to get done. My stock answer is that I never sit down and think, "I have to write a novel today." I sit down and think, "I have to write a chapter," or "revise a chapter," or "finish the chapter." That way, it's only ever 2,500-5,000 words that are the immediate goal.

As a further motivational gimmick, I always use the word-count utility when I've finished typing a chapter, and write that down, with a running total of words and the date in the front of my first notebook for the current work. . . . I also write down the music I've been listening to as I write and anything else that might be interesting to look back upon. . . .

The word count is a relatively small thing, but it has an amazing psychological effect, particularly as more and more chapters appear and the word total grows. I find it very encouraging, particularly in the first third of the book, which always seems to take me half the time.

Nix says that he writes chapter outlines "so I can have the pleasure of departing from them." An outline is a "discipline for thinking out the story; it also provides a road map or central skeleton you can come back to if lost. I often write the prologue or initial chapter first to get the impetus for the story going and then write the outline."

He offered this comparison of his first chapter outline for *Sabriel* with the second:

Outline 1
Prologue
1. Midwinter at the School. Abhorsen's present.
2. Departure. Oracle.
3. To the Wall.
4. Beyond the Wall.
5. The House of Abhorsen.
6. Flight to the Estuary. Caves/Sinkhole.
7. Ship's Prow. Sea's Son. (Touchstone)
8. The Travellers (salt gathering, frame tents . . .)
9. Among the Dead.
10. Into the Old City.
11. By Reservoir to the Palace.
12. Abhorsen and Kerrigor.
13. Escape.
14. Last Speech with Abhorsen.
15. The Raft People.
16. The House of Abhorsen.
17. Idrach the Necromancer.
18. Safe behind the Wall?
19. Kerrigor.
20. Touchstone's Past.

Below is a revised outline, "written after I'd finished chapter seven, and only looking ahead about seven chapters." You can see the forms starting to solidify, ideas spreading, thoughts growing more complex—like coral building on coral.

Outline 2
1. Wyverley College. Abhorsen's message.
2. To the Wall. Colonel Hongse.
3. Talking with Hongse. Crossing the Wall.

4. Skiing. Dead soldiers.
5. Cloven Crest. Sabriel enters Death.
6. Thralk. Sabriel's Flight. Mordicant.
7. The Cliff Tunnel. Abhorsen's Bridge. Mogget.
8. Abhorsen's House. Discussion with Mogget. The Study.
   Books on Chapter Magic. The Book of the Dead.
   Re-outfitting. Observatory—Mordicants, Lesser Spirits,
   Warped-folk. Men building a pontoon bridge. No way out.
9. Paperwing. Dead crows. Mogget's owl-shape.
   Crash into the estuary salt-flats. The Travellers.
   Underwater river, against the current.
10. The Caves. The Sinkhole. Ships. Touchstone.
    Interrogating Mogget. Belisaere's clue.
11. Journey to Belisaere.
12. Belisaere, the frightened city. Detective work.
13. The Reservoir. Abhorsen's Body. Kerrigor.
    Sabriel's Choice.
14. Flight. The Clayr? Clayr's Roost.

An outline helps with another concern: when to stop working on one scene and move on to the next. An outline can remind you that you've written enough at this point—that there is a later scene with another chance to return to the same setting or theme.

RESEARCH

Research happens at all stages, from initial ideas to final revisions. Early on, serious research often is needed. If the story requires it, you will need to take some time to visit local libraries or Internet websites.

When author Midori Snyder wrote her novel set in Italy, *The Innamorati*, she and her husband spent part of a year there; she writing, he on a teaching assignment. Snyder's plan for her novel was to base it loosely on the Commedia dell'arte street plays—early pantomimes. She would create numerous characters, afflicted by curses and unlucky in love, who enter a magical labyrinth. There, they would interact, meet mythical creatures who lived in the maze, and eventually discover their rightful partners.

From the beginning, Snyder immersed herself in the Italian folkways, learning the patterns of street life, the celebration of food and language, the complexities of gestures. She studied books on the Commedia traditions, on mask-making, on men and women's culture of the period. As she worked, she made color photocopies of pictures from art books—noblemen and women, street people, Commedia characters, gods and mythological creatures—all gathered into a looseleaf notebook.

Eventually, after several months of collecting information and images, Snyder began to write. As she did, she discovered questions that led her back to the library. Her work was much like the meandering, circular walk of the labyrinth itself, following paths that turned back on themselves, places that seemed to be encountered more than once, but always making gradual progress to the center of the story.

As she wrote, Snyder referred often to her photocopied art images. Soon, specific images in her notebook became portraits of characters in her novel. She also referred to tourist guidebooks she had collected. Real-world guidebooks, she discovered, are rich in details that can be adapted to your storytelling needs—from the kind of materials used to construct a building to local history and folk legends connected to a particular site.

Franny Billingsley also set her novel, *The Folk Keeper*, in an exotic place: the Orkney Islands, north of the Scottish mainland. However, Billingsley stayed at home to write—and to research the details needed to create a realistic setting for her magical novel.

> I got guidebooks on the Orkneys and looked at pictures of the gigantic cliffs rising from the sea, so I could describe them for myself. I read about the birds that were there so I could fill my fictional air with their cries. I found out what the weather was like. I discovered there are very few trees there, because the air is so salty and the wind is so strong. It's also a rocky world—just kind of place, I decided, where the "Folk" [her supernatural creatures] would thrive.
>
> I also did a lot of research on the sea. I learned that the tempo of life beneath the sea is slower than on land. I found out how incredibly dense water is, almost as dense as our own body, which is why it holds us up, of course. I learned all about seals: they close their ears when they dive, and they exhale all the air from their lungs when they dive. They use their whiskers to feel currents in the water, to alert them that a fish might be near.
>
> To create the geography of the manor where most of the story takes place, I needed something real to go on. I set the story

roughly 225 years ago, late 18th century, so I got a book on English country houses, to research what they looked like and what was in them. I sketched little diagrams of the house—what the wainscoting would look like, what people would wear.

When I got to writing, I didn't use most of it. But I could just put in little details to evoke the whole feeling of the place.

After many drafts, I added the caverns and the cellar. To get the feeling for a spooky, underground place, I got a book on caves, all about bats and spiders and underground fishes with no melanin—pale and white because there was no sun.

I didn't have a cave I could go into, so I would just go into a basement and ask myself: What does it smell like? What is the smell of wet stone? What do you feel when you put your hand on the wall?

Same thing with describing the sea. I don't live near one, but I live in Chicago near a big lake. You can stand on the edge of it and not see the other side. It has a sense of infinity. And it has a tremendous temper.

And I knew the moonlight shining over Lake Michigan on a calm, summer evening surely would look like the moonlight shining over the sea on a similar evening. So I would take myself to real places and collect data to use to describe the sights and sounds of the sea or the cellar in my book.

—Franny Billingsley, from interview with Philip Martin, 2001

CREATE A MAP

Susan Dexter recommends creating a map to keep you, the author, "from getting lost." Maps can also suggest creative ideas for plotted action, emerging visually in a way different from the ideas that spring from a written outline.

Maps are more than endpaper decorations, and you should start drawing one before you ever start writing your fantasy. Maps can suggest plot solutions. In the real world, things are where they are for good reasons. . . .

As I began to write *The Wind-Witch*, I had established in an earlier book that my Esdragon had a cliffy coast and treacherous seas. Now I needed it to suffer an invasion—by sea. Where could the invaders strike? Well, the Eral are after plunder, so they want towns. And

Esdragon's towns—as in the real-world region of Cornwall, on which I based my fictional duchy—are mostly at the mouths of rivers that drain the upland moors and reach the sea as broad estuaries.

I put rivers on my map, decided which were navigable for any distance—and *presto!* I had many places for my raiders to plunder, distant from one another, spots for Druyan to try to protect from the back of her magic-bred horse.

. . . You can't draw a straight line without a ruler? Relax! There are few straight lines in nature anyway. Now get yourself a real map. Any continent or a bit of one will do. Put tracing paper over your selection. . . .

Change the scale. Use an island to make a continent, or vice versa. Turn your map upside down. When I designed Esdragon and Calandra, I basically used Europe—but I stood it on end, balanced on the tip of Portugal. . . .

Study actual maps. Where do rivers flow? How do they look? Mountain ranges trap rain and alter climate. . . . Your band of unicorn hunters needs to cross the Dragonspike Mountains. Where are the passes? Are they open year-round or only seasonally? The threat of being trapped by an early winter can add drama. A map will remind you of that.

God, as Mies van der Rohe said, is in the details.

—Susan Dexter, in "Tricks of the Wizard's Trade," *The Writer*, November 1997

Whatever method of planning you may use, stay flexible. As you begin to write, you are sure to discover surprises or problems—"creative opportunities"—that will cause you adjust whatever map, outline, storyboard, or other planning aid you are using, to suit the emerging needs of your story.

As avant-garde music composer John Cage said: "Ideas are one thing. What happens is another."

CHAPTER TEN

START WRITING

AT SOME POINT, THE WRITING MUST BEGIN IN EARNEST. As he worked on his great retelling of Mallory's *Morte d'Arthur*, John Steinbeck took a research trip to England to visit sites connected with the legends of Arthur. In the Appendix to his book, *The Acts of King Arthur and His Noble Knights*, he described the moment just before the writing commenced.

> A curious state of suspension has set in, a kind of floaty feeling like the drifting of a canoe on a misty lake while ghosts and winkies, figures of fog, go past—half-recognized, and only partly visible. It would be reasonable to resist this vagueness, but . . . I do not.

He also admitted, "Now that I come to doing the actual writing I must admit to an uneasiness approaching fright."

Terry Pratchett gives some good advice on how to get the writing underway. He calls his first version of a novel: Draft Zero. In an interview with Claire E. White (see p. 219), Pratchett says that he just tries to let it all flow out:

> The thing now is to get as much down as possible. . . . It's all a technique, not to get over writer's block, but to get 15,000 or 20,000 words of text under my belt. When you've got that text down, then you can work on it. Then you start giving yourself ideas.

Pratchett describes this stage much as Steinbeck did. Pratchett's term for that floaty, misty feeling is "The Valley Full of Clouds"—reflecting the writer's need to start a story before everything is clearly seen. The trepidation this causes is common to all writers, but it can be overcome: by starting to write.

SET TANGIBLE GOALS

Most professional writers set goals. Usually, this consists of writing either for a given period of time every day or until a specific goal is met. The most disciplined writers set word goals, to write 1,000 or 2,000 words a day, and not to leave until that is done, whether it is noon or midnight. Ray Bradbury says that he has written a thousand words a day since he was twelve.

This means writing regardless of whether what is written is inspired or insipid. The important thing is to write. Hemingway said that the secret to being a writer was having the ability to apply the seat of the pants to the seat of the chair. In the same vein, Stephen King, in his book *On Writing*, said, "You need the room, you need the door, and you need the determination to shut the door."

Dorothea Brande called this "a debt of honor." If you decide to write every day at a certain hour, you must, she says, even if you what you write is nonsense or petulant complaints about being forced to write. Learn to apply yourself to your writing with consistency. Writing gets better with practice. As you absorb the rituals of sitting down each day to write and become determined to write in measurable quantity, you will also gradually be able to focus more on the quality.

Let's say you set a goal of just 500 words a day. With 250 words to a double-spaced typed manuscript page, this means writing just two pages a day. In a week, you have 2,500 words. It's starting to build up! In just 30 weeks, you will have 75,000 words—the first draft of a novel.

Some novelists got their start writing late at night, after their families had gone to bed. Some write on a daily commuter train, or on their lunch break. Most, though, write by finding a place to write, setting a time in which to do it, setting measurable goals, and respecting that daily "debt of honor."

RITUALS OF WORK

Some writers name their offices. John Steinbeck built a house and called it Joyous Garde, from the Arthurian legends. Wallace Stegner named his typewriter Old Bedlam. Why? Perhaps, as in fantasy itself, to know a name is to call forth its power. Ritual is important. Names solidify the idea of a writer's relationship with a friendly, familiar place to work and favorite tools.

Many writers have favorite implements: pens, pencils, styles of notebooks, the computer, the typewriter. Neil Gaiman said that when he wrote his novel *Stardust*, he chose a fountain pen, because he

I thought, when I was going to be a writer, maybe I'd go live in the south of France and write in the mornings, and then in the afternoon I'd go down and lie on the beach and have a blonde, a brunette, and a redhead in string bikinis come down and slide the scented oil all over me. Now I work 60 or 80 hours a week, and the only time I get near the beach is if my wife pokes me out of my study with a stick!
—Robert Jordan, in Locus magazine interview, 2000

wanted the flavor of that old-fashioned implement to pervade that story.

What motivates you to sit down at that place to start writing each day? For Garth Nix, it was his precious word count, growing slowly but surely. For some, it is taking a nice cup of tea to the computer desk. For some, it is isolation—a quiet place free from interruptions. For others, like J.K. Rowling, writing can be done in a café, the half-heard conversation and background noise providing a peaceful setting for turning inward.

Hemingway was convinced it was best to stop in the middle of a piece of writing; that way, he felt, it was easier to return the next day and resume. This method helps the writer avoid having to stare at a blank page or featureless monitor the next morning.

Stephen King's book *On Writing* contains an outstanding collection of straightforward advice on what it takes to be a successful writer. In his characteristic style, King says:

> There is a muse, but he's not going to come fluttering down into your writing room and scatter fairy-dust all over your typewriter or computer station. He lives in the ground. He's a basement guy. You have to descend to his level, and once you get down there you have to furnish an apartment for him to live in. You have to do all the grunt labor, in other words, while the muse sits and smokes cigars and admires his bowling trophies and pretends to ignore you. . . . He may not be much to look at, that muse-guy, and he may not be much of a conversationalist (what I get out of mine is mostly surly grunts, unless he's on duty), but he's got the inspiration. It's right that you should do all the work and burn all the midnight oil, because the guy with the cigar and the little wings has got a bag of magic.

—*On Writing*, Stephen King, 2000

King states that your job as a writer is to be working at your desk, keeping regular hours. That way, the muse knows where to find you. And he will, King assures us.

OVERCOMING WRITER'S BLOCK

In an interview with Claire E. White, award-winning author Neil Gaiman described his strategies to overcome writer's block. Every

There is almost no wrong way to write fiction; there are only ways that, for a given person, are more efficient or less.... Write in any way that works for you: write in a tuxedo or in the shower with a raincoat or in a cave deep in the woods.
—John Gardner, On Becoming a Novelist, 1983

writer needs a way to keep writing, even on those difficult days when the muse seems uncooperative. As Gaiman notes, he was later amazed at how well the results fared with audiences—even the passages eked out on those days when he felt a little off his game.

Strategy number one is that I always, or almost always, have at least two or three different things that I'm writing at any one time. In my experience, writer's block is very real.

You'll be writing something and suddenly it stops. The characters stop talking. You've been happily just transcribing everything they've been saying, and suddenly they sit down and shut up. Suddenly, you are in deep trouble. It does happen. It's very real.

It's not something (in my experience anyway) that happens on everything at the same time. It's just that sometimes a project needs a little time to think, a little time to breathe.

So . . . I always have two or three other things that I'm doing at the same time. I can just go to one of the ones that's working. Which is how I give this appearance of being prolific. I'm really not. I think of myself as a very lazy author. But it's very nice for me to have more than one thing that I'm doing at a time, and being able to bounce between them.

The other thing that I would say about writer's block is that it can be very, very subjective. By which I mean, you can have one of those days when you sit down and every word is crap. It is awful. You cannot understand how or why you are writing, what gave you the illusion or delusion that you would ever have anything to say that anybody would ever want to listen to. You're not quite sure why you're wasting your time. . . .

I would also note that on those days (especially if deadlines and things are involved) is that I keep writing. The following day, when I actually come to look at what has been written, I will usually look at what I did the day before, and think, "That's not quite as bad as I remember. All I need to do is delete that line and move that sentence around and its fairly usable. It's not that bad."

What is really sad and nightmarish (and I should add, completely unfair, in every way. And I mean it—utterly, utterly, unfair!) is that two years later, or three years later, although you will remember very well, very clearly, that there was a point in this particular scene when you hit a horrible Writer's Block from Hell, and you will also remember there was a point in this particular scene where you were writing and the words dripped like magic diamonds from your fingers—as if the Gods were speaking through you and every sentence was a thing of beauty and magic and brilliance.

You can remember just as clearly that there was a point in the story, in that same scene, when the characters had turned into pathetic cardboard cut-outs and nothing they said mattered at all. You remember this very, very clearly.

The problem is you are now doing a reading and you cannot for the life of you remember which bits were the gifts of the Gods and dripped from your fingers like magical words and which bits were the nightmare things you just barely created and got down on paper somehow!! Which I consider most unfair. As a writer, you feel like one or the other should be better.

I wouldn't mind which. I'm not somebody who's saying, "I really wish the stuff from the Gods was better." I wouldn't mind which way it went. I would just like one of them to be better.

Rather than when it's a few years later, and you're reading the scene out loud and you don't know, and you cannot tell. It's obviously all written by the same person and it all gets the same kind of reaction from an audience. No one leaps up to say, "Oh look, that paragraph was clearly written on an 'off' day."

It is very unfair. I don't think anybody who isn't a writer would ever understand how quite unfair it is.

—Neil Gaiman, interview with Claire E. White, in *The Internet Writing Journal* (www.writerswrite.com), March 1999

> Sometimes your story seems to come to a halt. There is nothing much you can do about it. You just have to wait, every now and then taking a look to see if anything is happening. Sometimes you are waiting for a new, necessary idea to float up from the depths of your mind and lock the whole thing together.
> —Joan Aiken, in "Plotting the Children's Novel," in The Writer, May 1982

TELL IT TO ME

What do you do when you're stuck, when the words won't flow or those that do seem uninspired? Let's turn to that masterful spinner of tales, Rudyard Kipling. One of his stories is titled "The Finest Story in the World"; it is about an aspiring writer who comes to the narrator, a professional writer, for encouragement and help.

"What's the trouble?" I said, knowing well what that trouble was.

"I've got a notion in my head that would make the most splendid story that was ever written. Do let me write it out here. It's such a notion!" . . .

There was no resisting the appeal. I set him a table. . . . For half an hour the pen scratched without stopping. Then Charlie sighed and tugged at his hair. The scratching grew slower; there were more erasures; and at last ceased. The finest story in the world would not come forth.

"It looks such awful rot now," he said mournfully. "And yet it seemed so good when I was thinking about it. What's wrong?" . . .

"Read me what you've done," I said.

He read, and it was wondrous bad, and he paused at all the specially turgid sentences, expecting a little approval; for he was proud of those sentences. . . .

—Rudyard Kipling, "The Finest Story in the World"

What solution does Kipling's protagonist propose to his hapless friend?

"Tell me the story as it lies in your head."

Remember, you are telling a story. You are not trying to impress your old English teacher, your friends, or yourself with literary backflips. As Scheherazade (the gifted teller of tales in *A Thousand and One Arabian Nights*) discovered, telling a good yarn will keep them coming back for more.

Every evening after my sister Lucy and I had gone to bed, my father would walk slowly up the stairs, his bones creaking louder than the staircase, to tell us a story. I can see him now, leaning against the wall of our bedroom with his hands in his pockets looking into the distance, reaching into his imagination. It was here, in our bedroom, that he began telling many of the stories that later became the books you know.

—Ophelia Dahl, daughter of Roald Dahl, author of *James and the Giant Peach*, *The Witches*, and many other beloved children's books (posted on the website www.puffin.co.uk/Authors)

Isaak Babel, that superb short story writer, describes somewhere how he cut two hundred pages down to seven before he got a story which satisfied him. . . . I learned the hard way. By telling stories on busy crossroads, in doctors' waiting rooms, at the hairdresser's—stories of which my children asked always and only one question: "What happened then?"
—Eva Ibbotson, in The Writer, February 1974

CHAPTER ELEVEN

REVISING

A s Diana Wynne Jones says, in rereading what you have written, if you encounter a passage that seems a little odd, and you try to convince yourself that it's not so bad—it probably is. You need to fix it. Unravel that sentence, or paragraph, or page, and reweave it back into the pattern.

Don't worry, everyone has to do this. Good stories aren't written, says bestselling novelist Phyllis A. Whitney; they are rewritten.

Here are six simple ideas for revising that will improve your writing.

1. PUT IT ASIDE

A lot of great novelists from Mark Twain to Stephen King suggest that you need to put aside what you write for a period of time before you look at it. The periods recommended range from two to six weeks. The idea is to be able to read it with a fresh eye. You can't do that a few days after you've written the blasted thing.

Put it away and let it rest.

If you must write, work on something else.

2. LESS IS ALWAYS MORE

J.R.R. Tolkien's story, "Leaf, by Niggle," is a humorous tale about an obsessed artist, named Niggle, who desires to paint a simple leaf. He adds more and more until he ends up with a gigantic tree, filling a canvas so large he has to keep it outside in a special shed. Everything he does is sucked into the project; other pictures he tries to paint end up getting stuck around the borders of the enormous work.

It was a tongue-in-cheek reflection of Tolkien himself, the great niggler. His modest children's tale intended as a sequel to *The Hobbit* grew into the large epic of *The Lord of the Rings*. While a laudable result, this is not the best way to conduct a professional career. Sometimes, you need to quit while a leaf is still a leaf.

"The pattern," he murmured, frowning … somehow it doesn't please me."
"Now then, Wanderer," replied Dwyvach, "no man put a sword to your throat; the choice of pattern was your own."
"That it was," Taran admitted, "But now I see it closely, I would rather have chosen another."
"Ah, ah," said Dwyvach … "in that case you have but one of two things to do. Either finish a cloak you'll be ill-content to wear, or unravel it and start anew."
—Taran Wanderer, 1967, by Lloyd Alexander

Did something you wrote grow to unwieldy proportions? Get out the pruning shears. If you can't find the more elegant form inside your story gone wild, ask a friend to read it. Give a scene to your writer's group for feedback.

Tighten your writing. "The adverb is the enemy of the verb," said Mark Twain.

Franny Billingsley's novels are models of tight, image-rich writing. She says sometimes she goes over her manuscript and as an exercise, tries to take out one word per sentence. Often, one leads to two or three. You'd be surprised at how many words prove unnecessary. As a novelist, you aren't getting paid by the word. If you are writing short stories, editors don't want to pay for extra words that don't contribute. Less is always more.

3. LOOK FOR A BETTER START

Does the story start at its most enticing point?

Go through and pick several other points where your story could start. Isn't one of them more exciting?

Many times the best start for a story is found a page or two later than you first think, at a point when the action is really underway. Look carefully through the first chapter to consider a place that would provide a stronger, more enticing start. You can always use brief flashbacks or other devices to pick up the earlier moments—if they are really essential.

> This typically—but not always—happens at the beginning of a story. Instead of getting action, or the story, we get background, told from no particular point of view. Sort of an encyclopedia entry on the subject in question. For some reason, fantasies are particularly prone to this flaw. The story will open with a long explanation of how the castle (or fortress, or bus station) came to be there, and who all the ancestors of the current duke (or king, or wizard, or head chef) were, and how the magic (jewel or ring, or crown, or polo mallet) came to be imbued with its powers and then stolen (or lost, or locked in a spell, or pawned). We then spend the rest of the book in search of the map (or book of spells, or claim ticket).
>
> —Roger MacBride Allen, in "The Standard Deviations of Writing" (posted on website, www.sfwa.org)

You don't want a complete description of everything. That just serves my ego as the author. Even as the reader is looking up to say, "Oh, that's really nice," he or she is distracted from the story.

So I really try to prune it down as much as I can, to give the readers just a whiff of it, because that's all they need. Because then, they create a whole world for themselves, and they're off.

—Franny Billingsley

4. WITHHOLD INFORMATION

This is a corollary of the "less is more" approach, with a specific goal: to increase tension. The trick is to hold back something, while letting readers know that there you are doing this. They will quickly sense a mystery whose secret has not yet been revealed. As readers speculate, they pay more attention from then on to each small item, wondering if it holds an important clue.

> Sir Benjamin looked startled. "White? No. Dapple grey. Had you especially set your heart on a white mount?"
>
> "No-o," said Maria, not quite truthfully. "Only—I thought I saw a little white horse in the park as we drove through."
>
> If she had startled her relative before, she had now dumbfounded him. He set down his wineglass rather suddenly, spilling a little of the beautiful claret, and gazed at her with the queerest expression on his face, a mixture of astonishment, relief, and profound tenderness. . . . She was glad when he stopped staring at her, drained his glass and got up.
>
> "Two such weary travellers . . . must be longing for their beds," he said.
>
> They had been abruptly dismissed, Miss Heliotrope and Maria realized. . . .
>
> —*The Little White Horse*, 1946, Elizabeth Goudge

Joan Aiken is a master of the supernatural novel, and she has carefully studied the work of past practitioners of the genre.

> M.R. James, who might be called the Grand Old Man of ghost-story writing, said that *reticence* was just as necessary in a ghost story as horror and malevolence; and with this I most emphatically agree. It is always a mistake to ladle on the grue too fast and too lavishly; just a delicate touch achieves a much stronger effect.
>
> Henry James, the other old master of the supernatural, likewise advised that the writer should make use of what he called his "process of adumbration," that is, making the reader use his own imagination to envision the horror that threatens the hero. . . .
>
> This is brilliant advice.
>
> Of the stories by M.R. James that after nearly a hundred years still hold great potency, the most terrifying is "Oh Whistle and I'll

Come to You." Yet, what happens? The hero picks up a whistle, and has a dream of a half-glimpsed creature chasing a terrified man through the dusk along a wintry beach. At the climax of the story, the bedclothes from the unoccupied bed in his hotel room assemble themselves into a shape and come at him. He sees a face of *crumpled linen* (James's italics).

But what could a creature made out of bedclothes really do to an active, golf-playing professor? The secret of the story is that the reader is not given time to ask such a question; he is completely caught up in the carefully assembled and graded action: first, the character of Parkins, a fussy, fidgety, old-maidish academic; then the detailed description of the English east-coast area, the hotel, the "pale ribbon of sand intersected by black wooden groynings" [breakwaters], and the monastic ruins where Parkins picks up the whistle.

The story seems to proceed at a leisurely pace, but all along the way, small hints are dropped. Parkins, having picked up the whistle, glances back and sees "a rather indistinct personage who seemed to be making great efforts to catch up with him but made little if any, progress. He makes little of this glimpse—though the reader makes more—but it serves to remind him of the moment in *The Pilgrim's Progress* where Christian sees a foul fiend coming over the field to meet him.

And from there, the tension builds steadily. When Parkins tries to blow the whistle, there is a sudden gust of wind, and an image comes into his mind of a desolate, windswept landscape, with a solitary figure. He then has the frightening dream, and the reader is conned into thinking that perhaps all the fear, all the threat, is in Parkins's own mind.

But no; the bedding on the second bed is disturbed at night and a local boy, outside, is terrified by the sight of a white figure—"not a right person"—in the hotel bedroom window. Notice that all through the story the impressions given the reader are always as observed by one of the characters in the story.

And even in the final climax, it is through Parkins's eyes that we see: "The spectator realized, with some horror and some relief, that it must be blind, for it seemed to feel about it. . . ." (The fact that the creature is blind makes it *more* frightening, not less.)

—From "Writing Ghost Stories," by Joan Aiken, in *The Writer* (February 1994)

5. BEWARE STEROETYPES

As you look over your manuscript, are your characters stereotypes? Are they archetypes? Or are they original characters in their own right?

Learn the difference. Archetypes are the originals from which the mold was made. The heroes of Greek myths are archetypes. Merlin is an archetype, as is the wicked witch in Sleeping Beauty. These are core models, and they tend to act out their role unflinchingly. Merlin cannot act otherwise; nor can the heroes of myth or the evil witch.

Steroetypes, on the other hand, are shorthand knock-offs, like the hunchbacked old crone with a crooked nose who cackles shrilly as she plots to do evil. We know she is a witch, but there is little new about her to attract our interest. This is the mark of a lazy writer. Why not envision a witch in another form? Why not make a witch with a soft heart who is compelled to report any fellow witches who use puppy-dog tails to the ASPCA?

True, sometimes an author does need a shorthand version of a character type, as with minor characters who are brought in and out of the picture to perform a stock role without interfering with the flow of the narrative. You cannot always take the time to develop each character to his or her fullest potential. Minor characters are sometimes called "flat," in comparison to major characters who tend to be "round" or multidimensional.

Good characters are neither stereotypes nor archetypes. They may have some portion of the archetypal character in their nature, but they lead their own lives, follow their own passions, make mistakes, learn and grow.

Many beginning authors fail in particular to create in-depth characterizations of members of the opposite sex. They tend to paint these characters with a flat palette of colors; the characters lack the complex shadings that could help them come alive.

One mark of a beginning writer is to create heroes that are too much like themselves. The mark of an accomplished professional is the ability to create characters that are different from the writer's own nature. Diana Wynne Jones believes an author can create more complex characters by creating protagonists that are of the opposite gender than the author; this allows a writer, she feels, to consider more facets of a character's personality, rather than relying too heavily on comfortable self-knowledge.

With one stroke of his fifty-pound sword, Gnorts the Barbarian lopped off the head of Nialliv the Wizard. It flew through the air, still sneering, while Gnorts clove two royal guardsmen from vizor through breastplate to steel jockstrap.... Easily outrunning pursuit, he took a few sentries at the gate by surprise.... Seeing a magnificent stallion tethered, Gnorts released it, twisted the rope into a bridle, and rode it off bareback.... Winter winds lashed his body, attired in nothing more than a bearskin kilt....
—Poul Anderson, "On Thud and Blunder," a critique of overwrought adventure fantasy (from the SFWA website, www.sfwa.org)

This same reasoning applies to good and evil characters. Are your bad guys all shallow, while the good ones are intriguing? Does this mar an otherwise strong story?

Look closely at characters you do not identify with—because of their gender or other aspects—and challenge yourself. Do they meet your own high standards of writing? Do you understand them in all their complexity? Do they bring anything new to their roles? Or are they convenient, lackluster, forgettable?

What would make them more memorable? What would make them surprising? What would make them shine?

Have you added anything new?

Arguably, in order for a fiction to be fantasy it must be prepared to dance with Tygers; it must take risks by exploring precisely those dangerous territories where no one has ever ventured before. . . . It must meddle with our thinking, it must delight in being controversial, it must *hope* to be condemned by authority (whatever authority one chooses to identify), it must be at the cutting edge of the imagination, it must flirt with madness, it must *surprise*, it must be doing things that other fiction *cannot*.

—John Grant, in "Gulliver Unravels: Generic Fantasy and the Loss of Subversion" (posted on Infinity Plus website, www.users. zetnet.co.uk/iplus/nonfiction/gulliver.htm)

CHAPTER TWELVE

SUBMITTING WORK FOR PUBLICATION

AT THE BEGINNING OF A CAREER, important feedback comes in the form of rejection slips. You are sure to get many, sometimes several on the same day. Don't despair. This is part of the education of a writer. It is how every great writer got started. The secret: they persisted and kept writing and submitting their work.

Some of the greatest works were rejected many times by publishers. Madeleine L'Engle submitted *A Wrinkle in Time* to several dozen publishers before she found one that would take it on; it won a Newbery Award and launched her wonderful career. Pearl S. Buck is said to have gotten a rejection slip for a story on the same day she was notified she had won the Nobel Prize for Literature. Everyone gets rejections slips.

EDITORS AND REJECTION SLIPS

Rejection slips serve a purpose. Writers need to learn that those horribly polite form letters do not necessarily mean the work is not good; it just means that those particular words on paper are not what the publisher desires to buy. There is a crucial difference. The sooner that a writer learns this revealing lesson, the better.

Editors receive many manuscripts, far more than they can ever publish. They search through submissions for work they think their customers might want to buy and read. Naturally, they look first at work submitted by agents—unsuitable work has already been filtered out by the agents, who represent mostly authors who have already been published. Then, in any time left, acquisitions editors or their assistants browse through the first few pages of manuscripts found in their slush piles. These are towering piles of unsolicited manuscripts that arrive, relentlessly, day after day.

How do you beat those odds? First of all, the first few pages must be compelling. Ask yourself the tough question: Would I buy this manuscript based on the first several pages? Editorial assistants seldom glance at more, unless those early passages show exceptional promise.

When you get rejection slips—and you will—use that as motivation to go back and improve your writing. Strengthen your beginnings. Give your characters more dimensions. Break free from stereotypes and offer something new—yet recognizable.

Read again the work of authors being published by the publishers to whom you are submitting your work. You can be sure it represents the tastes and business interests of those publishing houses.

Read trade magazines like *Locus*. It gives advance information about awards, conferences, and key trends—and details about which publishers (and which editors) are acquiring specific types of manuscripts. This insight into the business side of the publishing world is invaluable for a working writer.

AGENTS

Whether to seek an agent is a topic of debate. Once a writer begins to be successful, an agent can be a valuable partner. An agent's job is to pitch new work to the right publisher—and then to negotiate a good contract when serious interest in shown. Writing well and selling well are very different skills. A few writers can do both; others should focus on writing and let an agent do the rest.

Agents earn their fees by getting better advances, reserving key rights, and winning small victories in contract language. However, aspiring but unpublished writers will find it difficult to find an agent. Also, few agents are interested in handling short stories; the small amount they would get as a percentage of a sale is not worth their time. They are looking for writers who write novels.

Agents and publishers alike are looking for authors who show signs of being able to produce good work over time. They hope that an author has the potential to write more than one piece of work. They are looking for authors who have achieved some small indicators of success. Story prizes, writing fellowships, or inclusion in well-respected short-story anthologies are visible, valued signs of professional commitment and ability.

Some agents offer a combination of business advice and psychological hand-holding. Others take a hands-off approach; they do their work, and let you do yours. The relationship is best when you find an agent who fits your style as an author, who appreciates a similar level of communication and support, and who has realistic expectations.

I went from publisher to publisher and literary agent to agent....They all said, in effect, the same thing: "Older children wouldn't like it because it's about rabbits, which they consider babyish; and younger children wouldn't like it because it's written in an adult style...." I thought, "Who's talking about children? This book is for readers of all ages."
—Richard Adams, Watership Down, introduction to Perennial Classics Edition, 2001

It comes down to the quality of your work. Agents only make a sale when they have good work to offer. If they don't, they don't want to jeopardize their good contacts with publishers by talking them into reading work that won't be of interest to them or their customers.

Some agents offer limited editorial advice. Listen to them; they are trying to shape your work into something they can sell.

SUBMITTING YOUR WORK

Ultimately, it's your work. Whether it's an editor, an agent, or a friend giving you advice, you need to develop your own style that is good, that readers enjoy, and that offers some unique aspects.

Have you written something you think meets those criteria? Then don't wait. Send it in.

The submission process is straightforward. Publishers' websites have specific directions on how to submit work to them; they explain the kind of work they are looking for, ideal word-length, payment terms, and where to send the material.

You may want to refer to one of the many books for writers on submitting fiction; these provide a wealth of specific tips and important steps to follow. *The Complete Idiot's Guide to Publishing Science Fiction* (see Appendix A) is one of the better examples; it's full of lots of practical advice, plus sample cover letters, contracts, and more. It also offers a good list of literary agents who are interested in speculative fiction.

Another good source of advice and market listings is found on the website of the Science Fiction and Fantasy Writers of America. The SFWA is an important professional organization which works to support speculative-fiction writers. Their website offers articles on writing technique, sample contracts, markets, and industry news. Membership is available to those who have published several short stories or a novel. Check their website (www.sfwa.org) for details.

When you submit materials to a publisher, follow instructions carefully. A simple cover letter will suffice. Don't try to oversell; it is always transparent. The publisher's job is to read your stories and determine if they meet their needs. Just introduce yourself, convey the manuscript, and give a short summary of your qualifications. See the above-mentioned *Complete Idiot's Guide to Publishing Science Fiction* for a good example of a cover letter.

> Innovation has no place in manuscript format.
> —George Scithers, et al., in On Writing Science Fiction: The Editors Strike Back, 1981

For your manuscript, print it double-spaced, using a "plain vanilla" typeface (Courier is good), with one-inch margins on all four sides. After the first page, place your name and an abbreviated title at the top right of each page. A copyright notice is not needed; your work is automatically under copyright protection the moment it is written down.

For short-story submissions, include the entire story. For novel-length works, usually a one-page summary, with three sample chapters will suffice. Editors or agents won't read more unless they are interested, and if so, they will request the balance of the manuscript.

Don't send more than they ask for. It is a sign of unprofessionalism (i.e., you don't know how much to send). Worse, it suggests a weakness in your story—it indicates you're afraid that the first three chapters won't convince them to want to read more. If they don't, why would readers?

A writer should follow the sound advice given by Tor Books in their guidelines:

> We'd have sworn our submissions guidelines covered all the necessary information, but a few questions keep turning up. Like: How much detail should there be in the synopsis? And: if the book has a prologue, does that count as one of the three sample chapters, or can the writer send the prologue plus the first three chapters? And so forth.
>
> The answer is simple: send us whatever you think is necessary and sufficient to sell the book to us. This isn't a class assignment.
>
> The question that puzzles us the most is, "What are the odds of getting published by Tor? That is, what is our ratio of acceptance to rejection . . . ?
>
> Answer: for very good books, the odds are excellent. For books we don't like, the odds are abysmal. No other measurement is meaningful. If we have a month in which we don't see any manuscripts we like, we don't buy manuscripts we don't like just to keep up our acquisition rate.
>
> If you absolutely have to have a rough estimate of our rejection rate, the answer is that we reject most of them. But look at it this way: if you don't send us your manuscript, the odds that we'll publish it approach absolute zero. It's your call.

Check publishers' websites carefully and follow their guidelines closely. If you don't, you risk making a poor impression when an editor picks up your envelope and glances over the contents briefly. On the other hand, absolutely nothing pleases an editor better than getting a solid, well-written synopsis that doesn't over-promise, but provides the requested information, along with a good outline of the book and a couple of sample chapters—with writing that is really fresh and exciting. Editors have a job to do, and one of the most pleasurable parts is discovering a promising new writer.

If that's you, they want to see your work. Submit it.

TAKE A STEPPING-STONE APPROACH

It is most realistic for a new writer to plan a stepping-stone approach to developing a career. First, pitch your work directly to publishers. Keep writing and keep sending it in. Try to get some short stories published. Build up a track record, however modest, of prior publication. If your writing is good, you will start to sell the occasional story here and there. At the same time, your writing will improve as you gain experience, read the work of others, and hone your style.

Yes, you will also build up a pile of rejection slips. If you don't build up a considerable pile, you probably aren't trying hard enough.

For novels, while you may try the big publishers first, you may want to consider small publishers. Check, however, their credentials. Good small publishers exhibit several key traits: first, their catalog shows a track record of publishing well-respected work that has gotten good reviews. Second, look to see if they advertise in genre publications. Be cautious with smaller publishers who do neither—they have not yet shown signs of success and may not be able to provide the marketing help needed to reach your most important audiences. They may be good, but it will be hard for you to tell.

On the positive side, smaller publishers may be able to provide more hands-on editorial feedback. This is helpful to those authors who are on the verge of breaking into print, but who really need some realistic criticism and editorial expertise.

Avoid self-publishing. Yes, it can be done and yes, it will get your book in print. But is also a red flag; it will suggest that no regular publisher was willing to accept the work. It might be better in the long run to stick that manuscript away in a drawer. Go write something else. If you have the talent, you will eventually get published by a real publisher. Then, you can pull out that old story, dust it off, and

Myth is universal experience. Fantasy is personal experience.
—Joan Aiken, The Way to Write for Children, 1998

maybe improve it (since you've become a better writer). To your surprise, the publisher who accepted your other work will look very closely at that earlier work, perhaps even eagerly. You may find there is more to be gained in that way than in self-publishing that story. Self-publish if you must, but be realistic. It will get your book in print, but it is less likely to advance your career.

When you have had some work published, consider looking for an agent. Ask other writers you know for recommendations. Study the acknowledgements pages in books by authors whose work is similar to yours; often they mention their agents in their thanks.

You can go to conferences to make direct contacts. But agents, like publishers, are good at brushing off the direct inquiry. You won't win positive attention by buttonholing them at an event. The way to get them interested in you is to develop publication credits—and most of all, write work that is compelling.

Go back to short stories to focus on refining your writing style. Look at the careers of great writers of fantastic literature: Ray Bradbury, Kurt Vonnegut, and others who have continued to write short stories, sometimes publishing novels which are really linked series of short stories.

To succeed, an aspiring writer needs to develop a thick-enough skin to persist, yet a thin-enough skin to listen to criticism and learn from it. Keep writing, keep submitting, and you will be following in the footsteps of every great writer.

Pay absolutely no attention to those stories in the news about how some author made it big on his or her first try. Those are in the news because they are rare events. Your success will come the way it came for most authors: from hard work, persistence, and steadily improving your writing skills.

Commit to writing every day. Keep your goals in sight—getting better step by step.

The green fields of fantasy await you. Welcome to the community of writers who believe that stories that draw on the powerful, eternal patterns of fantasy are worth our time to tell—as well as we can.

Learning to avoid triteness, not only in word and phrase but also in ideas, plots, characters, and settings, is easily half the task of becoming a good writer.
—George Scithers, et al., in On Writing Science Fiction: The Editors Strike Back, 1981

HUMOR, LOGIC, AND FANTASY

Interview with Terry Pratchett
by Claire E. White

Beginning with his 1983 novel, The Colour of Magic, fantasy author Terry Pratchett's many Discworld novels have sold over 20 million copies in 27 languages worldwide. The past ten have been the number-one bestsellers in the United Kingdom. Discworld is peopled with Pratchett's imaginative characters: the bumbling wizard Rincewind; Captain Samuel Vimes, the beleaguered head of Ankh-Morpork's City Watch; the Igors with their interchangeable body parts and perfect servant's manners, the iron-willed Granny Weatherwax, and many others. Full of wit and humor, the Discworld novels are brilliant parodies of absurd things and attitudes found in our world today. Here, in an interview held April 2000 with Claire E. White, editor of The Internet Writing Journal, Pratchett talks about ideas, characters, and the craft of writing.

(White) In *The Fifth Elephant*, Captain Vimes is up to his neck in conspiracy, diplomacy, vampires, and werewolves. Let's start with werewolves. Why werewolves?

(Pratchett) A lot of the humor (and possibly a lot of the power in the *Discworld* series) comes from thinking logically about those things which we don't normally think logically about.

For example, in a horror story we just accept the idea of werewolves and vampires without going a little deeper into it. It seemed to me that a thinking creature that spends part of its time as a wolf and part of its time as a human is going to be a very interesting creature, with a very interesting psychology.

So I invented a female werewolf who is a vegetarian as a human being—but for one week per month is a wolf—with everything that entails. Her name is Angua.

I suppose it's a terrible thing for an author to say, but an author likes characters who are screwed up: Angua is screwed up, Granny Weatherwax is screwed up. They are not at ease with themselves, and that makes their heads very interesting places for the author to be.

I was having a lot of fun with Angua and then I thought, "What would a werewolf family be like? How would the genealogy of werewolves work? What would the politics of werewolves be?" One thing just led to the other, but they all started from the basic idea of thinking seriously about werewolves in a modern society—or what passes for a modern society.

(White) Vimes gets into a great deal of trouble in this book. I especially liked the chase scene. It's sort of *The Most Dangerous Game*, but played out in the background of a Chekhov play.

(Pratchett) Well, I'm glad you noticed that because I get fan mail from some of the younger fans and they say, "What was the bit with the three old ladies?" And I say, "Haven't you heard of Chekhov?" "Yes, wasn't he the first officer on the Enterprise?"

I put that sequence in the story as sort of an Easter egg: the little treasures (literary or other jokes) hidden throughout the story. I didn't want to do just a straight chase scene. And I thought, "This is the right kind of landscape, it's the right kind of weather, so let's have a couple of pages of mock Chekhov." The nice thing about Discworld is you can do that kind of thing.

(White) It seems to me that the *Discworld* novels have gotten a touch darker, perhaps with a few more serious bits in them. Is that accurate?

(Pratchett) First off, I have to say that I simply hate it when reviewers call my work "wacky" or "zany." Those people are going to be hunted down by the Mafia! Seriously, I suppose around the fifth or six *Discworld* book, I discovered the joy of plot. I think it was Esther Friesner who said you have to have tragic relief. If a book is nothing but funny, then it is nothing but funny. There is no contrast and it's hard to take anything seriously. It's hard to worry about the fate of a character. You do need those moments when you bring people down to earth.

In *Jingo*, there was a theme of what you might call quantum confusion (and only in fantasy can you get away with this kind of thing). Vimes picks up his personal organizer just at the moment when the Universe is splitting into two. So he picks up the personal organizer that belongs to the Vimes that makes the decision in a different way—he gets a personal organizer which is effectively telling him what would have been happening in his life had he not made a particular decision.

There is a scene where he's actually seeing (as if it were notes in an organizer) all his colleagues dying (although in his universe they are around him and alive). There is a war going on and in the section of the organizer that says "Things To Do Today," the entry says "die." This was quite chilling to see. These terrible things happened because he made a small decision which had a profound effect.

(White) I'd like to talk a bit about the practical side of being a writer. You've said you are from the Carpentry School of Writing. Could you expand on that?

(Pratchett) I have to say that I change the metaphor about once a week. But it may help if I give you an idea of how I go about writing.

I'm about 10,000 words into my next book. Do I know what it is about? Yes, I do—it's just that I'm not telling myself.

This is what I call Draft Zero. This is private. No one ever, ever gets to see draft zero. This is the draft that you write to tell yourself what the story is. Someone asked me recently how to guard against writing on auto-pilot. I responded that writing on auto-pilot is very, very important! I sit there and I bash the stuff out. I don't edit—I let it flow.

For the first month or so of writing a book I try to get the creative side of the mind to get it down there on the page. Later on, I get the analytical side to come along and chop the work into decent lengths, edit it, and knock it into the right kind of shape. Everyone finds their own way of doing things. I certainly don't sit down and plan a book out before I write it.

There's a phrase I use called "The Valley Full of Clouds." Writing a novel is as if you are going off on a journey across a valley. The valley is full of mist, but you can see the top of a tree here and the top of another tree over there. And with any luck you can see the other side of the valley. But you cannot see down into the mist.

Nevertheless, you head for the first tree.

At this stage in the book, I know a little about how I want to start. I know some of the things that I want to do on the way. I think I know how I want it to end. This is enough. The thing now is to get as much down as possible.

It's all a technique—not to get over writer's block, but to get 15,000 or 20,000 words of text under my belt. When you've got that text down, then you can work on it. Then you start giving yourself ideas.

(*White*) Do you think that you must be a good observer to write really great parody or satire?

(*Pratchett*) For many years I was a journalist, and so I was trained to observe in a journalistic way. What I always say to people is that when it comes to inventing characters, don't base a character on someone you know.

But it may be a good idea to base the character on a type of character that you know, because lots of other people will know people like that. And if they know people like that, then half the work has been done for you.

People say, "I know someone just like Granny Weatherwax!" The reader is simply inserting that person that they know into the story. A great deal of character work lies not in describing the characters, but in describing the shape that they leave in the world. How they react to other people. How they face things. When they keep silent. The manner in which they say things.

Character does not consist of telling the reader what color a person's eyes are and how tall he is. You do not need pages and pages of physical description to get a character. You can get nearly all the physical description you need by one thing that character says that makes people think, "Aha! I know exactly what kind of person would say something like that!"

(*White*) Let's talk a bit about the book you collaborated with Neil Gaiman on: *Good Omens*. How did it work on a practical basis?

(*Pratchett*) When two people work on a book, it isn't a case where Terry Pratchett and Neil Gaiman each does 50% of the work. Each one does 100% of the work.

There are some bits in *Good Omens* I know are mine. There are some bits I know are Neil's. Some bits we no longer know exactly whose ideas they were, or who wrote them.

We wrote it in the 14th century. We each had one phone line and a 1200-baud modem. We'd work it out: "OK, you send, I'll receive." Sometimes it would take 20 minutes to half an hour before we could send the stuff. It would have been cheaper and easier to have rung each other up and sneezed out the text in Morse Code.

I was the Keeper of the Disks. I insisted that there should only be one official version in existence at any time. The moment it split into two, we would be in dead trouble. But Neil would sometimes send me a disk with 2000 words, saying "This is the scene with so and so—insert it here." It more or less worked. It took us about six weeks to do the first draft.

It's not that we didn't take it seriously. But we were relaxed. We thought we would earn some holiday money by doing it. The nice thing about collaborating is that there is one other person in the world who is thinking about the exact same thing that you are.

When Neil Gaiman and I were doing the *Good Omens* tour it was great fun because I was suffering with one other person. We were actually interviewed by a very well-known interviewer in that particular city who hadn't even read his notes, let alone the book. The subtitle of the book was "The Nice and Accurate Predictions of Agnes Nutter." He thought that this was the real title of the book—that it was a nonfiction book about predictions.

Neil and I could see the engineer in the booth doubled over with laughter; he happened to be a fan. We looked at one another, and the unspoken thought was, "We'd better not wipe the floor with this guy." So we had to find a way of giving answers that would be technically correct, but somehow sending the message that the host was conducting the wrong interview.

(White) I understand that you interact a great deal with your fans. How much fan mail and e-mail do you get?

(Pratchett) It's overwhelming. I don't count it any more. I don't get as neurotic about handling it as much as I used to. These days, if I open a letter which begins, "I bet you won't read this letter..." I now think, "Well, fair enough then. I'll put this one back on the heap." But I do my best to answer it.

(White) I can't imagine that you have a great deal of free time.

(Pratchett) It depends on how you define free time. I recently said to a relative of mine, "We're having a holiday this year." And she said, "From what, exactly?"

(White) Are there any misconceptions you'd like to set straight?

(Pratchett) There is one thing that I get asked all the time—on a daily basis actually—by aspiring writers who contact me. They say, "I keep starting things; I don't know how to finish them. I don't seem to be

able to find time to write. I don't seem to be able to get my ideas down on paper."

What I always say is, "Consider, just consider for a moment, that although you want to be a writer, being a writer may not be where your particular genius lies."

When I was a kid, I really, really wanted to be an astronomer. I have no real mathematical abilities whatsoever. I'm fine when it comes to the numbers, but when you show me a quadratic equation I'm completely lost. What I wanted to do was to stare in wonder at the universe—which is not exactly what an astronomer has to do.

I think what a lot of people who want to be writers really want is to have written. That is harder.

What I tend to say is, "Look, if you wanted to be a boxer you would listen if someone like Mike Tyson said to you, 'Ok, you've gotta go down to the gym. You've gotta eat the right kind of stuff. You've gotta do your road work. You've gotta work at it for years and years, and it's going to be quite hard.' You'd say, 'Yes, Mike.'"

So to writers I say, you're going to have to read a lot—so many books that you're going to overflow. You've got to hook into the popular culture of the times. You've got to keep your mind open to all sorts of influences. You've got to sit down for hours at a time in front of the computer. And you must make grammar, punctuation, and spelling a part of your life.

What seems to be happening more and more (and I don't know why this is so) is that a lot of people labor under the misapprehension that if they cannot write it's because some kind of outside influence is preventing them from doing so—as if the universe itself is conspiring against their natural destiny of writerdom.

—From an interview with Claire E. White, editor of The Internet Writing Journal (www.writerswrite.com).

HOW TO BE MADDER THAN CAPTAIN AHAB

by Ray Bradbury

Ray Bradbury is a master of speculative fiction whose work epitomizes the madness of love for literature that excites the soul and stirs the heart. His credits date back to the 1930s and leap across science fiction, fantasy, horror, and mystery categories. Titles include famous works of American imaginative fiction such as The Martian Chronicles, Fahrenheit 451, Dandelion Wine, and Something Wicked This Way Comes. Many of his books are collections of short stories, sometimes strung together in a framework like the stories of The Illustrated Man, presented as the stories of a tattooed man's colorful body images. In 2000, he received the National Book Foundations Medal for Distinguished Contribution to American Letters.

His enthusiasm is contagious; he has inspired countless young writers with his passionate exhortations to write about anything that moves you, whether that is space travel to Mars, summertime memories of childhood, or "the thing at the top of the stairs." Some of his essays on writing imaginative fiction are collected in his 1994 work, Zen in the Art of Writing.

Here, in an article published in The Writer in February 1974, Ray Bradbury gives a timeless message to writers.

How does one go about becoming a writer?

Well, you might as well ask, how do you go about becoming human, whatever that is!

I suppose you fall in love, early, with all kinds of things.

I fell in love with books when I was five or six, especially the way books looked and smelled.

I have been a library jackdaw all of my life, which means I have never gone into that lovely holy place with a book list, but only with my beady bright eyes and my curious paws, monkey–climbing the stacks over among the children's, and then again where I was not allowed, burrowing among the adults' mysterious books.

I would take home, at the age of ten, eight books at a time, from eight different categories, and rub my nose in them and all but lie down and roll on them like a frolicsome springtime dog. *Popular*

Mechanics and *The Boy Mechanic* were my bibles. The encyclopedia was my open meadow-field where I rambled and muttered: "Curiouser and curiouser!" and lay down with Jules Verne's robot pups only to arise with Edgar Rice Burroughs's Martian fleas.

I have run amuck ever since in libraries and bookstores, with fevers and deleriums.

Hysteria must be your way of life, then, if you wish, any of you, to become writers. Or, for that matter, painters or actors or any other crazy lovely things!

If I emphasize libraries it is because school itself is only a beginning, and writing itself is a continuation. But the meat must be found and fed on in every library you can jump into and every bookstore you can pole-vault through.

Even as I did not prowl there with preconceived lists, so I do not send you there with nice dry tame small indexes of my taste, crushing you with an iron-anvil dropped from a building.

Once started, the library is the biggest blasted Cracker Jack Factory in the world!

The more you eat, the more you want!

And the more you read, the more the ideas begin to explode around inside your head, run riot, meet head-on in beautiful collisions so that when you go to bed at night the damned visions color the ceiling and light the walls with huge exploits and wonderful discoveries.

I still use libraries and bookstores in the same fashion, 40 years later. I spend as much time in child's country as I do over the corseted adults'.

And what I take home and browse and munch through each evening should give you a relaxing view of a writer tumultuous just this side of madness.

I may start a night's read with a James Bond novel, move on to Shakespeare for half an hour, dip into Dylan Thomas for five minutes, make a fast turnabout and fasten on Fu Manchu, that great and evil Oriental doctor, ancestor of Dr. No, then pick up Emily Dickinson, and end my evening with Ross Macdonald, the detective novelist, or Robert Frost, that crusty poet of the American rural spirit.

The fact should be plain now; I am an amiable compost heap. My mind is full of moron plus brilliant trash, shoved in my eyes and sticking out my ears and elbows. For I learned, early on, that in order to grow myself excellent I had to start myself in plain old farmyard blood manure. From such heaps of mediocre or angelic words I fever myself up to grow fine stories, or roses, if you prefer.

I am a junkyard, then, of all the librarians and bookshops I ever fell into or leaned upon, and am proud and happy that I never developed such a rare taste that I could not go back and jog with Tarzan or hit the Yellow Brick Road with Dorothy, both characters and their books banned for 50 years by all librarians and most educators. I have had my own loves, and gone my own way to become my own self.

I highly recommend you do the same. However crazy your desire, however wild your need, however dumb your taste may seem to others . . . follow it!

When I was nine, I collected Buck Rogers comic strips. People made fun. I tore them up. Two month later, I said to myself: "Hold on! What's this all about? These people are trying to starve me. They have cut me off from my vitamins! And the greatest food in my life, right now, is Buck Rogers! Everyone, outa the way! Git! Runty Ray is going to start collecting comic strips againI"

And I did. For I had the great secret!

Everyone else was wrong. I was right. For me, anyway.

What if I hadn't done as I have done?

Would I ever have grown up to become a writer of science fictions or, for that matter, any kind of writer at all?

No. Never.

If I had listened to all taste-mongers and fools and critics I would have played a safe game, never jumped the fence, and become a nonentity whose name would not be known to you now.

So it was I learned to run and leap into an empty swimming pool, hoping to sweat enough liquid into it on the way down to make a soft landing.

Or, to change metaphors, I dropped myself off the edges of cliffs, daring to build myself wings while falling, so as not to break myself on the rocks below.

To sum it all up, if you want to write, if you want to create, you must be the most sublime fool that God ever turned out and sent rambling.

You must write every single day of your life.

You must read dreadful dumb books and glorious books, and let them wrestle in beautiful fights inside your head, vulgar one moment, brilliant the next.

You must lurk in libraries and climb the stacks like ladders to snuff books like perfumes and wear books like hats upon your crazy heads.

I wish for you a wrestling match with your Creative Muse that will last a lifetime.

I wish craziness and foolishness and madness upon you.

May you live with hysteria, and out of it make fine stories.

Which finally means, may you be in love every day for the next 20,000 days. And out of that love, remake a world.

—From The Writer, February 1974. Originally published in Literary Cavalcade. Copyright 1973 by Ray Bradbury.

PART IV

RESOURCES

TOP MARKETS FOR FANTASY FICTION

BOOK PUBLISHERS

Ace Science Fiction and Fantasy (Berkley Publishing Group)
Susan Allison, Editor-in-Chief
375 Hudson Street, New York, NY 10014
Telephone: 212-366-2000. Website: www.penguinputnam.com
Accepts submissions from agents only.

Baen Books (distributed by Simon & Schuster)
Toni Weisskopf, Executive Editor
P.O. Box 1403, Riverdale, NY 10471
Telephone: 718-548-3100. Website: www.baen.com

DAW Books (distributed by Penguin Putnam)
Peter Stampfel, Submissions Editor
375 Hudson Street, New York, NY 10014
Telephone: 212-366-2096. Website: www.dawbooks.com

Del Rey Books (Ballentine Publishing Group)
Shelly Shapiro, Editorial Director
299 Park Avenue, New York, NY 10171
Telephone: 212-751-2600. Website: www.randomhouse.com/delrey
Accepts submissions from agents only.

Margaret K. McElderry Books (Simon & Schuster Children's Div.)
Emma K. Dryden, Executive Editor
1230 Avenue of the Americas, New York, NY 10020
Telephone: 212-698-7000.

Tor Books (Tom Doherty Associates)
Patrick Nielsen Hayden, Senior Editor
175 Fifth Avenue, New York, NY 10010
Website: www.tor.com

Wizards of the Coast
Manuscript Editor, Books
P.O. Box 707, Renton, WA 98057-0707
Website: www.wizards.com
Work-for-hire projects; submit work samples for consideration.

SHORT-STORY MARKETS

Century
Attn: Robert K.J. Kilheffer, Editor
P.O. Box 150510, Brooklyn, NY 11215-0510
Website: www.centurymag.com/guidelines.html. Quarterly.

Interzone
Attn: David Pringle, Editor
217 Preston Drove, Brighton, England BN1 6FL
Website: www.sfsite.com/interzone/guide.htm

The Magazine of Fantasy and Science Fiction
Gordon Van Gelder, Editor
P.O. Box 3447, Hoboken, NJ 07030
Website: www.sfsite.com/fsf

On Spec
Attn: Diane Walton, Editor in Chief
P.O. Box 4727, Stn. South, Edmonton, AB, Canada T6E 5G6
Website: www.icomm.ca/onspec.

Realms of Fantasy
Attn: Shawna McCarthy, Editor
P.O. Box 527, Rumson, NJ 07760

Weird Tales
George Scithers and Darrell Schweitzer, Editors
123 Crooked Lane, King of Prussia, PA 19406-2570
Website: www.weird-tales.com

For additional market information, see *The Writer's Handbook* (The Writer Books), published annually, available in bookstores or at www.writermag.com.

OTHER RESOURCES FOR FANTASY WRITERS

BOOKS ON WRITING

BRADBURY, RAY. *Zen in the Art of Writing*. Joshua Odell, 1994. Stimulating essays, merging the thrill of writing with the hard-headed discipline of writing every day. This will make you want to jump up and start writing more creatively.

BRANDE, DOROTHEA. *Becoming a Writer*. First published 1934 by Harcourt, Brace & Co. Reprint 1981 by J.P. Tarcher, Inc. A brilliant book on becoming and being a writer; focuses on the core issues most aspiring writers face: motivation, discipline, creativity.

DOCTOROW, CARL, and SCHROEDER, KARL. *Complete Idiot's Guide to Publishing Science Fiction*. Alpha Books, 2000. Excellent advice on the business of getting published, from two up-and-coming writers. Includes a sample contract, short-story and book markets, good list of agents.

GUNN, JAMES. *The Science of Science Fiction Writing*. Scarecrow Press, 2000. Worth buying for the Appendix alone, "Notes from a Workshop," which summarizes in a dozen pages key elements of writing speculative fiction—an excellent outline for planning, editing, and revising a story.

KING, STEPHEN. *On Writing*. Pocket Books, 2000. Combines excellent advice with stories tracing his own career. King's advice penetrates deeply into the discipline and practice of writing. Insists that authors need to write daily, write plainly, and tell good stories.

LE GUIN, URSULA K. *Steering the Craft: Exercises and Discussions on Story Writing for the Lone Navigator or the Mutinous Crew*. Eighth Mountain Press, 1998. Emphasizes the role of change, not conflict, in stories. Includes good creative exercises, developed in her popular fiction workshops.

SCITHERS, GEORGE H., SCHWEITZER, DARRELL, and FORD, JOHN M. *On Writing Science Fiction: The Editors Strike Back!* Wildside Press/Owlswick Press, 1981. A practical collection of guidance from magazine editors in the speculative-fiction field, with samples of actual published stories, comments from the authors and editors of those stories, and lots of timeless advice for writing imaginative fiction.

RESOURCE BOOKS

Brewer's Dictionary of Phrase & Fable. "Curious or novel" bits of tradition, mythology, and lore, and odd facts. Available in many libraries.

BRIGGS, KATHERINE. *An Encyclopedia of Fairies: Hobgoblins, Brownies, Bogies, and Other Supernatural Creatures.* Pantheon, 1976. (Abbreviated 1979 version titled *Abbey Lubbers, Banshees, and Boggarts: an Illustrated Encyclopedia of Fairies*). A reference work on fantastic creatures, mostly British Isle/Celtic.

PAGE, MICHAEL, and INGPEN, ROBERT. *Encyclopedia of Things that Never Were: Creatures, Places, and People.* (Penguin Studio, 1998). Over 400 entries, (300 color illus.), on fantastic things from mythology, literature, and lore.

The Writer's Complete Fantasy Reference. Writer's Digest Books, 2000. Useful details on versions of clothing, trades, weapons, religion and magical beliefs, and such, from cultures around the world.

ON FANTASY WRITING & PUBLISHING

ANSIBLE. www.dcs.gla.ac.uk/SF-Archives/Ansible/. The award-winning online newsletter by David Langford, with an entertaining combination of news and commentary about the world of speculative fiction.

FANTASY WORLDBUILDING QUESTIONS. www.sfwa.org/writing/. A series of pages created by author Patricia C. Wrede, with very extensive lists of questions to help a writer think through the details of creating a fantasy world. Hosted by the SFWA website.

LOCUS MAGAZINE. P.O. Box 13305; Oakland CA 94661. Telephone: 510-339-9196. Website: www.locusmag.com. Reviews of new books and magazine issues, plus news on the business side of the fantasy and science-fiction trade. Website includes calendar of upcoming conventions for writers and fans, author interviews, and extensive list of links to speculative-fiction magazines.

SCIENCE FICTION AND FANTASY WRITERS OF AMERICA. www.sfwa.org. The leading professional organization for speculative-fiction writers; provides a variety of resources and services. Website offers market information and links, articles on writing, sample contracts, details on how to become a member, and more. Publishes the quarterly journal, *SFWA Bulletin*, with information, insight, and insider news on the field.

SF SITE. www.sfsite.com/map3.htm. Website covers the contemporary speculative-fiction scene: reviews, interviews, many links to book and magazine publishers (in print and online), and more.

WEBSITES FOR RESEARCH

BRIGHT WEAVINGS. www.brightweavings.com. Focuses on the work of contemporary author Guy Gavriel Kay, includes extensive links to sites on medieval studies and other historical topics.

CAMELOT PROJECT. http://www.lib.rochester.edu/camelot/cphome.stm. Database of Arthurian texts, images, bibliographies, plus numerous interviews by Raymond H. Thompson with modern authors of Arthurian-connected fantasy fiction.

ENCYCLOPEDIA MYTHICA. www.pantheon.org. Online encyclopedia of mythology, folklore, and legends, with over 5,000 entries on mythical animals, objects, gods, places, and supernatural creatures.

ENDICOTT STUDIO. www.endicott-studio.com. Outstanding site by a group of authors and artists with wide-ranging tastes in all things mythic. Links, online journals, art, music, literature, and more.

THE GOLDEN KEY. www.george-macdonald.com. Presents the work of George MacDonald, with resources and e-texts of his wonderful novels—*At the Back of the North Wind*, the *Curdie* books, and others.

GREY HAVENS. http://tolkien.cro.net. Extensive collection of commentary on Tolkien's Middle-earth.

INTERNATIONAL ASSOCIATION FOR THE FANTASTIC IN THE ARTS. www.iafa.org. Scholarly organization for the study of the fantastic in literature, film, and other media.

INTO THE WARDROBE. http://cslewis.drzeus.net. Devoted to the work of C.S. Lewis.

THE LABYRINTH. http://labyrinth.georgetown.edu. An enormous searchable collection of web resources for medieval studies.

MYTHOPOEIC SOCIETY. www.mythsoc.org. A nonprofit society for the appreciation of myth and genres of fantasy. Offers a quarterly journal.

MYTHS & LEGENDS. http://pubpages.unh.edu/~cbsiren/myth.html. Text and essays on myths from many cultures across the globe.

THE SCIENCE FICTION FOUNDATION. www.sf-foundation.org. Nonprofit organization, based in Britain, for speculative-fiction studies. Publishes the journal *Foundation: The International Review of Science Fiction*.

SELECTED AUTHORS OF SUPERNATURAL FICTION. www.creative.net/~alang/lit/horror/horror.sht. E-texts and biographical material on Lord Dunsany, H.P. Lovecraft, Edgar Allan Poe, and others.

SURLALUNE. http://members.aol.com/surlalune/frytales/index.htm. Text, commentary, and bibliography of variants of common fairy tales.

THE TOLKIEN SOCIETY. www.tolkiensociety.org. International society, based in the U.K., promoting the life and work of J.R.R. Tolkien.

SELECTED BOOKS ABOUT FANTASY

BOYER, ROBERT H., and ZAHORSKI, KENNETH J, editors. *Fantasists on Fantasy: A Collection of Critical Reflections.* Avon Books, 1984. Excellent collection of essays on fantasy written by authors from George MacDonald to C.S. Lewis, from Peter S. Beagle to Ursula K. Le Guin.

CARPENTER, HUMPHREY. *The Letters of J.R.R. Tolkien.* Houghton Mifflin, 2000; first published 1981 in Great Britain by George Allen & Unwin. Fascinating look into the creative mind of Tolkien, with many references to the writing process and themes in his own work.

CARPENTER, HUMPHREY. *Tolkien: A Biography.* Boston: Houghton Mifflin, 1977; first published 1977 in Great Britain by George Allen & Unwin. Authoritative study of the life of the man whose writings in great measure led to the resurgence of fantasy today.

CLUTE, JOHN, and GRANT, JOHN, editors. *The Encyclopedia of Fantasy.* (St. Martins Press, 1999). An erudite, 1,000-page reference work for readers of fantasy literature, with 4,000 entries on all aspects of the topic, by author and theme.

EGOFF, SHEILA A. *Worlds Within: Children's Fantasy from the Middle Ages to Today.* American Library Association, 1988. An insightful, sometimes opinionated look at fantasy books for children, by decade, with discussion of many individual titles and series.

KING, STEPHEN. *Stephen King's Danse Macabre.* (Everest House, 1981). An insightful, entertaining look at the wonderful world of horror in fiction, film, and television, by a master storyteller.

SHIPPEY, TOM. *J.R.R. Tolkien: Author of the Century.* A thoughtful book, written in a clear, readable fashion by a medieval scholar, presenting Tolkien's work in its wondrous complexity. Required reading for fans of Tolkien and literary fantasy. Houghton Mifflin Co., 2001.

YOLEN, JANE. *Touch Magic: Fantasy, Faerie & Folklore in the Literature of Childhood.* August House, 2000. Thoughtful essays on storytelling, fantasy, and folklore, by an award-winning fantasy author.

ZIPES, JACK DAVID, EDITOR. *The Oxford Companion to Fairy Tales.* Oxford University Press, 2000. A wonderful encyclopedia covering fairy tales in folklore, literature, and film, with many entries on fantasy authors from Maurice Sendak to Edward Gorey, Astrid Lindgren to Robin McKinley. Excellent resource.

ACKNOWLEDGEMENTS & CREDITS

ACKNOWLEDGMENTS

The editor would like to thank all those whose imaginative writings and conversations helped shape this book, especially the authors who kindly contributed their time to interviews on the subject of fantasy fiction. I am deeply indebted as well to the following authors who helped shape my thoughts: Joan Aiken for her many articles which have appeared in *The Writer*, also to Susan Cooper, Ursula Le Guin, and Jane Yolen for their essays on writing, and to Terri Windling and the Endicott Studio website for many good reading recommendations. Thanks also to Drew Kennedy, whose insightful Sunday sermon on Harry Potter got me thinking about all this; and to young consultant Ben Evans, who contributed his perspective on good fantasy books to read, and why.

Within this book, I have drawn many brief quotes from exemplary works of fantasy fiction and from some other selected works of criticism and commentary; I have tried to do this fairly and accurately, respecting the spirit of the original work while showing its relevance to the larger field of fantasy and its creation. I have acknowledged the sources of quotes by citing the author and title of the work (and in some cases, a unique edition or translation) in the text. Permissions granted to quote longer passages from critical works about fantasy and its writing are gratefully acknowledged below.

PERMISSIONS

The excerpt from an article by Joan Aiken, "Writing Ghost Stories," (previously published in *The Writer*, February 1994), copyright by Joan Aiken, is reprinted by permission of the author.

The article "How to Be Madder than Captain Ahab," by Ray Bradbury, is copyright © 1973 by Ray Bradbury, and is reprinted by permission of Don Congdon Associates, Inc.

The excerpt from "Escaping from Ourselves," from *Dreams and Wishes: Essays on Writing for Children* by Susan Cooper is reprinted with the permission of Margaret K. McElderry Books, an imprint of Simon &

INDEX